SHORT-TERM
ANXIETY-PROVOKING
PSYCHOTHERAPY

SHORT-TERM ANXIETY-PROVOKING PSYCHOTHERAPY

A Treatment Manual

PETER E. SIFNEOS, M.D.

BasicBooks
A Division of HarperCollins*Publishers*

Library of Congress Cataloging-in-Publication Data
Sifneos, Peter E. (Peter Emanuel), 1920–
    Short-term anxiety-provoking psychotherapy: a treatment
    manual
Peter E. Sifneos.
      p.   cm.
    Includes bibliographical references and index.
    ISBN 0–465–07802–8
    1. Brief psychotherapy.   2. Psychodynamic psychotherapy.
    3. Problem-solving therapy.   4.Anxiety—Therapeutic use.
    I. Title.
    [DNLM: 1. Anxiety.   2. Psychotherapy, Brief—methods. WM
    420 S573sa]
    RC480.55.S54   1992
    616.89′14—dc20
    DNLM/DLC
    for Library of Congress   91–55606
                                                    CIP

To the Memory of my Mother
"χ α ι ρ ε"

Contents

Contents

PREFACE

During the past fifteen years I have had the opportunity to present in workshops, conferences, and seminars all over North and South America and Europe my work about a kind of short-term dynamic psychotherapy called STAPP (short-term anxiety-provoking psychotherapy).

I am pleased to find that a great deal of interest has been aroused among the participants. There are two reasons for this. The first has to do with the many years of investigation surrounding this kind of psychotherapy of brief duration, as well as the systematic studies of the results obtained. Second, we have made extensive and systematic use of videotapes to demonstrate this work, allowing evaluation and techniques to be observed and outcome findings to be assessed objectively by the participants. It is they who watched critically the nature of the patient–therapist relationship and it is they who could decide whether the patients had improved.

At the end of my presentations many mental health professionals attending these conferences asked for training, to learn how to offer this kind of brief therapy to appropriately selected patients. Unfortunately, this need could not be met because the Department of Psychiatry at the Beth Israel Hospital of Harvard Medical School, where I work, has a small number of trainees and has no funds available to offer fellowships to other mental health professionals. Moreover, neither the government nor the insurance industry, which could benefit enormously by these short-term limited techniques that considerably reduce the cost of psychotherapy, has helped finance training programs.

I have written this book to address the crucial need for training in this highly effective form of short-term therapy.

The question at this point is, What is STAPP? It is a type of brief dynamic psychotherapy based on psychodynamic theoretical premises. It was developed nearly forty years ago in order to meet the demand for psychotherapeutic help which far exceeded the availability of trained therapists, and to counteract the prevailing—and I feel absurd—idea that long-term psychotherapy was the only way to change human attitudes and behaviors.

It was thought that if patients who were able to assign top priority to a psychological difficulty, whether a symptom or an interpersonal problem, could be identified, they could work with therapists on the understanding of the emotional conflicts and defense mechanisms surrounding a specific focus, and they might be able to resolve the conflicts successfully once and for all over a brief period of time.

An opportunity to demonstrate that such an approach was feasible came in the mid-1950s when a patient came to the psychiatric clinic of the Massachusetts General Hospital complaining of an acute onset of phobias for all forms of transportation, as well as physical symptoms, following his plans to get married in three months.

He was treated successfully for a total of six sessions and in subsequent follow-up he was found to be symptom free. This patient became our prototype for STAPP. Later, more patients were treated in the same manner and were likewise helped. As a result, it became imperative to develop criteria for selection, to describe foci around which the therapy should revolve, to use similar technical requirements, and to study carefully the outcome findings. This was achieved by several research studies, all of which demonstrated the value of this type of brief dynamic psychotherapy.

STAPP, then, takes place in a setting where patient and therapist meet once a week, face to face, for forty-five minutes. It usually lasts between six and twenty sessions. This means that its length varies based on the patient's ability to resolve with the help of the therapist the emotional conflicts underlying a specified and agreed-upon focus.

The foci found best suited for such a resolution are loss and separation issues, grief reactions, and unresolved oedipal problems. We have concentrated on the study of the latter to have a homogeneous enough population. This may explain why a great deal of the material which is to follow revolves around sexual material.

Some in the field question the value of picking up only one focus and working on its resolution, when there might be additional psychopathological issues that require the therapist's attention and assistance. This type of question comes up quite often among participants in my workshops: "What if there is another area of emotional conflicts which a patient may want to explore after he or she has resolved the focus which was agreed upon during the evaluation session?"

There are several parts to the answer. First, not every patient has early characterological difficulties that should be dealt with before therapy can come to an end. Because of our emphasis on extensive STAPP evaluations, we feel confident that the dynamic focus that was chosen is the correct one most of the time. Second, even if there are certain other areas of difficulty in the patient's character structure, it does not follow that they will not be resolved by the patients themselves once they have learned how to overcome one set of problems through STAPP. We discovered in the follow-up of our patients that problem solving indeed takes place after the termination of STAPP.

I think that the reason therapists are suspicious about their own patient's capabilities has to do with their own grandiose fantasies (namely, that they are indispensable to their patients, who are viewed as being weak and in need of perpetual support). Furthermore, it is usually true that therapists who are psychiatrists (who have been taught for years at medical schools about "pathology" and who have never had a course on "health") tend to discover new psychopathological problems and do not trust or give the benefit of the doubt to the healthy aspects of some of their patients. As mentioned already, we have discovered that when patients have been shown how to solve one set of emotional conflicts underlying the dynamic focus, they can use this knowledge effectively for the solution of other, less important, emotional problems entirely on their own.

This manual aims at helping therapists to learn how to conduct such a brief treatment, guide them through challenges that may arise, and provide them with a way to assist patients to overcome quickly a circumscribed set of psychological difficulties.

I present a systematic discussion of the evaluation process and techniques, by providing examples of various options available to the therapists when they are confronted with therapeutic challenges and when they have to deal with a variety of associations their patients present to them during the course of their treatment. A word of caution: It is not my intention to write a therapy cookbook. The individual personality style of the therapists determines how they interact with their patients and gives them the freedom to decide in their own way how they will respond to the challenges presented. A detailed presentation of case material and different technical possibilities will offer therapists several options to deal with their patients and enlarge and enrich their therapeutic armamentarium.

In sum, then, it is hoped that this manual will meet the needs of mental health professionals both theoretically and practically, as they learn to use this kind of short-term psychotherapy which is based on psychodynamic principles and which has been found to be effective on well-selected patients. By using their own therapeutic styles and following the technical guidelines, they will be able to relieve the suffering of many of these patients.

As I have done in my other books, first and foremost I want to express my deep appreciation to all my STAPP patients for their willingness to provide me with the clinical material without which this book would not have been possible. Changes have been made to protect their confidentiality and their anonymity without, however, destroying the relevance of the clinical observations about their psychotherapeutic process. Most important, they gave me the opportunity to witness their efforts to overcome their psychological problems and to admire their motivation to change despite experiencing anxiety and pain in the process of their therapy. Finally, I am grateful to them for making my professional life a worthwhile experience.

I am also especially thankful to all the mental health professionals whom I met during my workshops, seminars, conferences, and congresses in Europe and in North and South America and who, with their comments and questions, stimulated me to become self-inquisitive and to learn from their criticism.

I am indebted to all those who invited me to present my work and my videotapes to their staffs in university settings and in mental health agencies.

To my dear friend of many years and chairman of the Department of Psychiatry at the Boston Beth Israel Hospital, Fred Frankel, I want to express my thanks for giving me the opportunity to have the necessary time and freedom of action to devote to writing this manual.

Last but not least, to Marilyn Maynard, who despite her very heavy work responsibilities was able to read my handwriting and find the necessary time to type my manuscript, I want to express my appreciation and my gratitude.

PART I

EVALUATION

A thorough psychiatric evaluation is vital in understanding the nature of the patient's psychological difficulties and deciding on the type of therapy needed to alleviate them, because the patient who receives the wrong treatment will invariably get worse. The evaluation is especially important in selecting patients for short-term anxiety-provoking psychotherapy which is suitable for a limited patient population.

Division of labor is the best way to use the expert knowledge of each of the disciplines of psychotherapy. Psychiatrists know a great deal about medical issues from their many years of medical education. Psychologists have the most training in psychological testing and in research. Social workers know a lot about community organizations. Each discipline has a great deal to offer in helping to understand the complex psychological problems encountered in the psychiatric clinic of a general hospital.

When I directed the psychiatric clinic of the Massachusetts General Hospital in Boston in the mid-1950s and 1960s, I organized daily evaluation intake teams. Each team was responsible for the assessment of the problems of all the patients who came to the clinic on a particular day; we had five different teams. Each team was composed of psychiatric residents, psychology interns, and postdoctoral fellows as well as pre- and post-Ph.D. social workers. There were also students from the three disciplines. The team had ten to twelve members with a senior trainee in charge. Usually a two-hour conference was held in the late afternoon, and decisions were made about which patients to present to a senior consultant. The role of the senior consultant was to answer evaluation problems presented by the members of the team. These at times involved questions about a patient, such as the way he or she related to the evaluator, the nature of the symptoms, or his or her interpersonal difficulties. Often, however, the team wanted the consultants to interview a patient in front of the group. A general discussion usually followed and a consensus basis reached, which was communicated to the patient at the end of the day. A second interview was rarely necessary and had to be justified. For example, an essential question may have remained for investigation.

These intake evaluation conferences not only offered an optimal way to assess the psychological difficulties of clinic patients but gave members of the team the opportunity for a meaningful teaching experience.

There are five components in the psychiatric evaluation process:

• Assessing the presenting problems
• Obtaining a systematic developmental history
• Using the appropriate selection criteria
• Formulating a specific dynamic focus for the psychotherapy
• Obtaining an agreement from the patient to work cooperatively with the therapist in order to resolve the emotional conflicts underlying the specific focus which is considered to be responsible for the psychological difficulties.

It is important therefore to emphasize again the importance of taking a history about sexuality as an integral part of the developmental history. On the other hand, not taking it may become more of a problem to the evaluator than for the patient. Hesitancy or failure to ask specific questions about sexual fantasies not only during adult life but also during puberty as well as prepubescent childhood, reveals the evaluator's difficulties and embarrassment with this subject.

After taking the history, the evaluator will have a fairly good idea of the emotional conflicts underlying the patients difficulties and on the basis of the criteria for selection for STAPP, which will be described in detail in the following chapter, establish a dynamic focus around which the short-term dynamic psychotherapy will revolve.

Of course, one should not view the presenting problems, the history taking, the criteria for selection for STAPP, and the establishment of a dynamic focus as individual components of the psychiatric evaluation, isolated from each other. They are intertwined. Keeping all these factors in mind helps the evaluator to synthesize the patient's material, arrive at a thorough dynamic understanding of the patient's difficulties, and decide which type of therapy is appropriate for the patient. For practical reasons, however, the following chapters will treat each of the five evaluation components in turn.

CHAPTER 1

The Presenting Problems

THE MAIN PROBLEMS PRESENTED by most patients who turn out to be good candidates for STAPP are psychosocial in nature—predominantly difficulties in interpersonal relations. The evaluator may also hear complaints about specific, usually mild, psychological symptoms, such as anxiety, depression, grief reaction, obsessive preoccupation, and monosymptomatic phobia, as well as, at times, about physical symptoms. Although not very severe, these difficulties may nevertheless interfere with the patients' daily lives and complicate their relations with other people. As far as *DSM III-R* is concerned, they fall under the "Adjustment Disorder" category.

The first task of the evaluator is to inquire about the onset of the presenting problems. When did they start? How did they start? What was their duration? What was their timing in reference to other events in the patient's personal life? When symptoms are present, the evaluator should investigate them and ask if they are related to interpersonal difficulties. One should inquire about their intensity, duration, and onset. How much have they interfered with the patient's daily activities? Was there a precipitating factor that brought them about? Other pertinent information will also be valuable.

With few exceptions, patients are not very well organized in presenting their problems. They emphasize what creates the greatest discomfort, and thus they may fail to present a coherent account of the onset and development of their difficulties. The evaluator must help such patients organize the presentation of their chief complaints in a more cohesive and systematic manner, as the evaluator does in the following transcript.

A fifty-four-year-old engineer came to the psychiatric clinic because his wife had called and made an appointment for him.

EVALUATOR: What may I be able to do for you?

PATIENT: As my wife said when she made my appointment, she attended one of your workshops.

EVALUATOR: Yes, I know, but the question to us is, what is the problem that bothers *you* most?

PATIENT: I'm not so sure. You see, my wife says . . .

EVALUATOR: *(Interrupting) You* are here. Therefore it is most important for us to have your side of the story. [The evaluator wants to find out how motivated the patient is to pursue the understanding of his psychological difficulties.]

PATIENT: It is difficult for me to tell you. I don't know exactly how to proceed.

This type of answer may indicate that the patient is passive, un-motivated, ashamed, frightened, fearful, disinterested, or evasive, to name a few possibilities. It is up to the evaluator to decide which of these possibilities may be the right one. An attempt must be made to help the patient formulate the complaint by offering some suggestions.

EVALUATOR: Let me try to help you. For example, do you have any physical difficulties?

PATIENT: No.

EVALUATOR: Are you disturbed by any other problems, such as being anxious?

PATIENT: No, but . . .

EVALUATOR: Yes, please go on.

PATIENT: You see, doctor, the reason that my wife suggested that I come to the clinic and called to make this appointment has to do with some difficulties between the two of us during the last few months . . . *(Appears apprehensive)*

EVALUATOR: I see . . . I know it may be somewhat difficult to talk about intimate matters, but everything that is being discussed here is between the two of us. [The evaluator is supportive, trying to entice the patient to present his side of his problem.]

PATIENT: Recently I have not been interested in sex.
EVALUATOR: Can we hear about this?
PATIENT: It is a difficult subject.
EVALUATOR: I understand, but it might be helpful to hear more about it.

The patient was able to go on without too much difficulty. The evaluator by his empathic stance as well as by pressing the patient is able to obtain a clearer picture of the presenting problem. The patient said that because his wife had called to make the appointment for him, he thought the evaluator would want to hear his wife's side of the story. Once he was convinced that the evaluator was interested in his story, he became cooperative and proceeded to relate his point of view.

A divorced mother with two children came to the hospital psychiatric clinic complaining of "nervous feelings," "tension," "difficulty making decisions," and "headaches."

EVALUATOR: How long have you had these symptoms?
PATIENT: I don't know. I've had them for quite a while.
EVALUATOR: I know that you may be unable to say exactly, but approximately how long have you had them? Would you say one week, one month, one year? [The evaluator attempts to assist the patient by offering various lengths of time.]
PATIENT: I felt tense and anxious, and then I had the headaches. . . . Now, as I said, I procrastinated a lot.
EVALUATOR: You say now that you were anxious. Before, you told me that you were nervous. Are these two feelings the same? [The evaluator wants to know if anxiety was different from nervousness, and also wants to convey the importance of being precise.]
PATIENT: I think that they are the same.
EVALUATOR: OK, then. Now let us take each one of these symptoms separately. Which one did you notice first?
PATIENT: Well, it was when I noticed that I had difficulty making decisions. You see, I had to go to visit my son's teacher. I remember that clearly. I kept on postponing it week after week.
EVALUATOR: This is helpful in timing the onset of this indecisiveness and procrastination of yours. It must have been during the school year. [The evaluator encourages the patient to remember the onset of her difficulties.]

PATIENT: Oh yes, come to think of it, it was before the spring vacation.

EVALUATOR: That makes it about four months ago.

PATIENT: I guess so, more or less, but I can't say exactly or be absolutely sure.

EVALUATOR: That is good enough. Before we did not know anything about the timing. Now we know it was about four months ago. You see, it is important to try to be as precise as one can. [Again the evaluator is supportive of the patient's efforts to remember.]

PATIENT: Yes.

EVALUATOR: Now, what about the tension, the anxiety, and the headaches?

PATIENT: As I noticed that I procrastinated and that I was postponing the visit from week to week, I started to feel anxious. I started to worry about myself. I remember one night I woke up and I could not go back to sleep. I was thinking, "If Joe (my ex-husband) were around he would have gone to visit the teacher instead of me." But this thought made me angry. I said to myself, "Here you go, Lois, you were glad that you got rid of Joe and now you wish he were around to help you make a decision. You must be nuts." I couldn't sleep. I got very tense, doctor.

EVALUATOR: So, now we have the sequence of your difficulty deciding about visiting the teacher to find out about your son's progress in school, followed by becoming anxious, and then getting tense. How severe were the anxiety and tension?

PATIENT: Pretty strong.

EVALUATOR: So strong that you were in a state of panic?

PATIENT: Oh no, I don't want to exaggerate and say that I was panicky. Far from it. I certainly did all my housework and all that, but these difficulties upset me and they interfered once or twice with my sleep.

The evaluator was able to form a pretty good picture of the onset, the timing, the intensity, and the sequence of the symptoms discerning and inquiring about each symptom separately instead of allowing the patient to describe her presenting problems in a global and confusing manner. There are, however, two issues that must be addressed by the evaluator. The first one has to do with the remaining physical symptom—namely, the headaches; the other has to do with the patient's former husband. Although spontaneous information may be an important clue about the patient's psychodynamics, it is better at this point to inquire further about the headaches; after this subject is exhausted, the evaluator can explore the nature of the patient's relationship with her son and her ex-husband. In any event, the relationships will be further looked into when the evaluator proceeds to obtain a systematic developmental history.

Returning, then, to the questions about the headaches: the evaluator must determine whether they constitute a separate problem or whether they are associated with the procrastination, the anxiety, and the ensuing tension. If they are a separate issue, the evaluator should make sure that they are not part of an underlying medical illness.

EVALUATOR: You also mentioned that you had headaches. When did they start?

PATIENT: I'm not sure that I remember.

EVALUATOR: Let us look at this in a different way. Did you consult your family doctor or anyone else?

PATIENT: I was complaining about them to my mother, and I remember her saying, "Why don't you go to see our family doctor? He may be able to give you something to help you."

EVALUATOR: And when did your mother make that suggestion?

PATIENT: Oh, it must have been only a few weeks ago.

The evaluator is still unsure. On the basis of this information it seems likely to him that the headaches were related to the tension that followed the other presenting symptoms. Since the possibility of an underlying medical cause of the headaches hasn't been ruled out, the evaluator must ask a variety of medical questions regarding the headaches, such as about their intensity; their location; what time of day they occurred; and whether they were associated with any other physical symptoms, such as weakness, malaise, fever, nausea, vomiting, dizziness, and the like, or with any other illness, such as a cold or a stomach upset.

The evaluator received negative answers to all the questions that would point to physical causes. Still, it is wise at this point to rule out underlying medical pathology; the evaluator should refer the patient to an internist or to the hospital medical clinic for a complete physical examination. This advice holds whether the evaluator has an M.D. degree or not. It is essential to investigate a potential hidden medical problem that may be camouflaged by psychological difficulties. In the case of the patient whom I have described, the evaluator decided to refer her to the medical clinic because he was unsure whether her headaches were associated clearly with the psychological symptoms.

The patient mentioned procrastination as her first psychological problem. The evaluator was able to get information about the onset, duration, intensity, and precipitating events. As the interview progressed, it became clear that a second evaluation interview would be necessary.

EVALUATOR: Although we have a much better picture about your presenting difficulties, I think that it is necessary to make an appointment at the medical clinic for a checkup to see whether or not there is an underlying cause for your headaches. Is this agreeable to you?

PATIENT: Of course, doctor. I'll do whatever you recommend.

Once the medical clinic verified that the patient's physical examination and laboratory tests were all within normal limits, a second evaluation interview was scheduled for the systematic developmental history. How to go about obtaining such a history will be described in more detail later on.

In recent years there seems to have been an increase in the number of patients arriving at psychiatric clinics, health maintenance organizations (HMOs), mental health agencies, or private therapists' offices who present serious complaints and who suffer from severe mental illness. One reason, perhaps, is the failure of deinstitutionalization policies prevailing in the United States. But there may also be another reason: the message may have been given to the community at large that mental health professionals are more interested in patients with serious psychopathology, such as borderline or narcissistic personalities or even psychotic illness. As a result, many people with circumscribed psychosocial problems may feel that their difficulties are not serious enough or that professional help is unavailable to them—particularly those who are not very psychologically minded. These people either attempt to deal with their difficulties alone or seek help from friends or from nonprofessionals. Unfortunately, the problems persist or get worse. Interpersonal relations deteriorate, and a situation that could easily have been alleviated by a brief psychotherapeutic intervention may tend to become chronic and more difficult to deal with.

Patients who present themselves with interpersonal difficulties or mild psychological symptoms, such as anxiety, depression, grief reaction, chronic procrastination, and monosymptomatic phobia, may be good candidates for STAPP. Evaluators should attempt to assess their suitability for brief treatment. After determining the presenting problems, they should proceed to obtain a systematic developmental history, as discussed in the following chapter.

CHAPTER 2

Taking a Developmental History

T HE SECOND MAJOR TASK in the psychiatric evaluation is to obtain a detailed developmental history. Yet many therapists do not spend enough time during their evaluation on developing a systematic history.

Obviously, the roots of patients' psychological problems lie in their biological makeup and in the interpersonal experiences of early childhood. Unless early experiences are scrutinized and patterns of behavior and psychological functioning explored, therapists cannot gain an adequate understanding of patients' difficulties and thus cannot help patients fully resolve the emotional conflicts underlying such problems.

Areas for Investigation

In previous publications (Sifneos 1972, 1987), I have set forth a list of areas that must be investigated in the evaluation of potential patients for STAPP. Questions must be asked about patients' earliest memories and about childhood interaction with other family members—which parent did the patient feel closest to? and of which parent was the patient the favorite? Relations with siblings and other members of the family should be looked into; experiences during the early school years and the latency period should be explored; puberty is of particular importance because new material emerges in that period, and changes from earlier childhood, particularly during the ages of four and five, may be dramatic. Finally,

11

information about the adolescent period and adulthood should finish the developmental history taking. A systematic medical history of the patient should also be obtained.

Types of Questions

The evaluator learns about all these aspects of a patient's background through the judicious use of *open-ended* and *forced-choice* questions. In my experience, it is best to begin the history taking with open-ended inquiries, such as, "Tell me about yourself," or, "What do you remember about your childhood?" This type of inquiry gives the patient an opportunity to recollect the past without interruption and in detail. It also allows the evaluator to observe how well the patient presents past experiences.

If the initial inquiry does not produce much information, one may try to assist the patient by being somewhat more precise but continuing to use open-ended questions: "What is your earliest memory?" If the patient appears to be unsure or hesitates, then one can continue to help out by saying, "Go back as far as you remember. It may be a memory, an episode, a fragment of some experience." If open-ended questions produce no results then the evaluator may switch to a forced-choice type of inquiry. The evaluator may proceed as follows: "Let me put some questions to you more precisely. Do you remember the time when you were four or five years old?" The patient may answer yes or no. If the answer is no, then another forced-choice type of questioning is in order. The evaluator's questions might be as follows: "Did you have any brothers? Did you have any sisters? Were you your father's favorite? Was he yours? Were you your mother's favorite? Was she yours?"

If at any point the patient responds with a memory of a special event or with a spontaneous association, then the evaluator may switch back to open-ended questions, such as, "Now, please tell me a little more about what happened around the time when this event took place."

If there are no spontaneous memories or associations, the evaluator should continue asking forced-choice questions, such as, "You seem to have difficulty remembering events from your childhood. Did your father or mother or another relative ever tell you about some episode that you experienced or something that you said when you were very young?"

If the patient continues answering no, the evaluator should continue with forced-choice questioning about the patient's childhood until the patient finally starts to remember various experiences or events. At that point, the evaluator should again switch into open-ended questions.

Alternating types of questions not only is supportive to the patient and encourages him or her to cooperate but also is helpful to the evaluator in pinpointing episodes that may have been significant to the patient. Thus a working alliance between the two participants may start to develop.

Sequence

One of the commonest mistakes trainees make is not to follow the patients' history sequentially; instead they jump around from points in the past to episodes in the present. It may be that patients provide information that they want to emphasize or they feel is important to them; they may want to avoid areas of their childhood that make them anxious. It should be remembered, however, that history taking is the *evaluator's*, not the patient's, task. Like the physician, who takes a medical history that includes questions about chief complaints and systems reviews in order to arrive at a diagnosis, the mental health evaluator must take the lead in obtaining a cohesive picture of the presenting complaints and of the patient's life. Part of the task is to get the story straight. To clarify the sequence, the evaluator may have to interrupt a patient who remembers an event from childhood and then jumps to a memory from adolescence. In such a case the evaluator may say: "Of course what you remembered from your adolescence may be of importance, but let's not go so fast because there may be other significant episodes from your childhood which we do not want to miss."

Difficult Subjects

HISTORY OF PHYSICAL OR MENTAL ABUSE

When traumatic episodes have disturbed the patient's psychological makeup to the point of contributing negatively to his or her character structure, the patient may have developed problems that would immediately disqualify him or her from receiving short-term dynamic psychotherapy. For example, incestuous relations or severe physical abuse in childhood invariably have a catastrophic effect on a person's psychological structure because such children are not provided with a secure base from which to develop. As a consequence, a person may later on in life resort to the excessive use of alcohol or drugs in an attempt to overcome the trauma and to soothe its overwhelming impact.

Patients who have a childhood history of incest or severe physical or emotional abuse, especially combined with later chronic alcohol or drug intake, require long and supportive psychotherapy to avoid the kind of massive regressive deterioration that may lead to psychiatric hospitalization.

In an effort to be empathic, evaluators may fail to pursue their inquiry thoroughly with traumatized patients. It is difficult to prescribe a course of action under these circumstances. If the evaluator decides that investigating such events may lead to a regression or flight on the part of the patient, then the subject should not be pursued. If, on the other hand, the evaluator feels uncomfortable and avoids these subjects, the effect may be negative on the patient who would have liked to make a clear confession of what transpired and who may feel that the evaluator does not understand the need to do so.

A history of suicide attempts is another indicator of severe emotional conflicts. Thus patients who have made suicide attempts of any kind—impulsive, manipulative, or after considerable deliberation—should not be considered as candidates for short-term dynamic psychotherapy.

HISTORY OF SERIOUS PSYCHOPATHOLOGY

Patients who by virtue of biological, genetic, or environmental factors have not developed enough strength of character to deal with the realities of everyday life need long-term empathic and supportive psychotherapy in conjunction with psychopharmacological medications. Also, psychiatric hospitalization should not be ruled out. Again such individuals will not be helped by any dynamic treatment of brief duration.

Sexual History

The history of patients' sexual development is often investigated by inexperienced therapists in the wrong way. This is unfortunate, because childhood sexuality and attitudes developed about sexual matters during puberty and adolescence usually have a profound effect on interpersonal relations in adulthood. Incest, as mentioned, has long-lasting negative effects on character development, and a patient who has experienced incest invariably requires long-term psychotherapeutic support.

During the course of history taking the evaluator must inquire specifically about sexual experiences and attitudes during the preschool years, during the latency period, and in particular, during puberty. Answers to questions about the onset of menarche in girls and about physical changes in both boys and girls must be scrutinized carefully, particularly with regard to the effect the changes might have had on patients' relations with parents, siblings, friends, relatives, or others. This line of questioning was fruitful in the following episode.

A twenty-two-year-old student complained about difficulties in her relationships with her boyfriends which prompted her repeatedly to end them. During the history taking the following exchange took place.

EVALUATOR: When you were a young child, I mean around four or five years old, were you closer to your mother or to your father?

PATIENT: I was much closer to my dad.

EVALUATOR: [Switching immediately to an open-ended question] Could you describe some experience that you and your father shared?

PATIENT: My father was an excellent carpenter, and he loved to have me help him with his woodwork. He had his shop in the basement, and we used to spend hours down there together. I remember that he would ask me to bring this tool, that tool, those screws, nails, hammers, whatever. I loved to hear him talk and describe how to use special tools. It was just great *(smiling)*.

EVALUATOR: You smile. You must have really enjoyed these times with your father.

PATIENT: Yes, I really did.

EVALUATOR: Now, how long did this good time go on?

PATIENT: You see, my parents wanted to have another child but my mother had two miscarriages. *(Frowning)* Finally she became pregnant when I was thirteen years old.

EVALUATOR: How old were you when you had your first period?

The therapist has two options here. The first is to pursue the seemingly unpleasant subject of the mother's pregnancy. The second is to inquire about the patient's sexual history because her mother's pregnancy might have coincided with her menarche. He chooses the second.

15

PATIENT: When I was fourteen.

EVALUATOR: [He returns to his first option.] And when did your mother deliver?

PATIENT: When I was about fourteen. That was when my sister was born.

EVALUATOR: So how did you feel to have a sister?

PATIENT: *(Frowning)* I was glad to have a sister.

EVALUATOR: [One should always point out such paradoxical discrepancies.] Yet you frown. Why?

PATIENT: You see, what happened when my mother went to the hospital to have the baby—it was exactly the day that I started to menstruate.

EVALUATOR: Were you prepared for it?

PATIENT: Not in the slightest. My mother had not said anything to me. I did not know what was happening when I started to bleed. I was very scared, so I ran down to the cellar where my father was working to tell him what was happening. When I told him—I don't know, I don't know how to put it—he looked embarrassed.

EVALUATOR: Embarrassed?

PATIENT: Kind of . . . yes. He said it was OK and not to worry, but he said he was busy because he had to do a lot of work in the house now that my mother was in the hospital. I was surprised because he was working on refinishing a table, and when I persisted in asking him what was happening to me he became irritated and said that I shouldn't bother him since there was nothing to worry about. He also said that he was, and I should also be, happy at the birth of the new baby.

EVALUATOR: Go on.

PATIENT: You see, from then on things changed.

EVALUATOR: In what way?

PATIENT: *(Hesitating)* Well, my father's reaction upset me. It seems things became different between us. You see, my father liked babies and young children. He gave all his attention to my sister. When once I complained that he was spending too much time with her, he answered that now I was "a young lady," more mature, and I should not need to be taken care of any longer.

EVALUATOR: So the good times with your father were over?

PATIENT: Yes *(looks sad)*. Yes, our relationship changed completely.

EVALUATOR: Completely?

PATIENT: *(On the verge of tears)* Yes, we never worked together anymore in the basement. All my father's attention was on Clara, my sister.

EVALUATOR: I can see that you felt hurt. [The evaluator's words must be carefully chosen. The word *hurt* is more appropriate than the word *jealous*, which may be more correct. The evaluator, through empathy, tries to encourage the development of a working alliance.

PATIENT: I felt awful.

EVALUATOR: And then?

PATIENT: Then I started feeling more and more angry.

EVALUATOR: At the baby? At Clara?

PATIENT: *(Emphatically)* No. At my father.

EVALUATOR: So the birth of your sister and the onset of your menstruation ruined the good times that you had with your father.

PATIENT: I am surprised that you connect the two, but I guess that you are right. They are really connected.

EVALUATOR: And which one was more to blame?

PATIENT: At first, as I told you, it was my father's liking babies. In a way it was understandable that he would like Clara.

EVALUATOR: And then?

PATIENT: Later, I remembered that when I was worried about the bleeding, when I had my first period, my father didn't help me. He was too busy making preparations for the new baby. *(Becoming teary)* He rejected me when I was in trouble.

EVALUATOR: Do you think that your current relations with your boyfriends may in some way be associated with the onset of your menstruation and the feelings of being rejected by your father?

The evaluator at this point is ready to make a tentative confrontation by tying together the current difficulties with the episodes that have just been described. Appropriate responses to such confrontations indicate that the patient may be a good candidate for STAPP.

PATIENT: *(Looking pensive)* Well, possibly in an indirect sort of a way.

The evaluator must make sure that his confrontation is correct. Actually, he should not have made the confrontation before having asked the crucial questions relating specifically to the difficulty the patient had with her boyfriends.

EVALUATOR: What sets in motion the problems with your boyfriends?

PATIENT: Hmm . . . yes . . . it is when they introduce the subject of sex . . . I hadn't connected the two.

17

EVALUATOR: Of course you hadn't. That is why you are here. This whole area, it seems to me, should be explored if you are to get psychotherapy. What do you think?

PATIENT: Yes, of course.

The evaluator was taking a risk by making a confrontation regarding the father's rejection, the birth of the sister, the onset of menarche, and the patient's difficulties with her boyfriends. It is clear, however, that establishing such a connection is worth the risk. The patient's response confirmed the accuracy of the confrontation and is an early indication that she may be a good candidate for STAPP.

A history of the patient's sexuality is therefore an integral part of the developmental history. Not taking the sexual history may be more the evaluator's problem than the patient's. Hesitancy or failure to ask specific questions about sexual matters from childhood through adult life reveals the evaluator's difficulties and embarrassment with this subject.

After taking the history, the evaluator will have a fairly good idea of what emotional conflicts underly the patient's difficulties. On the basis of the criteria for selection for STAPP, which will be described in detail in the following chapter, the evaluator will be able to establish a dynamic focus around which the short-term dynamic psychotherapy will revolve.

CHAPTER 3

Selection Criteria

CLEAR-CUT CRITERIA FOR SELECTION constitute the third and probably the most important component of the psychiatric evaluation of STAPP candidates. If the patient fulfills these criteria, the patient possesses adequate strength of character to undertake a type of psychotherapy that encourages the patient to come to grips with and resolve the unpleasant emotional conflicts that underlie his or her psychological problems.

In my two books on short-term dynamic psychotherapy (Sifneos 1972, 1987), I have written extensively about criteria for selection and how we arrived at their formulation after many years of research in Boston. In addition, I was for many years a visiting professor at the University of Oslo. There, in cooperation with several Norwegian collaborators, I was able to establish that the selection criteria developed in the United States could be used to select candidates for STAPP from a culturally different population.

In this manual I want to instruct evaluators in more detail about using these selection criteria and alert them to the difficulties that may be encountered during their systematic assessment.

The following are the five STAPP selection criteria:

1. The patient must be able to circumscribe the presenting complaints.
2. The patient must have had at least one meaningful (give-and-take, altruistic) relationship during childhood.

19

3. The patient must relate flexibly to the evaluator, demonstrating that he or she can experience and express both positive and negative feelings appropriately.
4. The patient must be fairly intelligent and psychologically minded enough to comprehend psychotherapeutic interactions.
5. The patient must be motivated *to change* and must not expect only symptom relief through psychotherapy.

Criterion 1: Circumscribing the Presenting Complaints

To determine if a patient fulfills the first criterion for STAPP, the evaluator must attempt to find out if the patient can circumscribe his or her presenting complaints. The patient should be asked to assign top priority to the one problem that he or she considers to be the most important.

Let us assume that a patient comes in complaining of a variety of psychological complaints. How can the evaluator proceed to sort them out and help the patient assign top priority to one problem? After hearing the patient's presentation of complaints, the evaluator should ask which one is the most troublesome and will require the most effort to eliminate. Most patients respond that all their problems are bothersome and ask for relief from every one of them. This is, of course, understandable. But a brief psychotherapeutic intervention like STAPP allows too little time for handling all potential difficulties, and a compromise must be reached between evaluator and patient about which problem to resolve. If the most important problem is eliminated, there may well be a ripple effect of changes and improvements.

In addition, there is another, and possibly more important, reason why the patient should be placed in the difficult position of having to select one presenting problem for resolution. Such an ability to circumscribe denotes an ability to choose as much as to compromise. Such capabilities are important indications of strength of character.

A thirty-five-year-old man who had an adolescent daughter complained of being tense and irritable and worrying constantly about her. He also had fears of having a heart attack.

As we saw in chapter 1, the evaluator should help the patient formulate the sequence and timing of the various difficulties as well as identify their onset, duration, intensity, and so on. Such questions must be asked whether or not the patient fulfills the first criterion of selection for STAPP.

> EVALUATOR: You have complained about a variety of problems. As we have seen already, your preoccupation with your daughter's activities made you tense and irritable and then you started worrying about your own physical health. Now which *one* is the worst problem? Which prompted you to come to our clinic in an effort to try to solve it?
> PATIENT: Doctor, they all seem to be important to me.
> EVALUATOR: True, but which one is the most important?
> PATIENT: As I just told you, they all are.

There are two options for the evaluator. The first is to shift the questioning into another area to avoid annoying the patient. The second is to pursue the questioning to help the patient choose a problem to be solved. It is usually recommended that evaluators follow the second option and continue with their questioning.

> EVALUATOR: Let me see. If we could help you get rid of only *one* of these four problems, which one would you choose?
> PATIENT: You want me to compromise?
> EVALUATOR: Precisely.
> PATIENT: Well, the irritability is the worst. I get angry at my daughter, but I also get annoyed at people at work, and this can get me into trouble.
> EVALUATOR: So, if we can help you to be less irritable, will you be satisfied?
> PATIENT: More or less.
> EVALUATOR: More or less?
> PATIENT: You see, I'm not so sure now.
> EVALUATOR: We can give you some medication to help make you less irritable.

Since the patient seems to choose a symptom, by offering medication the evaluator tests whether this is indeed his choice. Since he seems to hesitate, there is the possibility that he is reconsidering.

> PATIENT: I don't know.
> EVALUATOR: Let us look at it in a different way. Isn't it more impor-

tant to find out what makes you irritable? If we eliminated your irritability, what was causing it would remain unknown, and at some future time that may again give rise to the same irritability. For example, if you had a headache and you took some aspirin the headache would improve for a few hours, but after this lapse of time it would return because the cause of the headache would not have been found.

PATIENT: I see what you mean.

EVALUATOR: Well?

PATIENT: If it weren't for my worries about my daughter, I don't think that I would be irritable.

EVALUATOR: So what you are saying is that your worries about your daughter were or are the cause of your irritability and therefore they are more important than this symptom.

PATIENT: I guess so, doctor. You see, now she is an adolescent. When she goes out I keep on worrying. You know, when I hear all about drugs, fights, drinking, rapes, how could a father not worry himself out of his mind—particularly since she is my only child?

EVALUATOR: Now, which one of all these things worries you most?

The evaluator has to investigate the sequence of the development of the problem in reference to the patient's daughter. This will again demonstrate the patient's ability to circumscribe problems.

PATIENT: All of these things are important.

EVALUATOR: There you go again, globalizing. Which one of all these worries—the drugs, the fights, the drinking, the rapes—do you think upsets you the most?

PATIENT: Well, I think, doctor, that sex can get her in trouble. She is not my little girl anymore. She is becoming a grown-up woman. She is tall, slender, attractive, and a good-looking woman. As you can see, I am afraid that I may lose her one of these days to one of these . . .

EVALUATOR: You were going to say?

PATIENT: Bastards . . . she may fall in love, drop out of high school, and get in trouble. You know, all that stuff that you hear about nowadays on TV.

EVALUATOR: So your fear of losing your daughter to another man makes you irritable.

PATIENT: I guess so.

EVALUATOR: You guess so?

PATIENT: No, doctor, I know that this fear eats me up.

EVALUATOR: OK, then, now what about your fear about your heart attack?

PATIENT: I always worry about it whenever I go through a time when I am upset.

EVALUATOR: So, now, going back to all your complaints, if we can help you solve only one, which one will you choose?

PATIENT: I see what you are driving at. The problem with my daughter is the one that bothers me most and causes all the other troubles.

In this systematic and patient way the evaluator is able to assist the patient in formulating his symptoms, and enables him to arrive at the most basic difficulty. Such an approach also helps the patient anticipate what is likely to transpire during his subsequent psychotherapeutic sessions.

In this way the evaluator is able to assess that the patient has the capability of circumscribing and assigning top priority to one of his problems and has therefore demonstrated an ability to choose. If the evaluator is satisfied that the patient fulfills the first criterion for selection then the logical second step is to proceed with the investigation of the second criterion and to see if this also can be fulfilled.

As far as this patient is concerned, one would say that despite his initial confusion about the priorities regarding the presenting problems, with the help of the evaluator he is able to come quickly to the crux of his difficulties: his worries about his daughter.

Criterion 2: Having Had at Least One Meaningful Relationship during Childhood

Making a sacrifice for another person at the expense of one's own pleasure is evidence of altruism. A child's demonstration of altruism at an early age denotes a capacity to interact flexibly with another person in a give-and-take way. Such a relationship is "meaningful."

Why should one go about investigating so thoroughly the existence of one meaningful relationship in early childhood? Altruism and the capability of expressing feelings for another person in a give-and-take way are evidence that the patient reached a level of psychological maturity at an early age. Such an individual is not likely to become psychotic or develop a borderline or narcissistic personality later in life. In this sense the second criterion attempts to rule out these more serious conditions and gives the evaluator an opportunity to pursue an investigation of the patient's character strengths and suitability for STAPP.

A particularly useful line of questioning begins: "When you were a child, to whom were you closer, your father or your mother?"

If the patient answers "both," the patient is evading the question, and the question should be repeated.

Once the patient names a parent, or a loved one, the evaluator may proceed in the following way: "Would you describe for me the nature of your relationship? Can you tell me about any special episode that characterized this relationship? For example, did you make any special sacrifices for your parents or for another loved individual?"

A simple yes to the last question is not enough: the evaluator should demand a specific example of sacrifice. A specific episode will confirm that a special relationship did actually exist.

What kinds of examples will satisfy the evaluator? The sacrifice of a favorite toy would be good evidence of altruism, for it is well known that toys play an important role in the lives of children. Other important things that a child may offer to a loved one include a favorite book, the last piece of cake, special clothing. Some patients mention that in their prayers they would ask God to be particularly nice to one of their parents or to a favorite relative, friend, or sibling. One can go on and on with examples. The patient should be able to do the same.

One evaluator asked an eighteen-year-old whether he would have made a special sacrifice for his mother, whom he had described as his favorite parent.

PATIENT: Of course. I would do anything for my mother.
EVALUATOR: "Anything" does not give me a clear-cut picture of what exactly you would do.
PATIENT: It may sound a bit melodramatic, but when I was seven, I prayed before going to bed, and I would ask God to please take care of my father, brothers, and friends. But when I got to my mother I would say "God, please subtract some years from my life and add them to my mother's life."

Another type of question for assessing this second STAPP criterion is about the existence of at least one good friendship during childhood. However, one should be cautious if the patient claims to have had many friends. On the one hand, many friendships may indicate good interpersonal skills; on the other hand, the patient may need repeated gratification, particularly if the friendships do not last. It is thus better to hear about the existence of a give-and-take, lasting relationship with only *one* friend.

Occasionally, a patient may be too self-sacrificing—masochism may be an ingredient of the patient's character structure. People who are willing to sacrifice *all* their sources of gratification for another may be insecure and overly dependent. These attributes are evidence of unsuitability for STAPP.

Another problem that may cause difficulty is a tendency on the part of the patient to sacrifice excessively because of feelings of guilt. If this happens to be the case, then of course the nature of the guilt should be investigated before a decision is reached about the second criterion.

A very religious twenty-two-year-old man responded to the evaluator's questions about his ability to make a sacrifice for another person:

PATIENT: You see, doctor, I was brought up very strictly in my family by my grandmother, who was very religious. My mother was divorced, and she used to work long hours. When I was nine years old, I was playing with another boy—he was a couple of years older than I. We were playing doctor. He was examining me, and then he started to masturbate me. I liked it very much, but somehow I knew that he shouldn't be doing it. After he finished he told me that what he did was bad and that I should never tell anyone else about it because then we should both go to hell. I was very scared. From then on, every time I masturbated I felt very guilty because I was afraid that if my grandmother were ever to know what I was doing not only would she stop loving me but also I would go to hell. So I used to pray every time I masturbated and promise that I would sacrifice something special, that I would do whatever my grandmother wanted me to do, in order to avoid her punishment and the ultimate horror of going to hell when I died. From that time on, therefore, I did everything that my grandmother asked for. You ask about a sacrifice? I would do everything for her. I would not go out to play with other kids if she did not want me to go out. I would sit and watch all kinds of stupid TV shows that she liked just to keep her company. You ask about sacrifices? I'd do anything for her just to avoid the fear of punishment because of my guilt feelings about my sin.

It is clear that this type of excessive sacrifice is masochistically determined because of guilt feelings, and it is not a good example of the patient's ability to demonstrate the existence of one meaningful relationship during childhood.

A relationship with another person is always unpredictable and sometimes causes pain. Obviously, the capacity to withstand a certain degree of anxiety is a crucial ingredient for STAPP; also, the person who has that capacity has attained considerable psychological maturity.

Criterion 3: Interacting Flexibly with the Evaluator

Having had a special and meaningful relationship during childhood usually teaches a person how to interact with other people. To test the capacity to interact, one should scrutinize how the patient is relating to someone whom he or she encounters for the first time: the evaluator. The patient's awareness and expression of feelings during the psychiatric evaluation denote the existence of such feelings in the past and indicate that both the second and the third criteria for STAPP have been met.

During the first interview, the evaluator will ask: "Can you tell me about your experience during this interview with me? I have been asking you many questions. Some of the things that we have been talking about may be difficult. How do you feel about all this?"

The feelings the patient expresses for the evaluator during the first interview do not need to be positive. What one should be looking for is an open and flexible expression of wishes, conflicts, and feelings.

A twenty-five-year-old woman who had considerable difficulties with her domineering and critical, yet also seductive, father, had displaced her resentment of his unpredictability onto men in general and onto her husband in particular. Although he loved her, she was considering divorce.

When the evaluator questioned her about her relationship with her father, she had seemed to become progressively more defensive. More and more, however, she was able to give examples of her own ambivalence about her relationship with her husband. The more the evaluator pressed her by asking about her father's or her husband's attitudes, the more resistant she became. Finally she exclaimed that the evaluator seemed to be as biased as her father was, and that she had not come to

26

have a psychiatric evaluation to hear about her father's or her husband's problems. This spontaneous and straightforward expression of her feelings of annoyance with the evaluator was acknowledged by him.

EVALUATOR: I understand that you are annoyed with me for insisting on trying to understand and investigate more closely your relations with your father, but don't forget that you may feel angry with me because I may be viewed as having certain traits which you point out are similar to your father's.

PATIENT: Well, yes, I can see that I may be displacing my feelings for my father as I did to my previous therapist, to my husband, and now to you.

Such a response is significant because it points to the existence of the patient's developing transference feelings even during an evaluating session. The next vignette presents a similar situation.

A twenty-eight-year-old man who had a very close relationship with his mother was being interviewed by a female evaluator. The evaluator met him in the waiting room and asked him to come to her office.

PATIENT: You know, I had expectations of what you would look like after I talked with you on the telephone when we made our appointment. I thought that you would be much older, let us say about my grandmother's age, but looking at you today I think that you look very much more like my mother.

EVALUATOR: So, what are your feelings for me?

Here is a situation in which questions relating to the third STAPP criterion can be asked immediately, even if the evaluator does not know much about the patient, because it was he who introduced the subject of transference at the onset of the session. The evaluator thought that more information of value could be gathered at this early point of the evaluation interview.

The patient proceeded to describe in detail his great attachment to his mother. As the session went on it became obvious that his feelings for the evaluator were similar to his feelings for his mother. He had expected the evaluator to look like his grandmother in an effort to avoid the embarrassment of experiencing positive feelings about someone whom he met for the first time, a professional person at that. It is possible that if the evaluator had not inquired specifically about the transference feelings a golden opportunity might have been lost in her attempt to assess the third STAPP criterion.

Sometimes the evaluator may not be as lucky and may experience some resistance on the part of the patient who asks immediately about transference feelings for the evaluator. Under such circumstances it may be advisable to ask the patient to think about what has transpired during the first session and to return the following week for a second interview. If the patient returns and maintains that he or she has forgotten what took place during the first interview and does not remember what was discussed, this is a bad sign. It may be that a working alliance has not been established or that the patient's defense mechanisms of avoidance or denial are strong and rigid and have been used in an attempt not to deal with anxiety-producing aspects of the evaluation. It may be helpful to give the patient another chance by offering an interview with a different evaluator the following week. Of course, this can be done only for patients who are seen in psychiatric clinics that use intake team evaluations. The therapist in private practice may recommend a second opinion. It may be advantageous for the patient's second evaluator to be of the opposite sex from the initial one, in order to determine specifically whether the difficulties have something to do with the patient's inability to relate to people of the sex of the first evaluator.

Although flexibility is an important ingredient in the patient's character, it should apply equally to the evaluator. Even if a patient's response to the first evaluation session seems to be negative, it should not be concluded immediately that he or she does not fulfill the third STAPP criterion. An attempt should be made to clarify the situation.

The patient may have misunderstood the evaluator's instructions about what to do between the first and second sessions. If so, the evaluator should recapitulate what took place during the first interview and repeat the points that he or she wanted the patient to consider. The evaluator might make one of the following statements:

- "You may remember that last week we discussed at quite some length your relations with men in authority, with whom you seem to have had some difficulties in your job. You mention today that you forgot what I asked you to think about. The question which must be raised then is whether your forgetting is related to your viewing me as one of these men in authority."
- "You tell me that you forgot what I asked you to think about or to remember from the past. Did you really forget, or did you forget

because my question made you anxious? If so, shall we try again and give the subject a second chance?"

To reintroduce the subject of potential transference feelings that might be the cause of such difficulties, the following question may be posed:

- "Is it possible that you have some feelings for me that may be either positive or negative and that have interfered with your thinking about what I asked you to consider during this past week?"

If the patient does bring in a significant recollection of a specific event, a fantasy, or a meaningful memory, then a positive working alliance has been established. This has stimulated the patient to reflect on the past and to continue the work that the evaluation interview has set into motion. If the patient's recollection is not related to what was discussed in the previous interview, he or she is not necessarily trying to avoid the issues. Everything should be done to investigate this newly brought-up information.

A twenty-year-old student who had serious academic difficulties had gone to his tutor, a man in his late sixties, asking him for some help in preparing for a quiz. The patient, despite his tutor's efforts and assistance, failed the quiz. This failure had made him very anxious and had stimulated him to seek psychotherapy. He said he feared that he might be asked to leave the university, and that he would view flunking out as an utter humiliation. He also said that this would be the straw that broke the camel's back, because it would signify to him that he was not as smart as his older brother, who had graduated from college cum laude. It would also confirm his father's opinion about him, namely, that he should have gone to a trade school instead of to college.

All this information had been gathered during the first evaluation session with an older psychiatrist, who asked the patient to think about events in the past as well as what had transpired between the two of them and to return for a second interview. The evaluator's impression was that the patient had related to him in a particularly obsequious manner and that he had demonstrated a tendency to agree with whatever was said in a somewhat passive and dependent way. The second interview began as follows:

PATIENT: I flunked the task you assigned to me.
EVALUATOR: What do you mean?

PATIENT: I did not remember anything of value after our talk here last week.

EVALUATOR: Nothing came to mind from the past, which I had asked you to think about?

PATIENT: Nothing of any significance.

EVALUATOR: Let us not decide about its significance in advance.

PATIENT: You see, I tried to think of something meaningful but nothing came to my mind. I am disappointed and I am sorry to disappoint you.

Here is a direct reference to the patient's interaction with the evaluator, who has an opportunity either to investigate the patient's feelings for him or to ignore them and proceed with the matter of what the patient considered to be significant or meaningful. Both are important issues, but since the third criterion had not yet been fulfilled, the evaluator chose to pursue the subject of what the patient thought about his being disappointed.

EVALUATOR: You don't have to worry about disappointing me. I am here to help you to understand yourself. You are not here to satisfy my curiosity. I noticed last time that you always seemed to agree with me and that you wanted to try to please me. I am not here to judge you or tell you what to do. This is not the purpose of our evaluation. I asked you to think about the past so as to help me understand you better and in turn to be of assistance in disentangling your problems and helping you to stand on your own two feet.

PATIENT: *(Smiling)* I am glad that you leave it up to me and that you don't tell me what to do or have special expectations from me. Really, I did spend quite some time trying to think of something special, something meaningful to help us out, but nothing came to my mind.

The evaluator here has three options: first, to continue clarifying their relationship; second, to ask about the words *special* and *meaningful;* and third, to comment about the patient's smiling.

EVALUATOR: You are smiling. What are you smiling about?

PATIENT: Well, I had thought that nothing important happened, except—

EVALUATOR: Except?

PATIENT: Well, some very insignificant event that took place when I was about ten, but it has nothing to do with what we were talking about.

At this point the evaluator cannot disregard the patient's saying "significant," or "anything of value," so he decides to make an open-ended inquiry.

EVALUATOR: Let us hear about this "insignificant" event.
PATIENT: It was an episode that took place when I went out hunting. I used to go out hunting quail when I was young, but I wouldn't be caught dead killing birds now. As you can see, this has nothing to do with my academic performance.
EVALUATOR: Let us not decide immediately whether it does or does not. Can we hear more about that hunting episode?
PATIENT: If you insist.
EVALUATOR: *Not* if I insist. You put me in the position of telling you what to do. We can both try to find out if this hunting memory of yours has in any way a remote association with the subjects which we had been talking about.
PATIENT: OK. I went hunting with my father. He was an excellent shot, and he had tried to teach me how to hunt. Although at that time I was somewhat interested in it, I was not very good at all. So as we were walking together, a rabbit jumped in front of us and kept running straight ahead. My father yelled, "Shoot at it, shoot at it!" I pretended that I was aiming in its direction, but I did not want to kill that little creature. *(Angrily)* It was the last thing that I was going to do. So, as I was saying, I pretended I was aiming in its direction, and I fired. Of course I missed it. I missed it on purpose. My father was disappointed. He said that I never followed his instructions. I think he sensed that I didn't want to kill the rabbit. He said, "Let's give up these hunting expeditions" because I was "not going to amount to anything at all."
EVALUATOR: All this sounds quite familiar to me.
PATIENT: In what way?
EVALUATOR: Well, doesn't your father say the same thing or use the same words about your schoolwork?
PATIENT: *(Pensive)* Yes, that is true.
EVALUATOR: You told me that your father wanted you to go to trade school instead of going to college.
PATIENT: Yes. He said that I was not smart enough for college.

31

EVALUATOR: He also told you that you were not a good hunter. [The evaluator has a chance here to tie in the father's attitude about intellectual issues with the hunting episode.]

PATIENT: Hmm.

EVALUATOR: Now, to me it is a paradox that you want to confirm your father's opinion about you.

PATIENT: I don't understand.

EVALUATOR: Come, now. By flunking your quiz you fail, and you tell me that you may flunk out of college.

PATIENT: This is interesting, because my tutor also said that maybe physics was too difficult a subject for me.

EVALUATOR: So you confirm his opinion as well, namely, that you are not up to par intellectually. I did not know, however, that he also gave you advice and told you what to do like your father.

PATIENT: I hadn't seen the connection up to now.

EVALUATOR: You told me last time that your tutor was an older person. Isn't that correct?

PATIENT: Yes.

EVALUATOR: So let us recapitulate. [This is a good way to solidify an interpretation.] Your father tells you that you won't amount to much as a hunter and also that you should go to trade school. Your tutor essentially agrees with your father's recommendations. "Physics," he says, "is too tough for you," or words to that effect. They both tell you what to do, and you don't like it a bit. Yet by your actions you confirm their opinion of you. You are a bad hunter and you fail your quiz. So are you going to please your father and your tutor and go to trade school?

PATIENT: (Emphatically) No.

EVALUATOR: No? But isn't that what you are doing?

PATIENT: I want both of them to like me.

EVALUATOR: You want everybody to like you by being obsequious and passive and agreeing with everyone. You did it here with me last time. Now, this is not what we are going to repeat here. As I said already, I am committed to help you stand on your own two feet, to help you do what *you* want, not tell you what to do. You will be surprised to find out that many people will like you if you are independent, strong, self-reliant, and able to decide what you like.

The evaluator takes an entirely different stance from what the patient may have expected. An attempt is being made to initiate what

Franz Alexander has described as "a corrective emotional experience."

During the evaluation interview, the patient was at first resistant. He described clearly a pattern of behavior with men in authority which he expected to be repeated with the evaluator during the first session. He was obsequious, passive, and agreeing, but in reality he was resisting. There are several ways in which the evaluator could have responded at the outset of the second session.

1. He could be supportive and sympathetic regarding the patient's inability to remember "anything of value" during the week, to avoid making the patient feel pressed. Such an approach—which, unfortunately, is often used by trainees—would immediately give the patient the message that he was weak and would confirm his father's and his tutor's opinion of him. Although such an approach is meant to be supportive, it fails by confirming what the patient already knows: that older people think that he is no good.

2. During the psychiatric evaluation, as during a medical evaluation, some discomfort will be aroused. The evaluator may choose to alleviate the pain immediately, which is palliative. On the other hand, the evaluator may wait, sending the message that he trusts the patient's ability to withstand the pain—and therefore to overcome his problem.

3. Giving the patient advice is fraught with danger because it puts the evaluator in the same position as the patient's father and tutor. The message will be, "I agree with them. You are weak, you need support, you must go to trade school."

Clearly, the evaluator must try the second option, even though it may cause some discomfort for the patient. By doing so, he appeals to a hidden strength in the patient's character. If this approach does not work, the evaluator must conclude that the patient does not fulfill the third criterion, that he is not a candidate for brief therapy but needs longer-term care.

In fact, the strategy seems to work. The evaluator appeals to the patient to stand on his own feet, and he declines to be a judge of the patient's behavior. The patient starts to smile, demonstrating that he obtains some satisfaction from that statement. Yet the patient continues to test the evaluator by clinging to his story of having thought of "nothing significant." But he smiles again, and then he says, "I had thought that nothing important happened, except . . ." Both the smile and the word *except* are of the greatest importance, and the evaluator confronts the patient with them. His confrontation opens the floodgates. The "insignificant" event turns out to be most significant because it reveals a basic aspect of his past conflicts with his father. From then on the evaluator needs only to encourage him to bring up more material from the past: "Tell me more."

The patient is on the verge of falling into an old pattern. He says he will go on "if you insist." The statement might be completed: "If you insist like my father, then I would be subservient to you so that you would like me." The evaluator must try to convince the patient of his sincerity and remind the patient that whether to go on is his decision to make. In this way the evaluator emphasizes the patient's importance in their joint venture.

By the end of the session the evaluator has created a corrective emotional experience by undermining the patient's expectation that he must be obsequious and passive in dealing with an older person in authority. He may begin to learn that by being independent he can also be liked and achieve what he wants.

The third criterion for STAPP has a great deal of value not only because it gives the evaluator an opportunity to assess whether the patient has experienced a meaningful relationship, but also because it prepares for the development of a working alliance. A working alliance established early may be strengthened during treatment and eventually become a truly therapeutic alliance.

The assessment of the third criterion may be affected by countertransference feelings. Any positive or negative reaction on the part of the patient may influence the evaluator's ability to be objective. In a recent workshop I showed a videotape of the evaluation interview of a fairly complicated patient. During the discussion that ensued, several of the participants mentioned that the patient had reminded them of patients of their own who had been seriously disturbed and difficult to treat. They concluded that the same problems would be likely to be encountered with the patient shown on the videotape.

Such a reaction is understandable but dangerous, because it interferes with the evaluator's objectivity. The evaluator who has negative feelings about another patient and displaces them onto the patient who is being evaluated will not be able to make a fair and objective assessment.

If such is the case, the evaluator must bring to the fore his or her capacity for introspection. How much do these feelings emanate from past and possibly unpleasant experiences? How might they affect my judgment about the patient who is being evaluated currently? Such self-awareness will help reestablish objectivity. "I know that this patient reminds me of Mrs. J, but she is not Mrs. J, so give her another chance."

If the evaluator is unable to overcome such countertransference feelings, a consultation with a supervisor or colleague is in order. A presentation to an intake conference can also be helpful. If the evaluator is in private practice, a second opinion is of the essence.

When I was director of the psychiatric clinic of Massachusetts General Hospital, I happened to observe that several female patients who were being described as being "very beautiful," or "attractive" by male trainees had not been properly evaluated. For example, the history taking had not been complete and the criteria for selection had not been elucidated. During the discussions following their presentations, particularly those involving the assessment of the third criterion of selection, it was obvious that countertransference feelings on the part of the evaluators had been aroused by the patients' attractiveness or beauty. A second interview, by a female evaluator, brought to light a very different picture of the patients' psychopathology.

Evaluators must also pay attention to the patient's responses to tentative interpretations. If the patient demonstrates the capacity to associate appropriately by giving specific examples to the interviewer's questions or by bringing additional and pertinent information to some of the confrontations, the evaluation is proceeding smoothly and a working alliance is developing.

I have spent a good deal of time discussing the evaluation of the third criterion for STAPP. The basic transference–countertransference interaction during all forms of brief or long-term psychotherapy—dynamic, cognitive, behavior modification, interpersonal, and on and on—is *the* vital tool for achieving therapeutic change. The third criterion gives us a foretaste of the nature of the transference and is an important indication of the type of therapist–patient relationship that will develop during the course of treatment.

Criterion 4: Being Very Intelligent and Psychologically Minded

Some participants at my workshops have been surprised at the attention paid to the cognitive components of the patients' character structure, such as intelligence. They ask, "How can learning theory, which plays such an important role in behavior modification types of therapy, also be of importance in a short-term psychotherapy based on psychodynamic principles?"

The answer to such a question lies precisely in the value of a combination of both theories, learning and psychodynamic. Both approaches should be utilized flexibly and interchangeably to set into motion the process of self-understanding. Unfortunately, this point has not been made very clearly to our trainees. Psychology trainees are usually more familiar with learning theory; psychiatric residents and social work students, at least in my experience, are usually better acquainted with psychodynamic theory. One may expect a slant to appear in the evaluation of patients, depending on the background of the trainee, in favor of one or the other of these orientations. Both aspects are important. They may appear together: the resolution of a mathematical problem that involves considerable cognitive effort is usually followed by a profound emotional response. Evaluators therefore must be aware of the relationship between the two theoretical orientations, as well as of their own preference for one or the other.

Good candidates for STAPP are usually psychologically sophisticated individuals with a highly developed capacity to deal with complicated concepts. Experience with well-educated patients may play an important role in the way in which evaluators expect to deal with them. It also may bias them against less well-educated people who are not apparently sophisticated psychologically. What should the evaluator look for to assess the fourth selection criterion?

The patient's response to tentative confrontations and classifications plays the most important role in assessing this criterion. David Malan (1976) has elaborated his patients' responses during evaluation for his brief dynamic psychotherapy and considers them to be a criterion of selection in themselves.

Another important task for the evaluator is to pay special attention to the patient's language. A highly psychologically minded and well-educated patient is expected to use sophisticated language. But sophisticated language may not be a clear indication of psychological mindedness. Some people hear terms used on television or radio and use them without really comprehending their meaning.

Patients labeled alexithymic may use sophisticated language without being psychologically minded. These people have an affect deficit, in other words, an inability to associate fantasies and thoughts with their emotions and to describe them. Lacking the feelings and the words to express them, such individuals find themselves needing to act impulsively; they endlessly describe events surrounding an emotion (an emotion is defined as a biological state that can be aroused by stimulations of various limbic nuclei). In sum, they are stimulus-bound. Being vaguely aware of their deficits, they feel alienated from the world of people who talk about their feelings, and they tend to seek solutions for their isolation and loneliness by excessive use of drugs or alcohol. They are also prone to developing psychosomatic illnesses. Finally, they may try to use language they do not really comprehend. Such patients are encountered quite often in psychiatric and medical practices.

In the following vignette an evaluator deals with such an alexithymic patient during the psychiatric evaluation interview.

A sixty-year-old businessman had been admitted to the hospital complaining of difficulty in swallowing. The symptom arose a few months after his retirement. The internist, having ruled out every conceivable cause for this symptom, had decided that it could have a psychological etiology. He decided therefore to release the patient and referred him for a psychiatric evaluation. The psychiatrist who saw him speculated that the symptom was associated with the patient's retirement and that it represented a form of masked depression. Yet despite his repeated efforts to identify an emotional conflict that may have been associated with the patient's retirement, the psychiatrist failed to do so. The patient insisted that he had been looking forward to retirement and had been in fine health except for his swallowing difficulty. Still believing that the patient suffered masked depression, the psychiatrist placed him on antidepressant medication—but without success. When the patient was seen after a month and reported no improvement in his symptom, the psychiatrist recommended a second psychiatric opinion and referred him to the psychiatric clinic of a general hospital.

At the outset of the interview with the second psychiatrist, the patient described in great detail his experience with the internist, mentioning all the tests that had been done. He eventually talked about the first psychiatrist.

> PATIENT: I saw that doctor at the advice of my internist. You know, I thought that it was unnecessary because I was sure that I had no emotional difficulties, but he insisted, so of course I made an appointment.
> EVALUATOR: How did you feel seeing a psychiatrist, since you did not think that you needed to see one?
> PATIENT: Oh, since my internist wanted me to have a consultation, I was perfectly happy to do it.
> EVALUATOR: Were you pleased about it?
> PATIENT: I followed my internist's instructions.
> EVALUATOR: So, what happened?
> PATIENT: Well, the psychiatrist felt that I may be "introjecting" or

some word like that and this was the way that I had developed my dysphagia following my retirement. As far as I was concerned, I thought that all this psychiatric jargon had nothing to do with this physical symptom of mine. The psychiatrist continued to have theories he wanted to explore. Once, he told me, "You might be displacing your negative feelings on your esophagus while experiencing pleasure at being retired." Really, now! The only thing that I knew was that I had this unpleasant problem with my swallowing and that I was glad to have retired. Introjections, displacements, and all that stuff is Greek to me.

EVALUATOR: I see that you describe very well what took place, but I don't hear much about your feelings about this unpleasant situation.

PATIENT: But, doctor, I told you.

EVALUATOR: You described to me what transpired, but you did not tell me anything about your feelings. For example, did you feel annoyed that both of your caretakers had failed to help you?

PATIENT: Annoyed? Oh, I forgot to tell you that the psychiatrist put me on antidepressant medication. It was Elavil. I took 75 milligrams, then he increased it to 150, but that did not help. He is now considering an MAO inhibitor.

EVALUATOR: So you had another therapeutic failure. How did you feel about it?

PATIENT: Yes, that was another failure. Now you ask how I feel. I want the symptom to go away.

EVALUATOR: Of course, but how do you feel since the symptom persists?

PATIENT: But I told you I want it to go away. [The patient again describes all the laboratory tests his internist performed, then, switching to the psychiatrist, he repeats the Elavil story.]

EVALUATOR: *(Interrupting)* You have told me all this before. Didn't you feel frustrated by all these failures?

PATIENT: Of course.

EVALUATOR: Fine. Now what did you think when you were frustrated?

PATIENT: I told you that I wanted the symptom to be relieved.

EVALUATOR: Only that?

PATIENT: Yes.

EVALUATOR: Didn't you feel annoyed with the internist or the psychiatrist for not being able to help you? Didn't you worry that there might be something more serious? Did you have thoughts like that? [The evaluator is offering possibilities to encourage the patient to provide him with some information.]

PATIENT: I don't know what you mean. All this is for the doctors to think about. I am dependent on them.

EVALUATOR: *(Becoming frustrated)* Have you ever felt worried about anything?

PATIENT: Yes.

EVALUATOR: What do you think at such times?

PATIENT: What to do. Action.

EVALUATOR: Have you ever felt angry?

PATIENT: Rarely.

EVALUATOR: What are your thoughts when you are angry?

PATIENT: Thoughts—I don't have any. I take action.

It should be clear from this vignette that the psychiatrist fails to get the patient to talk about any fantasies or thoughts that he may have in reference to his emotions. The only thing the evaluator hears repeatedly is that the patient wants symptom relief; that plea does not give him any clues to the patient's difficulty. The evaluator feels frustrated, but he persists in his efforts to find an underlying emotional conflict responsible for the patient's symptom.

EVALUATOR: Was there anything specific which took place at the time of your retirement?

PATIENT: No.

EVALUATOR: Did you discuss it with your wife, for example?

PATIENT: No. My wife knew about it. I simply told her that I was planning to retire. She asked me some questions, but I said that it was my decision and that was that. She said it was OK with her.

EVALUATOR: Did you have any conflicts with anyone at work?

PATIENT: Now look, doctor. I worked hard all my life. I needed some rest.

EVALUATOR: Of course. Did you think about all the nice things that you could do when you retired?

PATIENT: No. I just thought I'd play a lot of golf.

EVALUATOR: Do you?

PATIENT: Yes.

EVALUATOR: Are you getting frustrated by all my questions?

PATIENT: Frustrated? No, you have a job to do and that is all. Maybe *you* are frustrated and you displace it on me.

EVALUATOR: I am impressed with your knowledge of psychiatric terms.

PATIENT: I learn quickly.

It is clear from this exchange that the evaluator is getting nowhere. It is also obvious that the patient uses sophisticated language; he is intelligent, but he is not psychologically minded. For the fourth STAPP criterion we are looking not only for intellectual capability but also for psychological mindedness. This patient passes the first test but fails the second.

Now consider the opposite situation: poorly educated patients who do not use sophisticated language to describe their difficulties. In such a case the evaluator must try to educate the patient about the nature of the psychotherapeutic interaction. On occasion an apparently unsophisticated or even illiterate patient may grasp very quickly what the evaluator is trying to explain about the nature of psychotherapy; the person may soon demonstrate the potential to become psychologically minded.

A poorly educated fifty-year-old woman who was mildly depressed about the prospect of facing a forced relocation from her apartment came to the clinic asking for medication to make her feel better. The evaluator explained to her that it might help if she were to talk about her feelings regarding the prospective move.

PATIENT: Oh, doctor, I am so glad you said that. I told my mother I don't need any pills, but she insisted that I had to come to get some. You see, she can't understand that I love this neighborhood where we live. We lived here all our lives. Now the city is relocating everyone. I don't know where all my friends will go. They say to the suburbs. We are poor—where am I going to find the money to go to see Janet, Sue, Joe, and all my friends? I am sad because I don't know how we can make it in the suburbs. I won't have anyone to talk with. My mother is old and does not understand. If I can come and talk about all that and about the relocation, I will be glad to. Thank you for understanding my problem.

The fulfillment of the fourth STAPP selection criterion requires both intelligence and psychological mindedness, the two basic ingredients of true psychological sophistication. The fourth criterion does not exclude patients who are older, poorer, or of lower status; those with physical symptomatology should also not be excluded. If patients from these groups are appropriately selected and treated, they too will achieve good results.

Criterion 5: Motivation for Change

The fifth selection criterion for STAPP is motivation for *change.* I have long been struck by patients' willingness to experience the unpleasant feelings related to their problems because they were convinced that the process was the only way to overcome the problems. Patients exhibit a considerable and active insistence on working to understand the emotional conflicts that underlie their difficulties, rather than sitting passively and expecting their therapists to cure them magically.

Other investigators in the field of short-term dynamic therapy, including Malan (1963, 1976), one of the pioneers in this area, consider this criterion essential. In his earliest work he defines motivation as a selection criterion for his brief dynamic psychotherapy; later he equates "motivation for insight" with our "motivation for change." He also (1976) emphasizes "motivation for insight being of value particularly if it is judged during the first four sessions, because as selection criteria, neither severity of pathology nor chronicity of symptoms seem to be contraindications in themselves."

Malan's observations correspond closely with my own findings. I view motivation for change as a problem-solving process that is based on the patient's curiosity, ability to recognize that the problems are psychological, participation actively in the treatment process, introspection, honesty, and willingness to explore and experiment. In addition, realistic expectations of the outcome of the psychotherapy and a demonstrated ability to make tangible sacrifices to achieve it are important components of this process. These components of motivation for change constitute in themselves subcriteria for assessing it during the first evaluation interview as well as for observing fluctuations during the course of the psychotherapy. It should also be pointed out that motivation for change is essential for the success of all kinds of psychotherapies, including psychoanalysis and other long-term therapies.

Motivation for change is associated with creativity and with a capacity for self-entertainment. This criterion represents a powerful drive to alter an unpleasant environment or an unsatisfactory lifestyle and propels a person forward to seek new solutions and broader horizons, even at the cost of some distress. Motivated patients in therapy are willing to experience some pain in the process of extricating themselves from the neurotic chains that tie them down and that keep them from expanding and using their talents.

Because motivation for change may fluctuate during the course of therapy, it should be monitored carefully by the therapist. Remaining high or increasing from one session to another is a good prognostic sign. On the other hand, any decrease is an ominous sign. For example, among fifty-three homogeneous patients who were treated by both short-term and long-term psychotherapies by a variety of therapists, thirty-six achieved successful psychotherapeutic results. Of these, 71 percent were rated as having good to excellent motivation for change (Sifneos 1971). From these and similar observations with STAPP patients, it was concluded that of the five STAPP selection criteria, motivation for change is probably the most important for prognosis of a successful outcome.

How does an evaluator assess motivation for change? He or she should assess the seven subcriteria:

1. Willingness to participate actively in the evaluation process
2. Honesty in reporting about oneself
3. Ability to recognize that the difficulties are of a psychological origin
4. Introspection and curiosity about oneself
5. Openness to new ideas and willingness to change, explore, and experiment
6. Realistic expectation of the outcome
7. Willingness to make a tangible sacrifice

In assessing these seven subcriteria the evaluator does not have to follow a rigid schedule of questioning. It is better to try to obtain a general impression of the patient's overall psychological functioning and insight into his or her difficulties. If the evaluator follows such an approach throughout the evaluation interview, he or she will be able to assess the seven subcriteria and form an overall impression of the patient's willingness to tackle difficult issues. In addition, the patient's ability to withstand discomfort and eagerness to seek solutions will point to motivation for change.

Certain types of questions will help the evaluator in assessing motivation for change:

- "Are you here on your own volition or at someone else's recommendation?"

- "Do you want to participate actively and answer my questions truthfully?"
- "Are you willing to discuss with me your emotional difficulties, even if it is difficult for you?"
- "Even if some of my questions seem unpleasant, are you prepared to answer them freely?"
- "Are you determined to talk honestly about yourself, even if it is somewhat embarrassing to you?"

Positive answers would indicate that the patient fulfills the first and second subcriteria for motivation for change. For the third, the ability to recognize that the difficulties are psychological in origin, the following sorts of question may be useful.

- "Do you think that your headaches are associated with the fights that you have with your relatives?"
- "Do your relationships with other people have any connection with the kinds of problems that make you seek help?"
- "Does your personality play any role in the kinds of difficulties that bring you here?"

Affirmative answers to such questions will demonstrate that the third subcriterion has been fulfilled.

Introspection and curiosity about oneself, the fourth subcriterion, can easily be assessed by the way in which the patient responds to some of the points that are discussed during the evaluation interview. The evaluator can be alert to these types of responses:

- "I have been trying to figure out why I behave the way I do under the circumstances that I have described to you."
- "I try to understand why I think and act the way I do."
- "Do I respond to others in some unusual way?"
- "When I'm having trouble, I withdraw from people and try to figure out for myself what's wrong."

The evaluator simply should be alert to evidence of the patient's self-examination.

To assess the patient's openness to new ideas and willingness to explore and to experiment, again the evaluator will gain a general impression of the patient's functioning. Appropriate responses to confrontations and clarifications will denote whether the patient is indeed

43

open to new ideas. The dynamic evaluator synthesizes information and presents it back to the patient in the form of confrontations and clarifications. These at first may appear to be alien, paradoxical, or downright absurd. If the patient is willing to consider them rather than reject them right away, the patient is most likely able to explore new ways of thinking, experiment with ideas, and take risks. The patient who handles confrontation and clarification well shows courage and strength of character.

The assessment of the patient's realistic expectations for the outcome of therapy is straightforward. The evaluator may ask something like this:

- "Assuming that your treatment is successful, what kind of person do you expect to be?"

Some patients do not answer realistically.

A thirty-five-year-old man was asked what he expected to achieve as the result of his treatment. He answered that he would like to be a concert pianist. When asked how many years he had studied the piano, he answered that he had never played the piano, but that he had always had a dream of doing so and being applauded by a large audience. He added: "It was always my dream. I hope that this therapy will help me overcome my inertia, learn how to play the piano, and achieve my life's ambition." This man certainly did not fulfill the sixth subcriterion of motivation for change.

On the other hand, another person who is asked the same question may respond as follows:

- "I realize as I have been talking about my problems today that I have complained about a variety of difficulties. Now, thinking about your question, I believe that the trouble I have with women in authority is the problem from which all the others follow. So I am willing to try to look into this difficulty, even if it causes me some discomfort, and I am confident that I'll overcome it once and for all."

Such an answer shows an ability to be realistic and a willingness to experience a certain degree of pain. It may be concluded, therefore, that this person demonstrates a willingness to change.

Other types of questions that may help patients specify clearly their expectations include the following:

- "Assuming that we could disentangle only this one chief difficulty out of your various complaints, would you be satisfied?"
- "Although you have asked for help with your procrastination, which has caused you so much trouble, in my opinion the difficulty in your relationships with your mother and your wife seems to be more important than the procrastination. In that case, do you want to try to disentangle these conflicts even if your symptom, which may be due to a different set of emotional conflicts, still persists?"

A patient who had been asked the second question acknowledged that he could recognize as a result of his discussion with the evaluator that his relationship with his wife was clearly a major problem in his life:

- "This procrastination of mine, which I complained about and which brought me to see you, may or may not be related to these interpersonal difficulties. If it is and it goes away, so much the better. If not, well, I have managed to live with it for a long time, so I can live with it a little longer. The problems with my wife now seem to have top priority, and I am willing to work to get rid of them here."

An answer of this sort points to an ability to compromise, to settle for less, to become less grandiose and more realistic.

The last subcriterion for motivation for change—the willingness to make a tangible sacrifice to overcome the difficulties that brought the patient for psychotherapy—is by far the easiest one to evaluate. Three areas can be used as a test of this subcriterion. The first is the patient's cooperation in finding an appropriate and convenient time to meet with the therapist. It is possible that an occasional problem may arise; yet if both patient and therapist are flexible, even at the cost of some inconvenience, then they both demonstrate evidence of an ability to compromise. The second area is financial. How much money is the patient willing to sacrifice to try to ameliorate emotional problems? How much is potential relief worth, even with no guarantees? Both clinics and private therapists usually have a sliding scale of fees to fit with their patients' finances. If a patient is unwilling to pay a realistic fee for professional services, perhaps the person is reluctant to become involved in the process of disentangling problems; the patient's motivation for change will be questionable.

The third area applies in psychiatric clinics of university teaching hospitals. Patients may be asked to participate in research. Thus, giving informed consent, spending time answering questionnaires, cooperating in additional interviews at no charge, or allowing sessions or interviews to be videotaped are tangible sacrifices and will satisfy the seventh subcriterion.

The subcriteria for motivation for change can be easily scored. Each fulfilled subcriterion is assigned 1 point. A score of 7 signifies that the patient has an excellent motivation for change; 6 is considered good, and 5 is fair. Any score below 5 is viewed as poor and the patient is thought to be unmotivated. For STAPP we accept only patients who have a score of 6 or 7.

The evaluator who has assessed the presenting complaints, has taken a systematic developmental history, and has determined that the patient fulfills the five criteria for selection must specify a dynamic focus around which the therapy will revolve and must present it to the patient for his or her agreement.

CHAPTER 4

The Dynamic Focus

Establishing a dynamic focus constitutes the fourth basic task of the STAPP evaluator. The task for the evaluator is to use information provided by the patient to arrive at a dynamic formulation of the nuclear conflict underlying the patient's psychological difficulties. The dynamic focus is an indication of the evaluator's capability to pull together seemingly unrelated pieces of information about the patient's past events, fantasies, memories, behaviors, actions, and so on, and to synthesize them into a meaningful whole.

The formulation is similar to the physician's diagnosis, reached after the practitioner has taken a medical history, performed a physical exam, and collected the results of appropriate laboratory tests. On the basis of this diagnosis a specific medical or surgical treatment, which is expected to relieve the patient's symptoms and perhaps cure the underlying illness, will be proposed to the patient.

Dynamic focus may be referred to by a different name: James Mann (1973), the developer of time-limited psychotherapy, calls it the central issue. All of us who work with brief dynamic psychotherapies agree that a focus is a basic prerequisite for such treatment. Although some differences exist in the way investigators go about arriving at a dynamic focus, these differences are mostly technical.

For example, others emphasize in a similar fashion gathering and synthesizing important and relevant information. The meaning of *impor-*

tant and relevant needs clarification. Experienced therapists tend to consider that everything that the patient says is relevant; it is easy to get bogged down, since some of the patient's communications may represent resistance to revealing information because it is anxiety provoking. It is important for the STAPP evaluator to recognize evasion on the part of the patient and to keep in mind the selection criteria. If the patient seems likely to be an appropriate candidate for STAPP, the evaluator should confront the patient with anxiety-provoking questions, avoid the patient's resistance to dealing with dynamic conflicts, and encourage the patient to face feelings, however painful. The patient's response to such challenges will signify whether a working alliance is developing. If motivated for change, the patient will overcome any hesitancy and concentrate on the resolution of his or her basic psychological difficulties.

A male patient had spent a great deal of his time trying to impress his evaluator with his mother's total rejection of him and her preference for his younger brother. He spoke with such vehemence about his feelings about his mother's "unreasonable behavior" that he made the psychiatric resident who was evaluating him question whether the patient was able to fulfill the second STAPP selection criterion—having had a meaningful relationship during childhood.

When the patient was seen by a senior psychiatrist for a second evaluation he again repeated that his mother had always rejected him and disapproved of him. It appeared to the evaluator, however, that the patient's criticism of his mother might be exaggerated. He decided, therefore, to explore that possibility.

> EVALUATOR: I understand that you had a bad time with your mother as a youngster, but I wonder if there was any time when you felt close to her or you thought that she might love you?
>
> PATIENT: *(Looking thoughtful, then smiling)* Well, you see, I remember an interesting episode. My mother was in the hospital for an operation, and my father and I went to visit her. My mother was happy to see us. She said, "I am glad that you came to see me. I thought that your brother would also come, but he called to say that he was too busy with his new job." She also said that she wished that he was as thoughtful as I was and would grow up to be like me.
>
> EVALUATOR: So, if your mother was happy with your visit, that means that she did not always reject you as you said.

PATIENT: Of course she was happy with my visit, but that took place only once.

EVALUATOR: Are you sure about that?

PATIENT: *(Looking sheepish)* Well, I do remember another time. While we were eating dinner my mother reproached my younger brother about his bad table manners, and she said, "Look at John [the patient]. He always has impeccable table manners—"

EVALUATOR: *(Interrupting)* For someone who was "always" rejected by your mother, you give me two excellent examples of your mother's approval of you.

PATIENT: OK.

EVALUATOR: Then let me put it this way. Is it possible that although your mother rejected you most of the time, she also loved and respected you, but that you have exaggerated her nasty behavior only to avoid your own positive feelings for her?

PATIENT: *(Looking thoughtful)* Maybe.

EVALUATOR: If so, can we concentrate on trying to understand all the aspects of your mother's behavior in reference to you, and not to see only the negative features which you emphasized so strongly? As I have already mentioned, you tend to exaggerate them.

PATIENT: OK. I'm willing to give it a trial.

From this example what constitute the relevant information are the examples that the patient produces in reference to his mother's behavior, and they shed light on the patient's insistence that he was "always rejected."

Edmond Gilliéron (1983), the preeminent Swiss developer of a brief psychotherapy based on analytic principles, uses a free-associative approach and allows the patients to formulate their own focus. Brusset (1983) "negotiates" a focus with his patients in the first two initial evaluation interviews. Habib Davanloo (1978) establishes "multiple foci." Some practitioners modify the focus as the psychotherapy progresses. All these differences, however, are relatively minor. Most therapists assume the responsibility of establishing the dynamic focus and presenting it to the patient for agreement.

In STAPP, because so much time has been spent on obtaining a systematic developmental history as well as on evaluating the patient according to selection criteria, once a dynamic has been established, the evaluator feels relatively sure that the focus to be communicated to the patient is the right one. Otherwise the evaluation process has been faulty.

In one of my books (Sifneos 1972), I compare the process of arriving at a formulation of the dynamic focal conflicts with putting together a jigsaw puzzle. It is an analytic-synthetic process. The patients have available to them all the pieces of the puzzle in terms of events, memories, fantasies, interactions, conflicts, feelings, patterns of behavior, and so on, but they are unable to synthesize them into a meaningful whole. The evaluator, on the other hand, by virtue of being not emotionally involved and having professional experience, is able to arrive at a formulation of the dynamic focus that can be presented to the patient for eventual resolution through joint effort.

Arriving at the correct focus and being able to help the patient concentrate on the emotional conflicts underlying it are usually associated with a successful outcome. In addition to presenting the focus to a potential STAPP candidate, the evaluator writes down criteria for outcome (that is, criteria that will demonstrate that the treatment is successful). Such information will turn out to be very helpful to whoever sees the patient in a follow-up interview; the findings of the follow-up interview can be compared with the criteria that were specified by the intake evaluator.

If an evaluator is unable to arrive at a dynamic focus after one or two interviews (three should be the maximum), the patient is probably too disturbed to face an anxiety-provoking type of psychotherapy.

Both Malan (1976) and I (Sifneos 1972, 1987) have discovered during our investigations of the results of short-term psychotherapies that focality plays a crucial role not only during the evaluation but also during the whole course of treatment. Malan (1976) furthermore emphasized that for selection neither severity of pathology nor chronicity of symptoms seemed to be contraindications in themselves; the only criterion of value was motivation for insight. Later he noted that "focality is highly related to outcome and is also related to motivation in a meaningful way." He concluded that "high motivation and high focality tended to lead to a short successful therapy."

If the evaluator can formulate a focus at the end of the evaluation interview and can observe that the patient responds appropriately to such a formulation, then a working alliance has been established between the two participants. This interchange also shows that the patient will be able to use this type of focal interaction during the course of the therapy; thus the patient is a good candidate for STAPP.

The foci that have been found to respond best to brief dynamic psychotherapies relate to unresolved oedipal or triangular relationships, grief reactions, and loss and separation difficulties.

The oedipal focus is a very common one. Yet the investigation of the vital role played by the Oedipus complex in the psychic life of every-one—which was dramatized by Sophocles and rediscovered by Freud—seems to have decreased during the past forty years. It is possible that Loewald's discovery of the early psychotic core of the Oedipus complex has discouraged interest in understanding its more adult and normal components. Furthermore, many people have a need to avoid the anxie-ties that may be aroused in dealing with the more adult components, which present to everyone the dilemma of having to choose one parent at the expense of the other when both are loved and admired. Interest in earlier, remote experiences can act as justification to avoid the difficult choices that complicate our adult lives.

There are certain subtle differences even in patients who are selected to receive STAPP and whose focus is an unresolved oedipal conflict. Patients who have an attachment for the parent of the opposite sex only in their own fantasies achieve the best results. Patients whose parent of the opposite sex was somewhat seductive, or at least demonstrated favoritism toward the patient, were somewhat more difficult to treat. Patients whose parent of the same sex had disappeared through death, separation, or divorce were the most difficult ones to help.

In all groups motivation for change helps patients overcome their conflicts with the help of their therapists.

The establishment of a focus is difficult to describe because the psychopathology of each case varies to a considerable extent. There are no particular types of questions to ask. Instead, the evaluator's ability to synthesize is vital for arriving at a dynamic focus. Other characteristics that are necessary include open mindedness, the motivation to learn about a new and somewhat difficult type of psychotherapy, and a thorough knowledge of psychodynamic theory. Both evaluators and therapists need these qualities.

The focus the evaluator decides on may not necessarily be associated with the presenting complaints that brought the patient to therapy. For example, the patient's symptoms may be only surface phenomena of a more basic disturbance in interpersonal relations. Once it has been understood, worked through, and resolved, the presenting symptoms may also be eliminated.

Finally, as mentioned already, the evaluator must present to the patient his or her formulation of the dynamic focus and of their agree-ment to work cooperatively at the resolution of the conflicts underlying it. Such an agreement constitutes the fifth and final component of the psychiatric evaluation process.

The following statements may be used by an evaluator to get the patient's agreement.

- "As a result of what we have talked about, it seems to me that there is a pattern of losses in your life which seem to dominate your relations, particularly with women. Are you willing to work on this subject during the course of brief dynamic psychotherapy?"
- "I think that your relations with your mother, which you described as distant and aloof, color your relations with women in general and your wife in particular. Are you willing to work on this subject in an effort to improve your relations with your wife?"
- "Your academic difficulties and your anxiety about them seem to be associated with your earlier experiences with your authoritative father. Do you agree, and are you willing to work on them?"
- "Although your phobias about flying may not be helped by brief psychotherapy, I am confident that the emotional conflicts relating to your interactions with men is a problem that deserves your special attention. Are you willing to work on it, even if your flying phobia persists?"

The patient's agreement to work on the resolution of such emotional conflicts denotes that a great deal has been accomplished during the evaluation interview and that a working alliance has been established.

Clinical examples of particular interventions to illustrate the evaluation of selection criteria as well as the establishment of a dynamic focus will be presented in the next three chapters.

CHAPTER 5

The Anxious Patient Who Lost Her Father: An Evaluation Interview

A THIRTY-FIVE-YEAR-OLD WOMAN who agreed to be video-taped came to the psychiatric clinic complaining of a variety of psychological problems. She was interviewed in front of an intake group after having been seen by a student social worker who had asked the consultant of the team to interview the patient so that the two of them could compare their impressions. The student mentioned that the patient had an older brother, and it appeared ostensibly that she had come to the clinic seeking help because she had become anxious after having found out about four months before that her mother was suffering from a serious illness.

The patient was rather tall and had a pleasant and somewhat sad face.

EVALUATOR: Good afternoon. I understand you have agreed to be videotaped and you have signed our informed consent form.

PATIENT: Yes. It is a bit embarrassing, but it is OK.

EVALUATOR: Thank you for coming also to our intake conference. I shall be asking you some questions so that we can evaluate your difficulties. It is important that you speak freely about your experiences and your feelings. Is this all right by you?

PATIENT: Yes, that is OK. I am eager to look into my problems and try to solve them with your help. [The patient already alludes to the possibility of working cooperatively with her therapist, indicating potential for a working alliance.]

53

EVALUATOR: So could you please tell us what made you decide to come to our psychiatric clinic? What is your basic problem?
PATIENT: I have been anxious. Maybe there are other problems.
EVALUATOR: When did you become anxious?
PATIENT: Oh, about last September.
EVALUATOR: Why did you come now?
PATIENT: My mother's illness precipitated my coming.
EVALUATOR: How long ago did you find out that your mother was ill?
PATIENT: About four months ago.
EVALUATOR: So why did you delay coming for so long?
PATIENT: Well, my mother's illness may have played a role in my coming, but these feelings existed before I found out that she was ill. As I told you, these feelings started last September. I had a job. I was finishing the work for my degree in college. Everything was OK. I had a good relationship with my boyfriend.
EVALUATOR: And then you became anxious. Now that is a paradox, isn't it?
PATIENT: It seems to be.
EVALUATOR: Now, let me see. You became anxious in September, when everything seemed to be going well for you. Then your anxiety started to increase after you found out about your mother's illness in December, to the point that you felt you needed help and you come to us today for it. Is this correct?
PATIENT: *(Hesitating)* More or less.
EVALUATOR: You hesitate. Do you think that these anxieties might be due to some physical problem?
PATIENT: Oh no, of course not. I do not think that I have a medical problem. I had a medical checkup recently and I was found to be healthy. This anxiety has something to do with my relating with people, but I don't know exactly how.
EVALUATOR: When did you have a physical exam?
PATIENT: Last month, but everything was all right, as I told you. It was in this hospital, in the medical clinic.
EVALUATOR: OK. Now, let us see, how anxious were you? Was this anxiety more or less continuous, or did you have panic attacks?
PATIENT: No panic attacks.
EVALUATOR: What do you think when you get anxious?
PATIENT: Well, anxiety is what I said, but I also felt irritable. Maybe that's the right word. I felt fatigued. I felt tired all the time. I had mood changes. I was worried.

In his efforts to investigate the onset, duration, and intensity of the patient's symptoms the evaluator is aided by the patient. She clarifies for him that what she thought of as anxiety was one of a variety of symptoms, such as irritability, fatigue, and mood changes. In addition he is presented with a paradox, namely that these symptoms preceded the patient's knowledge about her mother's illness by four months, when everything in her life was going well. So it appears that the timing of the patient's difficulties must be clarified and the paradoxical situation has to be investigated. In an effort to make sure, the evaluator tries to clarify the association of the patient's symptoms with the onset of her mother's illness. The fact that she had a medical checkup reassures the evaluator that the symptoms have a psychological origin.

EVALUATOR: Did you detect anything about your mother between September and December that made you worry about her health?

PATIENT: No, I didn't detect anything at all.

EVALUATOR: So, for the last six months you had a variety of symptoms not related to anything specific, but after you discovered that your mother was ill they became worse, and after you found out that they had no medical etiology you decided to come to the psychiatric clinic for help.

PATIENT: More or less.

EVALUATOR: More or less? What else?

PATIENT: My mother's illness was the precipitating factor. It was the end of my buffer zone *(becoming teary)* sort of . . . I tried so hard to figure out what was going on. I did a lot of thinking about all this, but I got nowhere, so I decided to come here . . . [The patient indicates that she is introspective, which means she is motivated to understand her problem.]

EVALUATOR: You are upset. What are you upset about?

PATIENT: *(Crying)* Well . . .

EVALUATOR: I know that it is difficult to talk about intimate things, in particular in front of a group of people. We appreciate your coming here and talking honestly about your difficulties, but I think that it is best to get them all into the open. [The evaluator, having been confronted with the patient's tears, feels that he has to be supportive, but he also encourages the patient to reveal new information. He also offers the patient a box of tissues.]

PATIENT: Yes, I know. I get upset because I can't control my feelings.

EVALUATOR: Maybe it is best not to have one's feelings in control all the time. Feeling appropriately sad is important, but we must of

55

course try to understand what is making you sad. I think there is more than just "not controlling" your feelings. [The evaluator here continues to be supportive about the expression of sadness, but he also tries to press for more information relating to what may be associated with this tendency to control feelings.]

PATIENT: *(Still crying)* I know that you are right, but as I told you, I thought a lot about all this.

EVALUATOR: I am sure that you did. Is there anything else that makes you sad?

PATIENT: I can't handle my feelings the way I usually did.

EVALUATOR: Handling feelings is one thing, acknowledging them is another. Anything else that comes to your mind? You say that you were in a good relationship with your boyfriend. Is there anything wrong with any of your other relationships? Is it again this issue of control?

PATIENT: I am better on my own, that's what it is.

EVALUATOR: Is that bad?

PATIENT: No, it's not. I am better alone. I have no choices as much as I did. I can think better when I'm alone, but in this way I can't get along as well with my friends as I used to be before.

EVALUATOR: Before? Before what?

PATIENT: Before the onset of these difficulties—during this recent period of time. I remember that I had these problems before, but not as bad. It is very different now.

EVALUATOR: You say before. When was that?

PATIENT: A long time ago. Fifteen years ago.

EVALUATOR: What was happening then?

PATIENT: The circumstances were not the same then. I didn't have a job. I was in Europe. Things were very different. I had left a relationship. I had financial problems. There were many reasons why I might have felt at a loss at that time. I felt lost and anxious.

EVALUATOR: So loss played a role then, as it does now. The potential loss of your mother?

PATIENT: No.

EVALUATOR: No?

PATIENT: This time my relationship with my boyfriend is good.

It is clear that the evaluator's preoccupation with the patient's mother's illness misses the information given to him by the patient. She was talking about the loss of her boyfriend in Europe; the relationship with him was not good, while the relationship with her current boyfriend is good. One wonders if the introduction of the relationship with her boyfriend is significant. The evaluator finally pursues that relationship.

EVALUATOR: Is it because it is good that it is a problem?
PATIENT: I'd hate to think that my problem is because I have a good relationship with my boyfriend . . . Maybe . . .
EVALUATOR: Does it remind you of anything? A good relationship with a man?
PATIENT: I don't know what you mean.
EVALUATOR: A good relationship in the past, when you were a little girl. Did you have a good relationship then?

Having been satisfied that the patient has a circumscribed chief complaint—symptoms she wants most to get rid of, which may be associated with a good or bad relationship—the evaluator is ready to start taking a development history as well as to assess the second criterion for STAPP, the existence of a meaningful relationship in childhood. He is rewarded accordingly.

PATIENT: With my father?
EVALUATOR: What about your father?
PATIENT: I had a very good relationship with my father, but an unreal one. When I was young we had great times together. There were never any problems, no conflicts whatsoever.
EVALUATOR: So, as you say, having a good relationship with your father, did you make any sacrifices for him?
PATIENT: Yes, I'd always—I gave up playing with my girlfriends, which I enjoyed very much, to go to work with my father.
EVALUATOR: Now, if I am not mistaken, you also have an older brother.
PATIENT: Yes, he is six years older than I, and he was always close to my mother.
EVALUATOR: How did you get along with them?
PATIENT: I wasn't close to either of them then.
EVALUATOR: Why?
PATIENT: Because I had my father at that time.
EVALUATOR: What do you mean?
PATIENT: I spent most of my time with my father before I went to school, as well as later on, as I told you. He took me to work with him. He introduced me to his friends.

EVALUATOR: What did he do?

PATIENT: He was a stockbroker.

EVALUATOR: Where was all this? Where were you born?

PATIENT: In Philadelphia.

EVALUATOR: So your father took you to work with him, and you had a good time together.

PATIENT: Yes.

EVALUATOR: Now, you say that you were not close to your mother.

PATIENT: There was no relationship. I didn't need her because I had my father.

EVALUATOR: Was it a bad relationship with her?

PATIENT: No, we were paired off, she with my brother and I with my father.

EVALUATOR: And what about your brother?

PATIENT: Close . . . I guess.

EVALUATOR: Why do you say "I guess"?

PATIENT: It is close now, as well as when I was an adolescent, but not when I was little. It wasn't bad by any means. The usual fights, etc., but it was my father that counted more. He was the most important person in my life.

EVALUATOR: What happened to your father? You said the relationship was "unreal."

PATIENT: He died when I was fourteen.

EVALUATOR: What did he die of?

PATIENT: In an automobile accident. He was hit by a drunken driver. He was killed instantly, just like that.

EVALUATOR: And how did you feel?

PATIENT: (Crying) Devastated.

EVALUATOR: It must have been quite a shock. How did you adapt? [The evaluator is again supportive, but he encourages the patient to go on. He is impressed by her spontaneity, honesty, and ability to express her feelings openly.]

PATIENT: (Continuing to cry) In a year I adjusted, more or less.

EVALUATOR: The rug was pulled out from under your feet. The person with whom you had the best give-and-take relationship as a child suddenly disappeared from your life. Did you become closer to your mother?

PATIENT: No. I became closer to my brother and to my two girlfriends at school. My relations with them were always good. As I told you, my feelings for my brother improved after my father died. My girlfriends were also very helpful to me.

EVALUATOR: Are you still close to them?

PATIENT: Yes, I did a lot for them when they had problems, and they helped me a lot throughout that very difficult period after my father died.

EVALUATOR: [The evaluator is satisfied that the patient has fulfilled both the first and the second criteria of STAPP, so he proceeds with the history taking.] How did you do at school?

PATIENT: Up to that time I was an excellent student.

EVALUATOR: At what time did you have your first menstrual period?

PATIENT: When I was thirteen.

EVALUATOR: So it was before your father died?

PATIENT: Yes.

EVALUATOR: Was there any change in your relationship with your father, since you were becoming an adult?

PATIENT: No, my father always treated me as an adult and not as a child.

EVALUATOR: Were you prepared for your menstrual period?

PATIENT: Yes, by cousins or my friends—I don't remember by whom.

EVALUATOR: Did you have any ideas about sexual matters?

PATIENT: Yes, I did. I had a good idea about sexual matters. I had witnessed several acts in animals—dogs, cats. I knew a lot by the time I was eleven.

EVALUATOR: Did you view yourself as a sexual person?

PATIENT: Yes, I did.

EVALUATOR: Did you view yourself as a sexual partner to someone in particular?

PATIENT: Yes.

EVALUATOR: To whom?

PATIENT: My brother, in play ways.

EVALUATOR: Why your brother? Why not another boy?

PATIENT: I didn't know any boys then.

EVALUATOR: Anyone else?

PATIENT: Probably—*(hesitating)*—my father.

EVALUATOR: Did you?

PATIENT: Yes. Yes, I did.

EVALUATOR: OK. Then that experience is also taken away from you. The good times with your father as a little girl are taken away, and now that you become a sexual person at thirteen or fourteen, that is also taken away by his untimely death. So you were left with a terrible loss.

PATIENT: Devastated . . . I was repulsed by sex for a while after my father died. *(Cries)*

EVALUATOR: I see. Now, how were things later on? Did you continue to be a good student?

PATIENT: Yes.

EVALUATOR: And you said you were closer to your brother at that time.

PATIENT: Yes, for two years before he went into the service.

EVALUATOR: So you also lost your brother when you were getting close to him, not exactly in the same way as you lost your father, but a loss nevertheless. He went away. You couldn't see him anymore. That was a second loss.

PATIENT: Yes. I was very fond of my brother then, especially since I was not close to my mother.

EVALUATOR: So we see a pattern of losses taking place. [The evaluator is seeking to establish a tentative focus of losses, particularly since by now it appears to be fairly clear that the patient fulfills STAPP's first four criteria. She appears to be interacting very well with the evaluator and she seems to be very psychologically sophisticated.]

EVALUATOR: Did you have any boyfriends after your brother left?

PATIENT: Yes, I did. I had several boyfriends. I had my first boyfriend when I was five.

EVALUATOR: So you started early? Were there sexual relations later on?

PATIENT: Yes, with some of them.

EVALUATOR: Were they satisfactory?

PATIENT: No, nothing—there was nothing special.

EVALUATOR: Did you go to college?

PATIENT: Yes, I did. At eighteen I had my first adult relationship, but it lasted only three months. That was long for me.

EVALUATOR: Why do you say that?

PATIENT: Because all my relationships were short-lived.

EVALUATOR: Was it because you expected them to end prematurely? [The evaluator tries to tie the pattern of the patient's short-term relationships to her trying to avoid the repetition of the pain of the loss of her father and brother.] Were you afraid that you would be abandoned, as you were by your father and your brother?

PATIENT: I suppose so.

EVALUATOR: You seem to agree with me. You don't have to. I mention these things because I seem to see a pattern of losses developing which may have had an impact on your current life. If you

60

disagree, however, let me know. It's OK. [The evaluator, to under-score the therapist–patient relationship, tries to undermine the patient's slightly passive streak.]

PATIENT: I haven't thought about these things in a long time.

EVALUATOR: It is important to think about these things. This is the reason why you are here.

PATIENT: Yes, of course. I am open to possibilities I have not consid-ered. I had looked at my father and brother separately, but you point out that I reacted in a similar way to my separation from them. That makes sense.

EVALUATOR: Well, to recapitulate, you seem to have had two very close relationships with men. The first and most important is with your father. It ends catastrophically. The second is with your brother. It is not as intense but it is also good, and it also ends. He goes away. From then on all your relationships with your boy-friends are short term. Do you have brief relationships to protect yourself from another loss? [The evaluator recapitulates.]

PATIENT: Yes, that's what happened at college.

EVALUATOR: What happened afterward? Did you continue to do well academically?

PATIENT: No. I felt that I was not interested in what was going on. I didn't do anything.

EVALUATOR: That's peculiar, when you had been such a good student in high school. Now, what were your relationships like while you were at college?

PATIENT: They were all short-term relationships.

EVALUATOR: Sexual relations?

PATIENT: Yes, with people who had been my friends previously.

EVALUATOR: What was your relationship with your brother and your mother like at that time?

PATIENT: My brother was in the army and then he got married and lived in the South. I saw him very rarely. My mother and I were not at all close. It involved my freedom.

EVALUATOR: What about?

PATIENT: My growing up. My sexuality.

EVALUATOR: Did your mother disapprove of your sexuality?

PATIENT: Oh yes, of course—if she understood anything about it.

EVALUATOR: Would your mother be very disapproving if she knew some of your sexual views we have been talking about?

PATIENT: Oh yes, she would.

EVALUATOR: When did you graduate from college?

PATIENT: I didn't. I dropped out after my sophomore year. I did nothing academically. I just finished my college work last summer; I went back to college two years ago.

EVALUATOR: So what did you do during the intervening fifteen years?

PATIENT: At twenty-one I went to Europe. I traveled around for a year. I worked off and on. It felt incredibly therapeutic. I was alone. I knew no one.

EVALUATOR: So you were happy to disappear?

PATIENT: Yes, exactly.

EVALUATOR: Were you looking for anyone?

PATIENT: No, I don't think so.

EVALUATOR: Are you sure?

PATIENT: (Starts to cry)

EVALUATOR: Where was your father from?

PATIENT: Sweden (continues to cry).

EVALUATOR: Where did you go in Europe?

PATIENT: All over—France, Germany, Italy, Greece—all over. I went even to Turkey. I went as far as I could.

EVALUATOR: But you didn't go to Sweden?

PATIENT: Of course I did.

EVALUATOR: Let's leave all the other countries out. What happened in Sweden?

PATIENT: It felt like home, despite the fact that my Swedish was very poor. I had several relatives there.

EVALUATOR: When you were in Sweden, was your father in your mind?

PATIENT: Yes, all the time.

EVALUATOR: Was your father born in Sweden?

PATIENT: Yes, in Stockholm. A great deal of my knowledge about Stockholm and about Sweden came from him. We went there when I was seven years old.

EVALUATOR: When did you come back here?

The evaluator, with his question about "looking for someone," has hit the jackpot. Not only does he arouse a great deal of affect from the patient but he also ties it to feelings for her father. Now he has the task of helping the patient understand her current psychological difficulties and symptoms and tie them to these past experiences.

PATIENT: I came back, but I didn't want to come back.

EVALUATOR: Why did you?

PATIENT: Because I was with a friend who wanted to come back.

EVALUATOR: What kind of a relationship did you have with this friend of yours?

PATIENT: It was a sexual relationship. But at first it was a friendship. It was good at first.

EVALUATOR: How did it end?

PATIENT: In a stupid way. We came back here and we both had a bad LSD trip. He was on drugs. It was a stupid move. The LSD trip was the precipitating factor. The relationship started to deteriorate after it became sexual.

EVALUATOR: So it had to end like the others?

PATIENT: Yes.

EVALUATOR: How old was your boyfriend?

PATIENT: Six months younger than I was.

EVALUATOR: What about other relationships during the last thirteen years?

PATIENT: They were all the same. They all lasted a short while. I had another one with someone who was also a little younger. It was a strange relationship.

EVALUATOR: Strange?

PATIENT: Well, he was addicted to drugs. I didn't realize it. After that ended, I had a lot of very short ones. All involved friends with whom I had sex, but it ruined the friendship.

EVALUATOR: Who ended these relationships?

PATIENT: Me. I always made the first move.

EVALUATOR: So you didn't want to get involved?

PATIENT: Yes.

EVALUATOR: What about this present relationship? You said it was a good one.

PATIENT: I've never seen anyone older during the past thirteen years. I've always picked younger guys because it was safer. My current boyfriend is older than I. He is nice.

EVALUATOR: How much older?

PATIENT: Six years.

EVALUATOR: Is this a sexual experience?

PATIENT: We were friends and then it became sexual.

EVALUATOR: So, is it going to be ruined now? You said that after a relationship becomes sexual the friendship is ruined. Isn't that what you said?

PATIENT: Yes. I am doing my best not to ruin it, but I don't know.

EVALUATOR: There is something very intriguing here. All your relationships were with younger men and they were short-term ones.

Your current boyfriend is older. Six years older—exactly your brother's age. Have you thought about it this way?

PATIENT: Now that you bring it up, it's so obvious. How can I be so incredibly dumb?

EVALUATOR: You are harsh on yourself. You are not fair to yourself. It is easier for an outsider like me to look into these extremely emotionally laden issues. You are emotionally involved, and that is why it is more difficult for you. Now, let's see. We have tied your father and brother together. Now you have a relationship, after all the short ones, which is longer lasting. It is with a friend, a relationship that becomes sexual, with someone who is six years older, exactly like your brother. Do you expect a loss to take place like the one that took place with your father and brother?

PATIENT: Hmm . . .

EVALUATOR: You see, it is important to see the basic patterns. Once this takes place you can free yourself from these problems.

PATIENT: Yes, I know.

EVALUATOR: Now, coming to your mother's illness—what are your feelings for someone with whom you did not have a good relationship?

PATIENT: Well, that is not exactly the case. After I came back from Europe we grew much closer. I felt that I protected my mother and she accepted me. She understood me.

EVALUATOR: And now are you going to lose your mother also. Another loss?

PATIENT: We'll see (crying).

EVALUATOR: So what we see is a continuous pattern of losses taking place.

PATIENT: . . . I know (crying).

EVALUATOR: The only question is what to do with all this information. It is understandable that parents usually die before their children. However, you have isolated yourself so as not to experience the pain of loss. You go out briefly with younger people to protect yourself. You cope by being alone. It is fine to cope alone. Aloneness is different than loneliness.

PATIENT: I know.

EVALUATOR: But is this pattern of isolation and coping . . .

PATIENT: (Interrupting) It is easier.

EVALUATOR: Easier, possibly, yet the repetitive fear of loss which you experienced when your father died and then again, to a lesser degree, when your brother left was devastating and still is. That is why you cope by isolation or by short-lived relationships.

64

The question we have not answered, however, is, what brings you here now? Of course, your mother's illness has something to do with it, but your symptoms started to appear before that. You found out later that she was ill, so we must suspect that it has something to do with your boyfriend—your boyfriend who is six years older than you like your brother is and who was a friend but lately a sexual partner. Was there any sexual aspect in your relationship with your brother? You mentioned that there was some kind of sex play between the two of you.

PATIENT: Yes, there was just before he left. We played doctor. Later on, when I was fifteen, he used to come to my room and climb in bed with me, caressing me and fondling me. I pretended to be asleep. There was no sexual intercourse.

EVALUATOR: When exactly did the relationship with your boyfriend become sexual?

PATIENT: In September.

EVALUATOR: Hmm!

PATIENT: And then I became anxious and irritable and I had my mood swings and was feeling fatigued.

EVALUATOR: So, don't we now have all the pieces of the jigsaw puzzle? The question that remains to be answered, however, is whether or not you are motivated to work on these emotional conflicts about the losses of your father and brother, even if they are unpleasant, with someone in a brief therapeutic encounter. Because if you wait another twenty years, it will be too late. Do you agree? Are you motivated to do it?

PATIENT: Yes, of course I am.

EVALUATOR: Is it realistic for us to expect that if we can help you achieve such an understanding about your relationships with men that you will be satisfied?

PATIENT: Yes, I will be very satisfied.

EVALUATOR: OK, then, I am very glad to hear it. Thank you very much for coming to talk about your difficulties so honestly with us as well as being willing to be videotaped.

PATIENT: Thank you. It was very helpful.

EVALUATOR: We'll be in touch with you to arrange for your psychotherapy. Good-bye.

In summary, the patient fulfills in her evaluator's mind the five selection criteria. The dynamic focus involves loss and separation issues, and she agrees to work on the resolution of the emotional conflicts involved. She is an excellent candidate for STAPP.

CHAPTER 6

Woman Complaining of Migraine Headaches: An Evaluation Interview

A THIRTY-TWO-YEAR-OLD DIVORCED WOMAN came to the clinic complaining of migraine headaches. She agreed to be videotaped and to be interviewed by an evaluator who had been told only that she was referred by her psychotherapist for a second opinion. She was seen at an evaluation intake conference attended by fifteen mental health professionals.

The patient looked anxious as she came in and sat down.

EVALUATOR: Please let us know what is bothering you.
PATIENT: Oh, I am a bit scared by all those lights and . . .
EVALUATOR: Do not pay attention to anything except telling us what your problem is.

The evaluator, not knowing anything about the patient's problem, is at first supportive so as to help her relax. This does not mean that he will continue to be supportive. As an opening reaction to a patient who appears to be anxious, it is always best to try to be reassuring.

PATIENT: My basic problem is migraine headaches.
EVALUATOR: How long have you had migraine?
PATIENT: The last one was four months ago. It went on for a long time and I had to be hospitalized. I hoped that they were going to find something physically the matter with me, but they didn't. They told me that the headaches must be associated with psy-

chological problems. They said that it was tension that might cause them.

This type of statement is often made by patients when their physicians are unable to find a specific physiological etiology for their difficulties. The physicians unfortunately jump to the conclusion that the problems are psychological in nature without really knowing whether this is the case. This type of diagnosis by exclusion is bad medicine. A patient who is told that "the problem is in your head"—even if it is true—will usually resent the statement. Furthermore, it is likely that subsequently the psychiatric evaluator will encounter a fairly uncooperative patient.

EVALUATOR: Let's not jump to that conclusion right away. You say that you suffer from migraine headaches. Is this the diagnosis they gave you?

PATIENT: Yes.

EVALUATOR: Could you describe to us what these headaches are like—where they are located, how intense they are, how long they last, what brings them about? You said that you had one for a long time. How long? Please try to describe them for us.

PATIENT: Well, the last one went on for two months—every day. I worked at a job where my boss was very demanding. I was always tense. He never took care of me. The headache was always on the left side of my face. I had a warning when it was going to come.

EVALUATOR: A warning?

PATIENT: Yes. There was a pounding at first, and then there was this sharp pain. I felt like crying.

EVALUATOR: Was there anything else besides the pounding? Did you see any lights or anything else?

PATIENT: Yes, lights—zigzag lights at the corners of my eyes. I felt bad. I knew it was coming. I took aspirin but it didn't help.

EVALUATOR: Did you have any nausea and vomiting?

PATIENT: Yes, of course. I didn't feel like eating, or anything.

EVALUATOR: How long did the headaches last?

PATIENT: On the average a week or more.

EVALUATOR: Were they as intense as in the beginning?

PATIENT: After the first day I got more or less used to them.

EVALUATOR: Who told you that these were migraine headaches?

PATIENT: A couple of doctors. I was sent to a hospital neurology clinic. They gave me several CAT scans, but there was nothing wrong, so they referred me to the headache clinic as a last resort. There they gave me tranquilizers.

EVALUATOR: Are there any kinds of foods that bring the headaches on, such as coffee, sugar, chocolates, and so on?

PATIENT: Everything I eat—coffee, sugar, chocolates, all of which I love. So I don't drink or eat them.

EVALUATOR: Is this a way to deny yourself pleasure in eating? [The evaluator ventures to make a tentative psychological confrontation.]

PATIENT: Yes, somewhat.

EVALUATOR: Hmm. That is interesting.

PATIENT: It is on my mind. I enjoy coffee and I used to drink a lot of it, and then I got the headaches, so I stopped.

EVALUATOR: [The evaluator ignores this important statement.] Since when have you had migraines?

PATIENT: Since I was fifteen.

EVALUATOR: Did you have them before?

PATIENT: No.

EVALUATOR: The first time that it happened to you, what was it like? Do you remember?

PATIENT: At first I didn't pay attention to it, but then it got worse.

EVALUATOR: From then on you have had headaches off and on until now?

PATIENT: More or less.

EVALUATOR: Even during your vacations?

PATIENT: I get them even on my vacations, which upsets me even more, because I want to have fun. I am a single parent. I have a son who is fifteen. He is an only child. I worry about him. You know, he is going through adolescence, going through all the different stages. [This is the second time that the patient gives evidence that there indeed might be psychological conflicts associated with her headaches.]

EVALUATOR: So, you have had this long-term symptom. But is this the first time that you have sought psychological help? You mentioned that you had extensive medical workups.

PATIENT: Oh no. I had psychotherapy for two years.

EVALUATOR: You did?

PATIENT: Yes, I expected miracles but nothing basic happened. I did learn, though, that it takes time.

EVALUATOR: Did you see a psychiatrist, a psychologist, or a social worker?

PATIENT: A psychologist.

EVALUATOR: What did you talk about?

PATIENT: About everyday problems. I talked all by myself because when I asked her advice about what to do, she would ask me what *I* wanted to do. She asked what choices I had, but she did not give me advice, which is what I wanted.

EVALUATOR: So she didn't answer your questions. How did you feel about that?

PATIENT: It annoyed me. I wanted answers. I felt that I was talking to myself. I wanted a friend. I wanted her to tell me what to do.

EVALUATOR: Why did you want to turn a professional relationship into a friendship?

PATIENT: It is hard to talk to a professional and get any answers.

EVALUATOR: So, have you given up your psychotherapy?

PATIENT: I am still in it, but she wanted a second opinion. I am thinking of moving. I am going to school and I am getting my college degree in economics. I want to get a good job when I finish next May.

EVALUATOR: All the things that you are telling us about are exciting. Are they as a result of your psychotherapy? Has this therapy helped your headaches?

PATIENT: Yes, a little. I have a headache now, being nervous about coming and talking to all of you here.

EVALUATOR: When did it start?

PATIENT: Yesterday, when I was thinking about coming here.

EVALUATOR: Is it as bad as you thought it was going to be?

PATIENT: Well . . . no.

EVALUATOR: OK, then, would you mind if I now asked you some questions about the past?

The evaluator is satisfied that the patient fulfills the first STAPP criterion. She has a circumscribed chief complaint. It is the so-called migraine, which has been thoroughly investigated medically and appears at face value to be associated with tension. He is therefore ready to take a developmental history.

EVALUATOR: How old are you?

PATIENT: Thirty-two.

EVALUATOR: Do you have any brothers or sisters?

PATIENT: I have a brother who is two years younger.

EVALUATOR: Were you born in this area?

PATIENT: Yes. I've lived here all my life except for six months while I was married.

EVALUATOR: Are your parents alive?

PATIENT: My mother is.

EVALUATOR: What about your father?

PATIENT: He died of a heart attack when I was twenty-five.

EVALUATOR: I see . . . Well, what was your earliest memory? Tell me, what was the first thing you remember about yourself when you were a very young child?

PATIENT: We were poor. I was often sick. I remember a doctor came. I was scared and I ran away, but my mother cornered me. He gave me a shot and I cried.

EVALUATOR: So the first memory of yours is associated with a medical problem: a doctor, a shot.

PATIENT: (Smiling) Yes.

EVALUATOR: When you were around four or five years old, were you closer to your father or your mother?

PATIENT: My father (smiling). He was an active man. When I needed him he was always there.

EVALUATOR: Can you give me an example?

PATIENT: I fell down once and I got hurt. He came to help. He bandaged my knee after he put iodine on the wound. It hurt but I didn't mind it. Once I was in the hospital and it was he who always came to visit me.

EVALUATOR: So you associate your father with medical problems. What about your mother?

PATIENT: My mother worked all the time. She was never at home that I can remember. She was unavailable. By the age of fourteen I was completely on my own.

EVALUATOR: Were you your father's favorite?

PATIENT: Well, yes. I didn't know it, but after he died my ex-husband told me that I was, but my father never said so. He felt guilty about my brother, so he tried to be nice to him.

EVALUATOR: If he felt guilty it means that you were number one!

PATIENT: Well, my brother was my mother's favorite. She babied him a lot. My father said that I was a go-getter and he liked that trait in me.

EVALUATOR: How did you get along with your brother?

PATIENT: I took care of him, because my mother was away for so long working. I was like a mother to him also.

EVALUATOR: So you took your mother's role?

PATIENT: Yes, I did.

EVALUATOR: Do you remember anything special that you and your father did together that was fun?

PATIENT: Oh, I'd do anything for my brother and my father. I wouldn't go to the movies, which I loved to do, if they needed me. I enjoyed being with them.

EVALUATOR: So you would make a sacrifice for them?

PATIENT: Oh yes, I would. I remember that on my fourteenth birthday my father took me out to a cocktail lounge. He bought me a drink. He introduced me to his friends. Later he took me to dinner. He danced with me as if we were out on a date.

EVALUATOR: Hmm, so it was like a date?

PATIENT: *(Smiling)* I got all his attention and I liked it.

EVALUATOR: I see. Now, in grade school did you have any good friends? Were you a good student?

PATIENT: I was an excellent student. I had a lot of friends, but Phyllis was my best friend.

EVALUATOR: Would you make a sacrifice for her also?

PATIENT: Sacrifice? You mean, would I help her out? Oh yes, of course. I would pay for her ticket when we went to the movies together out of my allowance. She was even poorer than I was *(smiling)*.

EVALUATOR: You sound as if you were a very happy child. [The evaluator is satisfied that the patient fulfills the second STAPP criterion.]

PATIENT: Yes, I was then.

EVALUATOR: When did you have your first menstrual period?

PATIENT: At twelve.

EVALUATOR: Were you prepared for it?

PATIENT: Yes, I was prepared by my father.

EVALUATOR: By your father? Isn't that somewhat unusual?

PATIENT: Well, I was a tomboy at that time. I wore his and my brother's clothes. I was not interested in boys, and my father didn't want me going out with guys. My father said, "It's time for me to talk to you." I said, "About what?" He said, "About woman things." I said, "Oh, no." He insisted, so I ran away and hid under the bed, but he came after me. He grabbed me. He said, "I'm going to talk to you whether you like it or not." I shouted, "No, no!" He said, "You are now old enough to have sex. If you get pregnant, I'll kill you."

EVALUATOR: Did you know what he was talking about?

PATIENT: Of course I did. I knew from Phyllis, who had her period already.

EVALUATOR: So you weren't interested in boys. You were a tomboy. Your father informs you about your period and gives you a warning as well. Isn't that interesting? [Occasional summarizing by the evaluator pulls the information given by the patient together.]

PATIENT: Oh, I remembered his warning.

EVALUATOR: Yes. He said, in effect, "Don't be interested in men." Did that mean that you should be interested in him?

The evaluator has an opportunity to investigate whether a focus on the patient's relationship with her father could be established, based on all the information she has provided to him about their relationship. He makes a tentative confrontation to see how the patient will respond to it.

PATIENT: In my father? Oh no.

EVALUATOR: [The evaluator is not willing to take no for an answer so easily. He insists.] Come on, now. Your father took you out on a date. He took you to a cocktail lounge, offered you a drink when you were fourteen, and . . .

PATIENT: He and my mother didn't get along at all.

It is interesting to observe this non sequitur answer, which reinforces the evaluator's opinion. Anyone who evaluates patients should pay attention to such spontaneous and seemingly unrelated associations. Being impressed by the patient's statement, the evaluator persists with his confrontation.

EVALUATOR: So, did he replace your mother with you? He warned you about getting pregnant. Did he want to keep you for himself?

PATIENT: Well, do you mean, was he jealous? The only one who was jealous was my mother. She was a cold woman. My father and I have the same personality. We are warm people. We express our feelings (smiles). Doctor, you know, my mother never kissed me. Can you imagine that? I kiss my son every day.

EVALUATOR: Did your father kiss you?

PATIENT: Yes, he did. (Smiling) Oh yes.

EVALUATOR: What are you smiling about?

PATIENT: He did things to get me mad (giggles).

EVALUATOR: Yet you giggle. [It is important for the evaluator to observe paradoxical behavior and bring it to the patient's attention.]

PATIENT: He used to french kiss me all the time. I didn't want him to do it, but he continued, to spite me. He used to laugh and laugh when I said no, when I resisted.

EVALUATOR: Why did you resist?

PATIENT: I am squeamish.

EVALUATOR: Was it that you are squeamish, or did you sense that your father had a special interest in you? He doesn't want you to go out with boys. He took you out on a date and all that. There seems to be a lot here. [Again the evaluator puts pressure on the patient as he is trying to establish a tentative oedipal focus.]

PATIENT: I didn't think so.

EVALUATOR: Don't run away from my point.

It is possible that some people will be annoyed, irritated, or shocked by the evaluator's insistence on confronting the patient with her attempt to evade her own feelings for her seductive father. It would be too easy to assume that the patient was the victim of a sexually abusive father and support her at this point. What is much more important and difficult is to point to her own desires for her father and at the same time her shame about them. The course that she took, to run away, was maladaptive.

In STAPP we view our patients not as weak victims but as capable of coming to grips with their own ambivalent feelings, of having the courage to face their experiences and the anxieties associated with them, and in the final analysis, with the help of their therapists, able to overcome these once and for all.

PATIENT: As I said, it was my mother who was jealous.

EVALUATOR: Yes, you told me about it. The question is, what was your mother jealous of? Of your relationship with your father?

PATIENT: When I grew up I was in love every day. All these guys were calling me all the time. My mother was jealous and I was only thirteen. Her friends would say, "You have a nice daughter," and she would downgrade me. She'd say, "Are you kidding, a nice daughter?" She used to hurt my feelings, but I wouldn't tell her because I knew my father was proud of me.

EVALUATOR: So it is clear that you had a special and very good relationship with your father, and your mother seemed to be jealous of you and downgrade you. OK. Did you graduate from high school?

PATIENT: Yes I did at seventeen. I was a good student in high school.

EVALUATOR: Did you have your headaches then?

PATIENT: Yes, they started when I was fifteen.

EVALUATOR: What happened then?

PATIENT: I went out with my boyfriend then and we had sex.

EVALUATOR: So you did what your father had told you not to do?

PATIENT: Yes, but I liked my boyfriend then.

EVALUATOR: What was so special about him?

PATIENT: *(Giggles)* It didn't work out later on, but then I liked him. He was like another father to me.

EVALUATOR: Hmm. This was not my statement. It was yours, and you giggle about it.

PATIENT: Yes, I know.

EVALUATOR: Another father, eh? Did he look like your father?

PATIENT: Well, their features were similar.

EVALUATOR: Why did you pick someone like your father?

PATIENT: To watch over me as my father did.

EVALUATOR: As your father did when you were hurt, when you were sick? Did you develop a headache so as to be taken care of like your father used to do? You see, I have two different pictures of you. I see you happy, active, independent, and successful, and then I also see you hurt, in need of help, sick and getting attention from your father and also from your husband later on.

PATIENT: I like someone to pick me up and to watch over me. I liked men when I grew up.

EVALUATOR: Is that what your father warned you about when you were under the bed?

PATIENT: Yes, when I was fifteen I went out with some soldiers and lied about it. My father found out. He was mad, and he kicked me on the behind and sent me up to my room.

EVALUATOR: What does this story tell us?

PATIENT: It says that I couldn't mess around.

EVALUATOR: Precisely. It also says that your father acted as a jealous lover. [Again some may think that the evaluator has gone too far by using the word "lover." This is not the case, however: by now he is fairly sure that he has a potential STAPP candidate who can withstand anxiety, so he is pressing hard to establish a focus.]

PATIENT: I had many boyfriends.

EVALUATOR: *(Laughing)* That's no answer. What I meant was that your

74

father acted as a jealous man, kicking you and so on, because he didn't like your being with those soldiers.

PATIENT: He did it to protect me!

EVALUATOR: Yes, and keep you to himself. Furthermore, he took you out on a date and he used to french kiss you, which you say you didn't like, but you went around pretending that nothing happened while everyone else observed all this. Your mother was jealous, your husband told you that you were your father's favorite, and I observe now the same things from what you are telling me. Is it because it is a difficult subject that you want to run away from it?

PATIENT: Well, last week I read an article in a magazine about fathers abusing their daughters and having sex with them. It is hard to imagine it's happening. It's sickening. My father never touched me except to pinch my behind sometimes playfully. He never made sexual advances. [Here is a good example of the patient's giving a truthful account of herself—a subcriterion of motivation for change.]

EVALUATOR: I never implied that your father made sexual advances. I simply say that there was a lot going on between the two of you which was more than a pure father–daughter relationship, even if it didn't come down to making sexual advances.

PATIENT: Hmm.

EVALUATOR: Furthermore, you got married to a man who had many characteristics of your father, if not all the good ones, unfortunately. By the way what was your sex life like with your husband?

PATIENT: I didn't enjoy it . . . I caught my husband cheating on me with my next-door neighbor a month after our marriage. I had a big wedding. I tried to make it go.

EVALUATOR: Did your father like your husband?

PATIENT: He didn't, but at that time I was also going with another guy whom my father couldn't stand because he drank too much, so he chose the lesser of two evils. So I married him, and six months after my son was born I asked myself, "What is all this mess about?" and so I threw him out. I divorced him, and my father was pleased that I did. He died a few years later suddenly of a stroke.

EVALUATOR: I am sorry to hear it. What was it like for you?

PATIENT: My world crashed (*looking very sad*).

EVALUATOR: So you see how important all this is. Your world crashed. Your husband couldn't fill your father's shoes. He couldn't take care of you as your father did.

PATIENT: Well, I had my son.

EVALUATOR: Yes, but he is not taking care of you. He is an adolescent and you worry about him.

PATIENT: I treat him as an adult, but he is lazy. I try to help him.

EVALUATOR: Does he ever see his father?

PATIENT: No. His father came to see him once in fifteen years.

EVALUATOR: OK. Now let's look at all this. You go to college, you plan to move, I get the picture that things are looking up for you, yet you have some problems, you have your headaches, and you have no one to take care of you.

PATIENT: I *do* have someone who takes care of me.

EVALUATOR: Oh, you do?

PATIENT: *(Smiling)* He does, just like my father used to do.

EVALUATOR: What does he look like?

PATIENT: *(Sheepishly)* He looks like my father, but he is married. We have been going together for many years, but as I said, he is married. He lives a double life. He doesn't want a divorce, so I ask myself where am I going and I conclude that I want to move and see whether I can make it on my own. All this gives me a headache.

EVALUATOR: There you are, you came to your own conclusion. Now what are you planning to do?

PATIENT: I want to go to New York to work on Wall Street. I want to be a stockbroker . . . and I know what you are going to ask: "What did your father do?"

EVALUATOR: You guessed right *(smiling)*.

PATIENT: Well . . . he was a stockbroker.

EVALUATOR: Now, let us see. I think that we have established clearly the importance of your relationship with your father, the conflicts about being on your own, or being taken care of as your father did. All this gives you a headache. Are you willing to work on the solution of this problem with your therapist?

PATIENT: Yes, I am.

EVALUATOR: One more thing, however. You shouldn't expect your therapist to tell you what to do or answer your questions and take care of you. Neither she nor we have any magic tricks, and even if we had and used them, it would be insulting to you if we did and if we treated you as a child. Psychotherapy is a joint venture and it strives to resolve a specific emotional problem. Would you like to try to work on these conflicts with your therapist?

PATIENT: Yes.

EVALUATOR: One more question: What are your thoughts about this interview here with me?

PATIENT: I liked it.

EVALUATOR: Did you learn anything?

PATIENT: It verified that I loved my father, that I want to stand on my own feet, and that the problems that I have with myself have something to do with him. That also gives me a headache. I expect I can succeed in resolving my difficulties.

EVALUATOR: Fine. I shall talk with your therapist and tell her about our interview.

PATIENT: Thank you. Good-bye.

This evaluation interview demonstrates that a patient who may not be sophisticated psychologically and who at first appears not to fulfill the fourth criterion for STAPP as the interview progresses becomes able to see that the focus presented to her by the evaluator, namely her conflict over a wish to be taken care of by her beloved father and by men in general is in conflict with her wish to be independent. This conflict makes her tense, and the tension leads to a headache.

The patient fulfills all the other STAPP criteria for selection, admirably. An oedipal focus has been established and the patient has agreed to work on its resolution either with her therapist or, if her therapist does not want to follow our recommendations, she may refer the patient back to the clinic for another therapist to be assigned to her for STAPP. The patient said that she was going to discuss our recommendations with her therapist. As far as we were concerned, she demonstrated all the STAPP characteristics.

CHAPTER 7

Man Complaining of Depression: An Evaluation Interview

THE PATIENT IS a twenty-five-year-old student. He is interviewed by a male evaluator.

> EVALUATOR: I have no information about you, so I would like to know what prompted you to come to the clinic. What is the one thing that bothers you most?
> PATIENT: I am depressed. That is what bothers me most.

The evaluator signifies that the patient must choose the most important problem. In this way he is helping the patient to begin to circumscribe his complaints, and he is assessing whether the patient fulfills the first STAPP selection criterion. He gets a clear answer to his inquiry.

> EVALUATOR: What is this depression like?
> PATIENT: I go in and out of depression. This symptom immobilizes me and it affects my relations with people.
> EVALUATOR: What else?
> PATIENT: I have a very low opinion of myself. I feel lethargic. I sleep a lot, or sometimes not at all.
> EVALUATOR: How is your appetite?
> PATIENT: It fluctuates. I gain weight easily, and then I lose it. This summer I lost twenty pounds, then I eat a lot of junk when I shouldn't and I put on weight.

EVALUATOR: Is this a self-destructive attitude?

PATIENT: Yes, because I don't like to be overweight.

EVALUATOR: If this is a self-punitive attitude, what are you punishing yourself about?

PATIENT: It is a vicious cycle. There are some things that happened recently which may contribute to my depression. I had trouble at school, my grades were not so good. My sister, to whom I am very close, got pregnant and had an abortion despite my advising her not to go through with it. Then my girlfriend accepted a job in the South so we were separated. Finally, my father took a job in England so my parents left for London last month.

EVALUATOR: All these examples that you gave me have something to do with losses. The abortion leading to the loss of the baby, your girlfriend and your parents leaving to go away. Are you sensitive to losses?

The evaluator, on the basis of information that has been given to him by the patient, raises the question of the patient's sensitivity to loss, which can become one of the foci for STAPP. So an evaluator should not hesitate to attempt even during the early part of the interview to make a confrontation based on information given by the patient.

PATIENT: Oh yes, I am. I have always been, as far as I can remember. Even with my father, who I never got along with very well, when he told me that they were going to be in London for two years, I felt upset. I felt the loss.

EVALUATOR: So this is paradoxical, because even if you were not getting along with your father, you felt the loss when he mentioned that he was leaving, and you were upset. [The evaluator repeats to reinforce the patient's statements.]

PATIENT: I sure was.

EVALUATOR: So is it possible that the depression and its subsequent complications are associated with these losses?

PATIENT: I think so. *Yes.* I gave it a lot of thought.

EVALUATOR: Why is it so? What is it that you lost in your early life that makes you sensitive to losses and contributes to your becoming vulnerable to similar circumstances in your adult life? [The evaluator raises the possibility that earlier experiences in life sensitize a patient and contribute to the development of difficulties in adult life.]

PATIENT: Well, I have memories from my childhood. I remember once when I was very little, my grandmother, who I loved very much, died suddenly. I cried and cried for days. My parents couldn't understand why I reacted in such a way to her death. They were worried. [The patient's immediate recollection of a childhood loss should signal to the evaluator not only evidence of an early working alliance but also evidence that earlier losses may have contributed to his hypersensitivity in this area.]

EVALUATOR: How old were you when your grandmother died?

PATIENT: Oh, I must have been about four.

EVALUATOR: OK, now, let me ask you a few questions about your past life, so that we can get a longitudinal picture of it. How old are you?

PATIENT: Twenty-five.

EVALUATOR: What is your earliest memory, as far back as you can remember?

PATIENT: I remember that my mother had taken my brother to the doctor and left me with a babysitter. I had a temper tantrum.

EVALUATOR: How old were you then?

PATIENT: I was three or so.

EVALUATOR: How many brothers and sisters do you have?

PATIENT: I have two older brothers and two younger sisters. My brothers are thirty-two and twenty-eight, and my sisters fifteen and twelve.

EVALUATOR: Were you born in this area?

PATIENT: Yes, in Maine. When I was four we moved here to Boston.

EVALUATOR: Do you remember the move? What was it like?

PATIENT: I was glad to move because there was an old woman—a neighbor across the street. I was very scared of her. To scare me, my brother told me that she was a witch and I believed him. I was very happy to move. I remember in our new house we had to go the cellar when they had air raid drills. There was my mother and my two brothers and I. [The evaluator should observe that the patient is giving spontaneous associations from the past, which signifies intensification of the working alliance.]

EVALUATOR: Were you closer to your father or your mother?

PATIENT: To my mother.

EVALUATOR: Did your mother have a favorite?

PATIENT: I have the feeling that I was her favorite. I did well in school.

EVALUATOR: How did you get along with your father?

PATIENT: (Smiling) He wasn't around much. Once I remember he took

80

me to a baseball game and we had fun. He took only me and not my brothers.

EVALUATOR: Were you competitive with them?

PATIENT: No. I did want to have a good relationship with my father, but I think he liked my older brothers better.

EVALUATOR: Since you were your mother's favorite, did the two of you do anything special together?

PATIENT: Yes. Once I helped my mother do the dishes. She was very pleased and took me to the movies that night. It was in the middle of the week, and I had to go to school the next morning. I was very happy. I felt I had a special relationship with my mother, but that made me aware that although I wanted to, I did not have a good relationship with my father. [The patient supplies evidence that he is capable of making a sacrifice, like doing the dishes, for someone he loves.]

EVALUATOR: Is it possible that because you had such a good relationship with your mother, you did not have such a good relationship with your father? In a sense, you had to choose one parent or the other?

PATIENT: Hmm.

EVALUATOR: In a sense, you had to be closer to one parent than to the other. In your case it was your mother.

PATIENT: My mother always took my side when my father was critical. Actually, my parents used to fight quite a bit. They even talked about divorce. I was scared when I heard them quarreling.

EVALUATOR: Another potential loss?

PATIENT: Yes, I remember being scared.

EVALUATOR: Now one of your sisters was born about ten years after you. Do you remember her birth?

PATIENT: Well, not exactly, but I do remember her being a young baby. I was curious about her because she was a girl. She was a plaything.

EVALUATOR: Did you have any thoughts as to where this little child had come from?

PATIENT: No. I don't recall. When my youngest sister was born, my mother tried to explain something about being pregnant, but I was thirteen then and I knew all about it. She was embarrassed.

EVALUATOR: Where had you obtained information about sexual matters, pregnancy, childbirth, and all that?

PATIENT: A kid had told me some years before, so I couldn't understand why my mother was embarrassed. I thought that she wanted to pull the wool over my eyes and did not want me to know much about sex and all that. I couldn't understand why she couldn't talk straight about it.

EVALUATOR: So it is clear that the whole subject of sex was avoided by your mother.

PATIENT: Yes, very much so.

EVALUATOR: How did you do in school? Were you a good student?

PATIENT: Yes, I was an excellent student, but my parents were never satisfied. I got an $A-$ and they wanted me to get straight As. They were both very rigid.

EVALUATOR: How old is your mother?

PATIENT: My father is fifty-three, and my mother is thirty—I mean, fifty.

EVALUATOR: So, given twenty years ago—

PATIENT: *(Interrupting)* She was an attractive woman.

EVALUATOR: I can imagine, because you made a slip of the tongue a minute ago and said that she was thirty.

PATIENT: Did I?

EVALUATOR: Yes, you did, so even now in your mind your mother is an attractive young woman of thirty.

It is important for the evaluator to pick up any slips of the tongue during the first interview, as in the course of psychotherapy. Such slips indicate unconscious wishes, and the evaluator's noting of them lets the patient know that the evaluator is aware of his or her unconscious processes.

PATIENT: She would visit me in school and talk to my teachers, and all the kids were impressed and whistled when she came in. They'd ask me, "Is she your mom?" and say, "Boy, she's something."

EVALUATOR: How did all this make you feel?

PATIENT: *(Smiling)* It made me feel good.

EVALUATOR: Furthermore, you were your mother's favorite.

PATIENT: At that time I was.

EVALUATOR: You mean, things changed? You lost your favorite position?

PATIENT: No, but she cared for me in a special way. We could talk. I could show my feelings in front of her. My father gave me hell when I cried, but my mother understood. She never put me down for crying.

EVALUATOR: So you had a good relationship with your mother during your early life! [The evaluator has further confirmation that the patient fulfills the second STAPP selection criterion. In his statement he reinforces what the patient has implied.]

PATIENT: Yes, I did. I haven't thought about all this for a long time.

EVALUATOR: Yes, of course. This is the reason why you are here now.

PATIENT: Yes, I know.

EVALUATOR: Now, what about your relationships with women? Did you have any girlfriends?

PATIENT: I had a girlfriend when I was eight.

EVALUATOR: Eight—hmm, that's pretty good *(laughing).*

PATIENT: *(Laughing)* Yes, I started early.

Humor may be appropriate during an interview. A sense of humor in both the evaluator and the patient is a good sign of a working alliance and an indication that the third STAPP criterion can be met. The evaluator must not laugh at the patient, however.

EVALUATOR: Any other girlfriends later on?

PATIENT: Oh yes, when I was seven I had a cousin with long, dark hair and I used to rub my hand on her hair. It felt very good. We used to play together in the cellar.

EVALUATOR: Seven! That is even better . . . hmm. The cellar? Like when you were going in the cellar with your mother during air raid drills?

PATIENT: Yes, right! right! right!

EVALUATOR: Very good . . .

The evaluator is moving away from a neutral therapeutic stance by rewarding the patient. Patients *should* be rewarded when they work hard and bring up spontaneous and important information, thus strengthening their relationship with the therapist. This type of interaction becomes intensified during the course of the therapy.

EVALUATOR: How old were you when you had your first sexual encounter?

PATIENT: I was eighteen.

EVALUATOR: What was it like?

PATIENT: It was terrible. It was with a girl I picked up in the movies. We had sex. It was awful. She didn't care for sex. I was hurt. She said that I was inexperienced. I had a premature ejaculation. I was humiliated. She wasn't sensitive.

EVALUATOR: So, it was a bad experience.

PATIENT: Yes, I thought that she didn't like me and I couldn't understand why she didn't.

EVALUATOR: Did that influence your relations with women, which up to that time had been pretty good or very good?

PATIENT: Well, not really, because between the ages of thirteen and seventeen I was involved with men. There was an older guy who taught me how to masturbate and introduced me to having sex with men. I ran away from home, and I was having relations with men who paid me.

EVALUATOR: How long did all this last?

PATIENT: About four years. Soon after, however, I got sick and tired of being involved homosexually and of getting paid for it, so I called my mother and asked her if I could come back home. She was glad that I called and said that if it was OK with my dad I could come back. It was after I returned that I had that bad first sexual experience with that girl I picked up in the movies. I didn't give women up, however, because I started having relations with women from then on and I completely stopped my sexual interactions with men. I got a job and I didn't need to make money that way anymore.

EVALUATOR: Where did that homosexual side come from? You say it was for financial purposes, but was it also an attempt to get close to men because of your yearning to have a good relationship with your father, which you didn't have?

PATIENT: Well, it had to do with running away from home.

EVALUATOR: Oh! Why did you have to run away from home?

PATIENT: I was out with my friends, and my parents disapproved of both my boyfriends and my girlfriends. When I was fourteen I ran away from home because they told me I couldn't go out. After I called my mother—that was when I was eighteen—she said that both my father and she wanted me to come home. I did return.

EVALUATOR: Now between fourteen and eighteen, did you continue going to school and being a good student?

PATIENT: No.

EVALUATOR: But again you haven't explained exactly why you ran away from home. I understand that you had some problems with your parents' disapproval of your friends, but I don't think that this was enough of a reason for you to run away. Was there anything else?

PATIENT: Well, my mother changed when I was thirteen.

EVALUATOR: She did? In what way?

PATIENT: Well, she used to get mad so easily. She would have a temper tantrum, so after that we couldn't talk as we used to.

EVALUATOR: So the good times with your mother came to an end? You gave me a description of the good relationship with your mother. You were smiling when you talked about it, but now I see you frowning. Something distasteful seems to come to your mind. What happened?

PATIENT: My mother can turn on you, from being nice, loving, and understanding to being mad, to being vicious. She withdraws from you as if you didn't exist.

EVALUATOR: "As if you didn't exist!"

The evaluator has found a valuable clue to the patient's sensitivity to rejection and loss, which may contribute to his depression. The evaluator's repetition of the patient's statements indicates that he is particularly interested in what the patient is describing.

PATIENT: We would come back from school and we would immediately identify our mother's bad mood. We would ask, "What have I done? What have I done?" We would walk on eggshells so as not to make her mad. We were terrified. She knocked plates off the table. She was so angry. We didn't know what the hell was going on. One time she was nice, then she would turn on you as if she didn't care about you.

EVALUATOR: So your mother was inconsistent, in contrast to your father, who, despite his attitudes, was always consistent.

PATIENT: Yes, my father was always consistent. He was very consistent.

EVALUATOR: Did these episodes with men represent an abortive attempt to establish rapport with a male in order to recapture or create a good relationship with a consistent father which you felt you lacked as a child, and did they come about because of your mother's changes in her behavior toward you?

PATIENT: Yes, very much so. I thought about it sometimes. I tried to piece it together. I tried to understand why I did what I did. I thought maybe I was looking for a father in all these men. I was looking for someone to like me, to smile at me, to accept me for who I was, not to growl at me.

EVALUATOR: In that situation, however, you went too far. The relations with these men who paid you could have become very

85

destructive. They could have led to a catastrophe in your life. You never knew what kinds of people you were getting involved with. So this urge to have a meaningful relationship with your father must have been a very strong one. Furthermore, the disappointment in your mother, who had changed and forced all of her children to walk on eggshells, must have been terrible in comparison with the old times, when you were so happy and so close.

PATIENT: Yes.

EVALUATOR: Did you continue to do well in high school?

PATIENT: No, I was too distracted. I couldn't work. I barely managed.

EVALUATOR: But you did graduate from high school, didn't you?

PATIENT: No, I didn't. I dropped out in my freshman year.

EVALUATOR: So all these difficulties we have talked about also affected your school performance. You had been such a good student before, as you told me.

PATIENT: Yes.

EVALUATOR: What did you do during the past nine years?

The evaluator has two options. The first is to pursue the important connections that have been made about the patient's disappointment with his mother. Furthermore, his dangerous search for a substitute for the missing relationship with his father might have been a reaction to his mother's rejection. The second is to obtain information about the patient's life subsequent to his dropping out of high school. He chooses the second option because he feels that the patient's relationship with his father and men is a complicated issue that should be left for further clarification and disentanglement during subsequent therapy.

The patient answered that he drifted from job to job. He described extensively his relationships with women, but he emphasized that these relationships were also short-lived and generally unsatisfactory. Finally, the departure of his parents for England and his sister's abortion contributed to making him depressed and prompted him to come to the clinic.

EVALUATOR: I understand that these two losses made you decide to seek help, but some of these problems have been going on for a long time.

PATIENT: *(Interrupting)* I got tired of the same ups and downs. Six months ago I was feeling good, now I am feeling depressed. I decided I had to seek help to break the vicious cycle.

EVALUATOR: Of the two losses—your parents' departure and your sister's abortion—which one had a greater impact?

PATIENT: Well, there was also the fact that my girlfriend moved out. She said that I was impossible to live with. She complained that I was angry with her, that I would withdraw my love from her. I wouldn't talk with her for days.

EVALUATOR: Why did you do what your mother did to you? Why did you identify with your mother?

PATIENT: Yes, my mother did it, but my father did it even more. He'd be depressed, he withdrew, he didn't talk for days—he was such a negative person.

It is clear that the evaluator has made a mistake by thinking that the patient identified with his mother during his puberty. This type of mistake is made often by evaluators or therapists when they do not wait to get all the patient's information. It is of interest how the patient in this case corrects him by emphasizing his identification with his father.

EVALUATOR: So, why did you do what your father did?

PATIENT: I hoped that by being like him he might like me more. In that way I would get close to him. We would have many traits in common.

EVALUATOR: You also said your grades were not good. Are you in school now?

PATIENT: Yes. I went back to school to get my diploma.

EVALUATOR: Oh, I see. OK. Now, what about this interview? We have covered very quickly so many important events in your life. Do you think that looking more closely at your sensitivity to all these losses, which may have contributed to your depressive feelings, will be helpful?

PATIENT: I sure do. I need to be encouraged to think, and I need help to solve these problems.

EVALUATOR: What did you think of this interview with me?

PATIENT: I liked it. I got some insights.

EVALUATOR: I am glad to hear it, but I think that a second interview to look into all these problems more carefully might be a good idea. Would that be all right with you?

PATIENT: Yes, of course.

EVALUATOR: What I had in mind was to try to understand what happened around the age of thirteen or fourteen, when you ran away from home and got involved with men and when your relationship with your mother changed.

PATIENT: OK.

EVALUATOR: Fine, so we shall be in touch with you. Thanks for speaking with me.

PATIENT: Thank you, doctor.

The need for a second interview is clear. Although the patient seems to fulfill several of the criteria for selection for STAPP, his psychological sophistication and his motivation for change have not been established to the evaluator's satisfaction. In addition, the cyclic aspects of his depressive feelings, his running away from home, and his homosexual acting-out period should be better understood and explored. He thus should consider the following options:

1. A second interview conducted by the evaluator himself to investigate these issues in an effort to understand what took place between the patient and his mother to alter their relationship and contribute to his running away from home.
2. A second interview conducted by a female evaluator to check further the third STAPP criterion. The patient seems to relate well to a male evaluator. The question must be raised, however, whether he will relate as well to a woman.

In this case a second interview with a female evaluator was decided upon. That interview revealed that when the patient was thirteen, his mother developed postpartum depression following the birth of his youngest sister. This depression was the cause of his mother's irritability and contributed to the change in her relationship with the patient. He interpreted her behavior as a rejection of himself. At first he tried to understand whether his mother's change was due to his behavior, then he tried to get close to his father; but his father's aloofness and withdrawal drove him to run away from home and to seek love and attention from men. Having discovered that this acting out was also unsatisfactory, he again tried to reestablish relations with his parents and with women, but he was again unsuccessful. His repetitive failures to have a meaningful relationship with a girlfriend led to his becoming more and more sensitive to separation and to losses and contributed to his depression. Every attempt at establishing a new relationship with a woman made him excited, but each failure led to another depression. Becoming tired of this pattern and suffering the double loss of his girlfriend and his parents precipitated his seeking help.

PART II

TECHNIQUE

The second part of this book deals with the techniques and the requirements of STAPP. I hope to offer suggestions on treating a patient who has been found to be an appropriate candidate for this kind of brief psychotherapy. The task is not easy, however: one of the most important components of therapeutic technique is the individual style of the therapist. That cannot be adequately described or taught.

What can be described are technical guidelines for the therapist to keep in mind. How the techniques are incorporated will be a matter of individual style. These techniques, which will be discussed at length, fall into the following categories:

1. The working alliance evolves into a therapeutic alliance.
2. The patient's positive transference feelings for the therapist are used early in therapy.
3. The therapist is very active.
4. Focus is maintained throughout.
5. Anxiety-provoking confrontations and clarifications are repeatedly used.
6. Feelings for key people in the past are linked to transference feelings for the therapist.
7. Regression is avoided.
8. A "transference neurosis" is not allowed to develop.
9. New learning, ways of problem solving, and partial insights about the focal conflicts must become evident.

10. At times of massive resistance recapitulation is used.
11. The patient whose motivation for change remains high, despite painful feelings, is supported.
12. Tangible evidence of changing attitudes must come forth.
13. Full insight about conflicts underlying the focus should be demonstrated.
14. Early termination will be achieved.

In addition to these technical aspects, the chapters that follow will include discussion of countertransference issues and characteristics (sex, education) of the patient.

STAPP imposes four requirements on the therapy sessions:

1. Weekly sessions take place at a specified time.
2. The therapist and patient are face to face in an office setting.
3. The session is forty-five minutes long.
4. That the therapy is limited in time is discussed, but no number of sessions is specified in advance.

If the patient's evaluator becomes the therapist, in the first therapy session it is still helpful to state again what the focus of the therapy will be and to remind the patient that he or she has agreed to stay with that focus. During the evaluation the patient should have learned that the resolution of the emotional conflicts underlying the focus will promote a rapid improvement of the patient's psychological problems.

The therapist and patient should agree on a mutually convenient weekly appointment time, which should be kept unchanged as much as possible. If a change is necessary, it should be discussed well in advance and a different appointment time should be agreed upon. Of course, emergencies are exceptions from this setup. Although the arrangement may seem to be on the rigid side, it is meant to discourage acting out and resistance in the form of repeated requests for a change of appointment.

Even with sophisticated patients, it helps to specify that the sessions are face to face and will last forty-five minutes, not the usual fifty minutes. This session length has been found to be satisfactory, and it also sends a message to the patient that the brief psychotherapeutic treatment is not psychoanalysis.

Finally, the therapist should discuss the duration of the therapy. The therapist must emphasize that although there is no specific limit on the duration of the treatment and no termination date is fixed, the therapy is expected to be brief. Patients usually ask how long it will last, particularly if they are aware of time-limited psychotherapy, which usually involves a set number of sessions. In STAPP the therapist and the patient determine when the patient's specific emotional conflicts underlying the focus have been resolved. STAPP usually lasts from six to fifteen interviews. If a therapist observes that an ostensibly well evaluated patient is taking much longer to make progress, then either the evaluation was faulty or the patient is resisting in order to prolong the treatment. Because the private practitioner evaluates the patient's problems alone, it is especially important to convey the concept of time limitation.

Gilliérion (1990) has placed special emphasis on the setting of short-term dynamic psychotherapy. He believes that the face-to-face, once a week, active interaction with special emphasis on a focal issue contributes to the brevity of treatment; in contrast, the open-ended, free-associative techniques of psychoanalysis and long-term psychoanalytically oriented psychotherapy lengthen treatment.

CHAPTER 8

Early Technical Issues

The Therapeutic Alliance

IF A WORKING ALLIANCE HAS BEEN ESTABLISHED with an evaluator other than the therapist, then the new therapist will have to reestablish it with the patient. The new therapist may have to review some of the issues that were discussed during the evaluation interview—for example, the patient's complaints and the dynamic focus—and he or she must find out whether the patient agrees to work on the resolution of the emotional conflicts involved. This type of a review will reassure the patient that the therapist is thoroughly familiar with the specific issues of his or her case.

A patient who has gotten along well with the evaluator may feel somewhat disappointed if another therapist takes on the treatment. It should not be forgotten, however, that patients who are accepted have fulfilled the third STAPP criterion—they can interact flexibly with the evaluator. The task, then, of the new therapist is to convince the patient that he or she is well trained and capable of helping disentangle emotional difficulties. In addition, the therapist should convey the idea that working together is a crucial ingredient of success. That notion arouses the patient's interest and increases his or her confidence in the new therapist.

In the following vignette the patient expresses hesitation at being treated by a therapist other than the evaluator.

PATIENT: I must admit to you a certain disappointment that the doctor I saw here in the clinic two weeks ago is not the person who is also going to treat me. I hope that this doesn't hurt your feelings; it doesn't mean that I don't want you as my therapist. I simply wanted to bring it up. You see, I had confidence in his ability to help me to deal with my problems.

THERAPIST: Of course, I understand what you are saying. I know that it might be somewhat difficult for you to have to change from one person to another, but there are two points that I want to emphasize. In this clinic there are many professionals who act in different capacities. Some are evaluators and others are therapists. Also, at times, although we may indeed want to treat the patient we have evaluated, our therapeutic time is all filled up and we must refer someone we have seen to someone else who has an opening. What is more important, in my opinion, is that you have been accepted to receive this type of short-term dynamic psychotherapy. You are thought to be capable of resolving your problems with the help of a therapist over a short period of time. It is this capability of yours that is the most important dimension in your case. Because of this it also was thought that you would be helped irrespective of who treated you, as long as the therapist was familiar with the requirements and the techniques involved in STAPP. I am such a person. I can easily see that you liked your evaluator and you might have preferred him as your therapist, but I am also sure that you are not a dependent person who needs someone to perform magic. In the final analysis it is your own capacity to resolve your own difficulties that counts. It goes without saying that you need some assistance. I am perfectly willing and capable to offer it to you.

This type of forthright and honest statement is persuasive to STAPP candidates whose primary aim is to resolve their emotional problems, not to have someone else do it for them.

For the establishment of a therapeutic alliance the new therapist must have reviewed the notes of the evaluation interview and be familiar with what transpired. That is one reason to review the focus of the therapy. If the patient, to test or to confine the therapist, wants to change the focus, the first therapeutic session must be turned into a second evaluation interview until the therapist feels confident that all the criteria for

STAPP have been fulfilled and that the focus is exactly what the previous evaluation specified. This additional evaluation will convince the patient that the therapist is as competent and familiar with STAPP as the previous evaluator was.

Rarely, the initial evaluation interview is faulty, so that a new focus must be specified. Under those circumstances the therapist should give the patient clearly the reasons why the focus must change. This type of explanation, will also help convince the patient of the therapist's competence.

This whole discussion between therapist and patient may be considered as educational. Yet patient education is considered controversial, and many therapists disapprove of it. Freud himself emphasized that the determining factor in psychoanalysis is whether the patient is educable. This applies just as much to STAPP.

The assumption that all patients are knowledgeable about psychotherapy is not necessarily correct. It is unfortunately true that the public does not have a positive picture of psychiatry or psychotherapy. It is therefore helpful for the therapist to explain to the patient what should be anticipated in the treatment. A clear presentation of the requirements is only a beginning. What is more important is a discussion of the potential conflicts that may develop during the course of the therapy as a result of the anxiety-provoking nature of the therapist's confrontations and clarifications. It may be helpful for the therapist to say something like this:

> THERAPIST: My role during the course of this therapy will be based on what you bring up. You may find me asking questions or raising issues that you dislike. I may inquire, for example, about your associations in reference to important events during your life, or insist on clarification about your feelings in reference to certain individuals. You may not want to experience these feelings. Finally, I may wish to point out how you go about dealing with such issues in ways that may be viewed as maladaptive.

In making this type of presentation, the therapist is educating the patient about what is involved in a brief dynamic therapeutic interaction as well as about what kinds of issues are likely to come up during the course of therapy.

The therapist may emphasize the anxiety-provoking aspect of the confrontations and clarifications:

THERAPIST: On the basis of information that you give me, the aim of my job will be to raise questions, ask for more associations about important events in your life, scrutinize your relationships with people, and inquire about your feelings and about the ways you deal with them. It is possible that times you will find my questions and my confrontations and clarifications unpleasant or even irritating. I do not enjoy making you uncomfortable, but my role as an objective observer necessitates my raising these points, which you may want to avoid precisely because they are unpleasant. It is possible, of course, that this very avoidance may be the reason why you have not been able to resolve your own psychological problems.

Similarly, the therapist may warn about resistance:

THERAPIST: During the course of the treatment you may at times feel resistance because of the unpleasant associations involved in some of the confrontations or questions which I raise. We both need to understand the nature of your resistance so as to get to the conflicts that underlie them and to help resolve them.

Finally, the therapist will talk about helping the patient learn to solve problems independently after the treatment has come to an end. This helps the patient keep a positive view of the outcome and of the possibility of being able to solve future psychological problems alone.

These statements are all educational. I believe the therapist should be an unemotionally involved teacher.

The difference between a working and a "therapeutic" alliance is only a matter of degree. One cannot expect a full-blown therapeutic alliance to become established in the first or second therapy session. A true therapeutic alliance involves the full and joint cooperation of both therapist and patient, as they try to understand and resolve the patient's psychological conflicts. This alliance stimulates the patient's ability to bring into the therapy session memories, fantasies, and episodes from the past. Furthermore, the feelings involved and the defense mechanisms used have to be understood. If better and more adaptive defense mechanisms and behavioral patterns can be developed, then psychological conflicts will be resolved once and for all.

Early Use of Positive Transference Feelings

The best way to strengthen the therapeutic alliance is for the therapist to discern and use the patient's transference feelings. *Transference* is used here to mean "a psychological interaction between two people having both conscious and unconscious components." Generally speaking, in psychoanalytically oriented long-term psychotherapy as well as in psychoanalysis, the patient's transference is usually not dealt with until it appears as a resistance.

Freud discovered the importance of transference, and he considered it the basic tool of psychoanalysis. He distinguished between positive and negative transference feelings and hypothesized that resistance was associated with the more erotic parts of the positive transference. He further divided positive transference into conscious, friendly, affectionate, trusting, sympathetic feelings and more sexual, unconscious positive feelings. Transference resistance, then, may result either from negative feelings or from the repressed erotic elements of positive feelings.

In STAPP the therapist takes advantage of the conscious positive feelings that predominate and ends the treatment before the development of a transference neurosis where both full-blown positive erotic and negative feelings which are repressed are usually resisted.

The therapist must pursue any indication of conscious positive feelings. The therapist might say: "Can you talk more about your feelings for me, since you have brought them up just now?"

Patients' responses to statements like this vary. Some change the subject to avoid talking about their transference feelings. If so, the therapist must insist on discussing the transference, even if the patient continues avoidance tactics. Patients may minimize the significance of what they have said and might even be or act annoyed at the therapist's persistence. Patients may say, "You make a big deal out of it," or "I was just making small talk," or "Oh, it was just a way to start my session today." If the therapist does not insist on clarifying the transference, the message will be given to the patient that the subject is of not great significance; later, when transference feelings come up they may not be verbalized.

Some patients understand the importance of talking about their feelings for the therapist and do not hesitate to do so. If this is the case, no problems will arise in investigating the significance of the transference feelings and the therapy will progress smoothly.

If a patient rarely experiences early negative or erotic feelings that he or she wants to avoid, the therapist will be in a good position to remind the patient that they have clarified transference feelings in the past.

Why is it so important to deal with the transference early? I have already mentioned the importance of avoiding the development of a transference neurosis, which will be discussed at greater length in chapter 10. In addition, there is another important technical point. The transference is used early to facilitate the development of past–present links. This aspect of treatment will be discussed in detail in chapter 9. Suffice it to say at this point that the word *present* involves the transference, the here-and-now feelings of the patient, which have been displaced from key people in the past onto the therapist and which give the opportunity to the two participants to experience them alive, so to speak, during the psychotherapeutic session.

In the following dialogue, the therapist's early use of transference feelings gives rise to some interesting associations.

A woman came in for her second STAPP session.

PATIENT: I am tired today. Last time I did most of the talking, so it is your turn today to talk.
THERAPIST: Can we hear more about your need for me to talk today?
PATIENT: I don't know. I came in today feeling kind of tired. I noticed that you were wearing a Harvard tie. This has nothing to do with my saying that I wanted you to do the talking, but the thought occurred to me immediately after I looked at your tie.
THERAPIST: Both issues, the talking and the tie, have to do with me. So, as I said, let us talk more about your feelings for me.
PATIENT: Oh, you are making too much about nothing. I remember an episode when—
THERAPIST: *(Interrupting)* As important as this episode might be, if we pursue it then we shall avoid hearing about your feelings for me.

The therapist disregards the opportunity to pursue a potentially interesting association, choosing instead to pursue the transference issues. Following the patient's association will be of no value unless the feelings associated with it have been transferred to the here and now of the therapeutic session. Then they will become available to be examined within the therapist–patient interaction.

PATIENT: There you go again.
THERAPIST: Come on, let us hear about your two spontaneous state-

ments about me, the need for me to talk and your observation of my Harvard tie.

PATIENT: *(Remains silent)*

THERAPIST: What are you thinking about right now?

PATIENT: Well, in a way your tie reminded me of a tie which looked a lot like yours, a tie my older brother used to wear.

THERAPIST: Can we hear more about your relationship with your older brother? You haven't talked very much about him.

PATIENT: You see, my older brother was on my side. He always tried to help me out. You know, we've talked about the competitive feelings I had for my sister, who was the darling of my parents, who were invariably biased in favor of her and who would criticize me many times unfairly. I always felt alone and rejected.

THERAPIST: And how did your brother come to your assistance?

PATIENT: He would always talk to them and try to see things more objectively. He also reassured me and explained things to me.

THERAPIST: Was he also wearing the tie which looked like mine?

PATIENT: *(Laughing)* There you go again. Don't make fun of me

THERAPIST: Oh, you are wrong. I am not making fun of you at all. Far from it. I am very serious about what I said. You see, my talking and my tie, which you brought up early, acted as a bridge from the past to the present. They brought here between us feelings which occurred at that time about the unfairness of your parents' attitude in reference to your competition with your sister. This gives us a golden opportunity to examine these past episodes and the feelings they aroused then, as well as to understand their significance at the present time.

PATIENT: I see. Now I understand why you were so insistent about your tie, which I thought was a picayune point. I can see its importance, now that you have explained it *(smiling)*.

THERAPIST: You are smiling. What about?

PATIENT: It may amuse you that when I first met you, I thought that in a way you looked a bit like my brother.

The patient's last statement seems to be a bonus. It is also very significant because it demonstrates that on occasion, transference feelings occur spontaneously even at the outset of a therapeutic encounter—even, sometimes, before its onset—and they reveal anticipatory feelings about the psychotherapeutic work. On one occasion a patient of mine mentioned having read a book of mine before we had met and before she knew that I would become her therapist. She had developed in her mind a picture of what I would look like, thinking that I would resemble her father. When she met me, she thought that this expectation had been met.

Dealing with transference feelings early is a technical aspect that many trainees, particularly during their first or second year of psychiatric training, find hard to manage. This difficulty has to do with their inexperience, which gives rise to feelings of anxiety, modesty, and shame. It is also possible that they may have an erotic attraction for the patient. All these issues should be considered, and acting out countertransference is to be avoided at all costs.

One example of how a male psychiatric resident dealt with a STAPP patient was discussed briefly in my book (Sifneos 1987), when I described the inappropriate use of videotaping. The basic difficulty lay in the transference and the resident's countertransference feelings for the patient.

The patient was a young, attractive, female student who was seen by our research group and was found to be a suitable STAPP candidate. She had fulfilled the criteria for selection. An unresolved oedipal problem with her parents was considered to be the specific focus underlying her difficulties. This information was conveyed to the resident to whom she had been assigned. Her therapy was to be videotaped.

In the second therapy session she complained to her therapist that their first session had been difficult because she had felt that he was as persistent in his confrontation of her as her mother used to be.

In his supervisory hour the resident asked if a mother–transference link was developing and how to go about dealing with it. The supervisor, who was also a member of the research group, thought that the patient was using her feelings for her mother to avoid discussing with the therapist her displaced and erotic feelings for her father. He advised the resident to note such feelings if they surfaced during the subsequent sessions. Indeed, they did. The patient missed her next appointment, and the therapist of course inquired about the reason for the missed session.

THERAPIST: What happened when you called last week to tell me that you were going to miss our session?

PATIENT: You see, when I called you I had just woken up from a long dream, and I was embarrassed that it was too late for me to come here to see you.

THERAPIST: Let's hear about this dream.

PATIENT: (Hesitating) You want to hear about it?

100

THERAPIST: Yes, indeed.

PATIENT: Well, I was on a beach. It was a beautiful summer day, and I was with this guy. We were making love from early in the morning until six in the afternoon. It was at that point that I woke up, and to my horror I found out that it was six o'clock, the time we were supposed to end our session. So I said to myself, "Jennifer, you blew it." Then I called you.

THERAPIST: Who was the guy?

PATIENT: I don't know. But he had some of your characteristics because he had a beard like you and also wore a light-colored coat like your white coat.

THERAPIST: So there might be some feelings that you have for me, as we know, because I remind you of your mother in the way I confront you as she used to do.

When the resident related this sequence of events to his supervisor, it was clear that he had missed completely the patient's erotic transference feelings, and because of his embarrassment he reminded the patient that her feelings for him were similar to those she had for her mother, which were irrelevant at that point. Actually, on the videotape it was evident that the patient was very excited as she related her erotic dream, while the resident, if anything, was embarrassed. Finally, when he mentioned that the patient's feelings for him were similar to her feelings for her mother, it was clear that she was very unhappy.

During the supervision the resident was told that he avoided his countertransference feelings for the patient and chose the subterfuge of using the "mother–transference" link to get away from the anxiety that such feelings had aroused in him.

In the next session the therapist was able to tie the patient's feelings for her father to feelings she had for men in general and her therapist in particular. The videotape documented the patient's visible relief upon receiving that interpretation. From then on, the therapy proceeded uneventfully.

The STAPP therapist must deal with the transference feelings early in the course of treatment, when they are positive and when they predominate. The therapist who is able to use the developing therapeutic alliance and to confront the transference early can set the stage for making past–present links (chapter 9).

Activity of the Therapist

To many patients a therapist is viewed as someone who listens attentively, is sympathetic, and talks very little. The majority of therapists would agree with this description. In the 1940s, many supervisors taught their students the principle of minimal activity, which consisted of the sound "hmm" if the patient brought up something the therapist thought to be of interest, "uh-huh" if the patient's association was viewed as very important, and finally a laconic "Tell me all about it" if the information was considered to be vital. This type of therapeutic interaction has been taught systematically over the years; many therapists have dutifully learned this lesson and have become passive and almost mute. It is a safe stance, but a wrong one.

There have been efforts to defy these educational attitudes. During the 1920s, Sandor Ferenczi (1978) introduced his "active techniques" of rewards and reinforcements of patients' associations similar to those being used in behavior modification therapy in order to shorten psychoanalysis. His and others' attempts at modifying technique did not have a lasting effect on psychodynamic psychotherapists, who in their efforts to be strictly neutral continued to say very little and did not attempt to shorten treatment.

I do not mean that the therapist should lecture, advise, manipulate, or impose values. The therapist's activity is used to pull together for interpretation the material that is brought up by the patient. For example, the therapist may point out how the patient uses maladaptive defense mechanisms so that underlying psychological conflicts may be approached. In addition, the therapist must explore new ways for the patient to approach conflict.

CHAPTER 9

Central Technical Issues

Focality

EVERY TECHNICAL ASPECT OF STAPP is intertwined with every other. The activity of the therapist is intimately associated with focality, which in turn is closely connected with the repeated use of anxiety-provoking confrontations and clarifications.

The technique of focality is used by all who offer short-term dynamic therapy. The patient must agree to a focus before being accepted for STAPP (chapter 4). During the course of the therapy, the patient should be encouraged to stay within the focus; confrontations and clarifications which may provoke anxiety are relentlessly used to perform this task.

Staying within the focus will invariably produce anxiety because the focus touches the patient's unresolved psychological conflicts. Despite their repeated efforts to deal with the conflicts, patients have been unsuccessful alone and have sought therapy.

It is obvious that a conflict is in the making: the patient is motivated to resolve the psychological difficulties but does not like to experience painful feelings; the therapist is eager to help but is aware that the necessary behavior will arouse unpleasant emotions in the patient. Thus, the more the patient wants to run away from the focus, the more the therapist must keep it in view. The patient and the therapist become friendly adversaries.

How can this paradoxical situation be overcome? The therapist is confident that because of the patient's excellent motivation for change, and despite the arousal of unpleasant emotions, the eagerness of the patient to get better will predominate and will become instrumental in keeping the therapy going.

The therapist can make various types of intervention to help the patient work actively on the focus, as in the following examples.

- "You seem to have talked for a while about issues which are not at face value associated with what you and I have agreed to concentrate on."
- "Although this episode that you mentioned today may have aroused some unpleasant feelings, I do not think that it should interfere with the main task of this treatment, which is centered on our agreement to help you resolve the difficulties in your relations with men."
- "It is of interest that you are bringing up this issue today, but is it possible that it serves to avoid further exploration of your feelings associated with the focus that we agreed on?"
- "Let us get back to the central focus of this therapy."

Of course, the therapist will phrase such confrontations or interpretations according to individual style. In any event, every effort should be made to communicate to the patient that *agreement* to work on the resolution of the conflicts underlying the specified focus is a basic requirement for the relief of difficulties.

It has been erroneously suggested that STAPP is offered only to patients who demonstrate unresolved oedipal problems. Grief reactions and loss and separation issues have also been the focus in successful treatments. We have systematically studied a group of patients with unresolved oedipal problems in order to have as homogeneous a patient population as possible; perhaps this requirement led to the misunderstanding.

Nonetheless, unresolved oedipal problems remain a common focus in STAPP. During the course of our investigation we discovered that there existed three categories of unresolved oedipal focus, each more difficult than the last to resolve. We designated them *A*, *B*, and *C*.

In category *A* it was only the patients' fantasies that indicated to them that they were the favorite child of the parent of the opposite sex. In reality, this had not been the case. During the course of STAPP it became clear to the patients that they disliked the idea of giving up that fantasy; but because they were realistic and because they saw the kinds of difficulties that their persistent fantasy had created for them, they became motivated to give it up. This type of STAPP patient reaction is entirely different from the attitudes of narcissistic patients who cling tenaciously to their fantasies and are unwilling to give them up despite the enormous problems the fantasies create.

The therapist must remain aware of the patient's resistances and must keep centered on the focus by confronting the patient repeatedly with the realities of the situation:

- "I understand that the fantasy of being your father's favorite gave you a great deal of satisfaction, but from what we know on the basis of your memories, you were not the favorite in reality."
- "Of course, there is clear evidence from what you say that your mother loved you very much, but it does not mean that she loved you more than your brothers."

If the patient objects to such confrontations the therapist may insist by saying:

- "I know that you don't like to hear me say what I did, that in reality you were not the favorite of your father, but what we are aiming for is the truth. From what I have heard from your associations, there is no evidence that you were the favorite."

Another approach to this problem is to emphasize the problems that the persistance of such a fantasy has created during the patient's adult life. For example, one could say:

- "You see, we may be able to understand that as a child you were longing to be number one, to be the apple of your father's eye. Continuing, however, to think this way now, and always finding fault with the men that you are dating because they are not up to your father's standards, creates many difficulties in your interpersonal relations with them."

Innumerable situations like these will occur and can be confronted in similar language.

Category *B* may present more complex problems: it usually involves a relationship with a parent of the opposite sex, when realistically the patient was that parent's favorite. Such a situation reinforces the patient's wish and so is more difficult to give up. Faced with a dilemma of giving up a pleasant and realistic relationship with the favorite parent, in exchange for the attention of a parental substitute such as a boyfriend, the patient may choose the former and resist any change. It should be evident why so much emphasis has been placed on the fifth selection criterion, the motivation for change. It is precisely this motivation for change that propels the patient to give up this incestuous, gratifying interaction in order to grow up.

Category C is the most difficult to resolve. The oedipal issues involve a situation in which the patient is not only in the favorite position but also has actually replaced the parent of the same sex as a consequence of divorce or even death. The patient continues to live with the parent of the opposite sex and assumes some of the functions and duties of the departed parent. This attractive realistic situation corresponds precisely with his or her wishes and is difficult to give up. Yet the patient realizes that something causes difficulties in interpersonal relationships or results in the development of symptoms; this realization prompts them to seek help. Here again the patient's wish to overcome inertia is based on the motivation for change, which comes to the rescue and helps the patient cooperate with the therapist, finally succeeding in giving up oedipal cravings.

The following vignette is an example of the technical use of focality.

A twenty-year-old female patient had been her father's favorite. She was unable to interact with men because she felt that they were always trying to "control" her. Two of her boyfriends, however, had broken off with her because they said *she* was "controlling." The question was, who controlled whom? Her father had died when she was fifteen. She had blamed her mother for his death and she had displaced her feelings of loss onto her boyfriends; she had tried to control them so that they would not abandon her. The agreed-upon focus for treatment was her attachment to her father and competition with her mother as well as other women.

In earlier sessions she had blamed her father for being seductive. In the sixth session, after she recognized her own erotic wishes for him, she became anxious. She felt a need to run away. She claimed that she did not hear what her therapist was saying when he confronted her repeatedly with her feelings for her father.

The issue to be dealt with during the following sessions was her competition with her mother and other women in general, and her sexual competition with them in particular. It was this aspect of the focus that the therapist wanted the patient to understand and to deal with.

The following exchange took place during the seventh STAPP session.

> THERAPIST: Let us get back to our focus. What did this discussion we had last week about your erotic feelings for your father have to do with your competitive feelings for women in general and your mother in particular?
>
> PATIENT: I'm not sure what you mean.
>
> THERAPIST: What did we talk about during last week's session? [The therapist, instead of repeating his previous statement, attempts to get back to it by asking the patient what she remembers. He hopes to bypass her resistance.]
>
> PATIENT: About sexuality.
>
> THERAPIST: Yes, sexuality. In reference to whom?
>
> PATIENT: In reference to my parents, which I don't like to talk about.

Again the patient is trying to avoid talking about the specific sexual feelings for her father, by lumping both parents together. Patients often use this technique to get away from anxiety-provoking confrontations. It is important therefore that the therapist insist on being specific.

> THERAPIST: Not your parents in general, but to what parent in particular? So, I repeat, sexual feelings in reference to whom?
>
> PATIENT: —for my father. Do we have to repeat all this?
>
> THERAPIST: Yes. Coming back to my question, what would experiencing sexualized feelings for your father make you be vis à vis your mother, with whom you had been competitive and whom you felt you had defeated?

The excerpt presented here shows how a therapist can concentrate on the unresolved oedipal focus despite the patient's anxiety.

Anxiety-Provoking Confrontations and Clarifications

As the preceding exchange illustrates, staying within the designated and agreed-upon focus increases anxiety and brings about resistance. When that happens, the therapist is faced with a dilemma. Should one persist in making the patient more and more anxious, and thus resistant, or should one become more supportive and try to diminish the effect—in short, become anxiety-suppressive?

The STAPP therapist persists in making anxiety-provoking confrontations and clarifications. Here again the therapist counts on the patient's motivation for change. Despite unpleasant emotions, the patient will understand the need to come to grips with the anxiety once and for all, for the sake of recovery.

The therapist's confrontations and clarifications must be based on information provided by the patient. It is vital, therefore, that the therapist use statements, words, phrases, or special terms mentioned previously by the patient. When the therapist is able to repeat the patient's exact words—"and I quote you now"—the patient is enormously affected and cannot deny the validity of the therapist's clarification.

Most often anxiety-provoking questions or confrontations are associated with the focal issue. Having heard a great deal about the patient's past as well as about emotions and conflicts, the therapist is able to zero in on the conflicts, to demonstrate to the patient that the origin of his or her difficulties is clearly associated with the focal emotional conflicts.

To be able to quote the patient verbatim, it is imperative that the therapist take notes. This is a controversial recommendation; many psychotherapists consider note taking antitherapeutic. Indeed, if note taking creates a wall between therapist and patient, it becomes counterproductive.

We once observed on videotape a young resident who was treating a rather aggressive patient. After a somewhat stormy session he could be seen using his writing pad as a shield in front of his face, as if he wanted to become invisible to the viewers and the patient. This sort of reaction can be dealt with in supervisory interviews, as part of the education of mental health trainees.

The advantages of note taking outweigh enormously the potential disadvantages. In STAPP, right from the beginning the therapy moves quickly and a great deal of material is brought up by the patient. It can be dealt with appropriately, particularly when the technical aspects of the therapy are followed correctly. Therefore, the timing of the material brought up by the patient should be clearly monitored. A busy therapist cannot be expected to remember exactly when some of the patient's associations came up. Notes help the therapist remember exactly how the session progressed and the exact words used by the patient in describing a special espisode, feeling, or person. Reviewing the notes of the previous session prepares the therapist for anything that happens in the forthcoming session.

Academic or research-oriented therapists make use of their notes to write up their cases for publication or for their research studies, rather than rely on their own memory. Note taking is clearly of great value to these therapists.

One last question may come up in reference to note taking: Do patients object? It is possible that with very severely disturbed or delusional individuals, the therapist may accede to a request not to take notes. But these are not STAPP patients. In many years, I have not encountered a single STAPP patient who has objected to my taking notes.

Returning to the subject of anxiety-provoking confrontations and clarifications: again the therapist has a range of statements to use. If the patient blocks or is silent for a while, inquiring specifically about what the patient is thinking can be helpful, but it can also be anxiety provoking.

- "You were talking, and now all of a sudden you stopped. What have you been thinking about?"
- "You seemed to block as a result of what I asked you. Can you tell me, please, what went through your mind?"

If a patient brings up information about some form of acting out which seems to be antitherapeutic, the therapist might say:

- "It appears to me that your action is completely contrary to what we have been talking about. Under these circumstances, therefore, I think that there is no need for us to go on, because it is clear that you are not interested in solving your problems if you act out against your own therapy."

Such a statement usually will produce a great deal of anxiety, because the patient's motivation for change has been challenged. Patients usually vehemently deny that they want to discontinue their therapy, and they also agree that acting out will be counterproductive.

If, on the other hand, the patient has used acting out as an excuse to terminate treatment because it is too anxiety provoking, it should be concluded that the original evaluation of the patient's motivation for change was faulty and that the patient was not an appropriate candidate for STAPP.

Anxiety-provoking confrontations and clarifications are also related to the patient's transference feelings, particularly if such feelings were not clarified satisfactorily in the early STAPP sessions.

A twenty-year-old male student had noticed that there were similarities between his mother and his female therapist. Both were viewed by him as being successful in their professions.

During the third session the patient emphasized how much he wished the therapist to tell him what to do.

THERAPIST: Can we hear more about why you wish for me to tell you what to do?

PATIENT: Well, you are the expert, you are the therapist to whom I have come for help.

THERAPIST: So, as we have already seen, you view me like your mother, who is also a successful professional person.

PATIENT: Yes, there is the element that both you and my mother are successful professional women.

The patient is acknowledging his transference feelings in a general way. The therapist can of course pursue and clarify the common characterization between herself and the patient's mother. On the other hand, she may feel that enough work has been done on that point, so she may decide to ask more about the patient's wish to be told what to do and, generally speaking, to be guided. Allowing the patient to remain passive would be counterproductive. She decides to challenge the patient's attitude, even if he does not receive her confrontation enthusiastically.

THERAPIST: Are you also saying that your mother used to tell you what to do in the same way as you want me to now?

PATIENT: Well, no.

THERAPIST: No?

PATIENT: You do have similarities with my mother, as I have already mentioned, but I never expected my mother to tell me what to do. If anything, my mother always complimented me about my independent thinking and she always respected my feelings.

THERAPIST: So who was the one who told you what to do, who do you associate with me?

PATIENT: It was my older brother. As you know, I lost my father when I was two years old and my older brother, who was ten years older than I, acted as the man of the house. He was always telling my sister and me what to do. Actually, he happened to give us good advice most of the time, but at times I resented it. We fought a lot.

THERAPIST: Do you want me to tell you what to do, to give you good advice like your brother used to do, or bad advice which you resented?

PATIENT: *(Remains silent)*

THERAPIST: You are silent. What are you thinking about?

PATIENT: Your statement. I don't like it. [Clearly the therapist's confrontation in this case was anxiety provoking.] I don't like to see you having traits of my older brother, because I am glad that you remind me of my mother, with whom I got along so well.

In this case the anxiety-provoking confrontation had a double positive effect. It informed the therapist of early competitive feelings between the patient and his brother, but it also reinforced the positive identification of the therapist with his mother.

Anxiety-provoking confrontations and clarifications can also sometimes be made in reference to paradoxical situations presented by the patient.

THERAPIST: You are telling me that you had angry feelings about both of your parents, yet at the same time you say that you didn't mind being angry at your mother but you felt upset when you were angry at your father. Now this is paradoxical, isn't it?

PATIENT: Yes. I had angry feelings about my parents.

THERAPIST: You always answer in reference to your parents. Let us clarify some more the angry feelings about each one of your parents separately.

PATIENT: You are always so precise. [The patient is unhappy about this clarification.]

THERAPIST: This is my job. My question is, for what parent separately, not for both.

PATIENT: OK, if you insist. With my mother. I felt angry when she gave me advice or tried to baby me as if I was a child who did not know what I really wanted. With my father it was different. I felt annoyed when he would spend a lot of time teaching my younger brother how to play baseball.

THERAPIST: So you were irritated by your mother's attitude, and you were jealous about your father's attention to your brother.

PATIENT: Oh, you!

Although the series of anxiety-provoking clarifications makes the patient uncomfortable, the statements serve the purpose of clarifying as well as deepening the therapeutic exploration. The therapist needs to be precise, which is exactly what the patient dislikes because it forces him to separate the angry feelings for his father from the angry feelings for his mother—jealously from irritation.

It is not only in reference to paradoxical situations that the therapist should be anxiety-provoking. Every kind of non sequitur, grandiose expectation, illogical association should be investigated and explored extensively because it may be used defensively to hide or to avoid the underlying emotional conflict. Bringing it into the open, although it may give rise to anxiety, helps to come to grips with it, work it through, and in the end resolve it.

All the technical aspects of STAPP described so far converge to arouse the patient's interest and to reinforce motivation. The therapeutic alliance, the early use of the positive transference, the activity of the therapist, the emphasis on focality, and the use of anxiety-provoking confrontations and clarifications all help develop possibly the most important aspect of STAPP technique, interpretation of the past–present links.

Past–Present Links

Making a link between the patient's past feelings for important people and the patient's transference feelings for the therapist constitutes one of the most important technical aspects of all brief dynamic psychotherapies. That is why the early interpretation of transference feelings is so important.

Past–present links allow the therapist to examine the patient's childhood emotional conflicts surrounding parents or parent surrogates, which create difficulties in interpersonal relationships later in life. Having been transferred onto the therapist, these same emotional conflicts can be investigated actively; the patient's maladaptive defense mechanisms can be shown to be responsible for the ensuing problems. Then a search can be initiated for better and more adaptive defense mechanisms and for new behaviors to be learned. In this way, it is hoped, subsequent difficulties encountered by the patient can be corrected.

According to Alexander and French's (1946) concept of the corrective emotional experience, an atmosphere is created within the therapeutic session in which better ways of handling neurotic problems can take place. This also occurs often in STAPP. The therapist should not manipulate the transference and act in a special way to model behavior, however.

In STAPP the therapist simply points out that links exist between the past and the present. Having reviewed session notes the therapist should clarify obvious connections between conflicts with people in the past and similar conflicts that have come up during the therapy session. The therapist must be able to collect systematically information about the timing of certain events, special memories, and feelings that were experienced by the patient in the past. If a patient recounts a special interaction with one parent and mentions that he or she felt exceptionally happy, the therapist should inquire about the circumstances surrounding the happiness, ensuring that the strong positive emotion was clearly associated with the specific interaction mentioned by the patient, not with a similar interaction at another time. It is possible, of course, that a similar feeling associated with a different episode has been added to the original memory and has reinforced it. In the case of feelings added together, the therapist should investigate why the patient merged two positive experiences into one and intensified the feelings associated with them. For example, perhaps the patient wanted to deny the second episode because when it took place relations with the parent had become worse. Transferring the first positive feeling to another time helps to deny the deterioration in this relationship.

The following statements can be made by the therapist who is investigating the exact timing of certain events and the emotions associated with them:

- "You describe that interaction with your father, but you don't mention when it took place. How old were you when it happened?"

If the patient answers in a nonspecific way, the therapist must persist:

- "As we know, this was the time when you and your father were close. You told me that later on your feelings for him changed. Do you remember when, exactly, your relationship changed?"

Questions like these help to pinpoint time so that a past–present link can be associated specifically with the event in question, and not with others that may have similarities but occurred at another time.

A thirty-year-old female patient had been talking about her love of sailing.

THERAPIST: How old were you when you started to sail?

PATIENT: Oh, my father taught me how to sail when I was seven. I was very happy because he told me that I was very good. Later on, however, he stopped sailing with me.

THERAPIST: And when did that happen?

PATIENT: When I was nine.

THERAPIST: Why did he stop?

PATIENT: I don't know.

THERAPIST: How did you feel about his not sailing with you anymore?

PATIENT: I was angry at him.

THERAPIST: So the good times of sailing with your father lasted only for two years?

PATIENT: More or less.

THERAPIST: What happened when you were nine?

PATIENT: Nothing special.

THERAPIST: There must be a reason your father stopped sailing with you.

PATIENT: Maybe it was his work. He traveled a lot. There were also some financial difficulties when my sister was born and—

THERAPIST: (Interrupting) You bring up too many memories all at once.

PATIENT: I don't really know.

THERAPIST: Let us find out.

PATIENT: OK.

THERAPIST: When did your father have financial troubles?

PATIENT: Oh, he did off and on. He always complained about finances, and that is why he had to go traveling.

THERAPIST: This was a chronic difficulty?

PATIENT: Yes.

THERAPIST: So we cannot blame it on something that happened between the two of you.

PATIENT: I guess not.

THERAPIST: Now, you mentioned the birth of your sister. When was that?

PATIENT: When I was nine.

THERAPIST: Did it have something to do with the end of the sailing?

PATIENT: I don't know.

THERAPIST: How did you feel about your father's no longer going out sailing with you?

PATIENT: You asked me already. As I told you, I felt angry.

THERAPIST: How did you get along with your sister?

PATIENT: OK. But, you know, we had a few fights.

THERAPIST: Fights about what?

PATIENT: Well, maybe I was a bit jealous with all this attention being given to the new baby.

THERAPIST: By whom?

PATIENT: By my parents.

THERAPIST: Let's keep them separate. What about your mother?

PATIENT: She was proud of my sister.

THERAPIST: What about your father?

PATIENT: She was his favorite when she was young.

THERAPIST: How did you feel about that?

PATIENT: I felt a little jealous.

THERAPIST: So you felt angry about the end of the sailing and "a little jealous" about your sister being your father's favorite.

PATIENT: Yes, that is true ... This is quite helpful, because I remember that my mom and I became quite close at that time, although we hadn't been too close before then.

THERAPIST: You say this is helpful. What do you mean?

PATIENT: You were able with your questions to get me to see a connection I had not thought of before.

THERAPIST: So you are saying that my questions help you?

PATIENT: Yes, they do.

THERAPIST: Does that remind you of anything?

PATIENT: It reminds me of my report card. I was a good student and my father was pleased with it. He used to ask me a lot of questions about school. This was at the time that we were going sailing together.

THERAPIST: Before the birth of your sister?

PATIENT: Yes.

THERAPIST: So your father and I have one thing in common. We ask questions which you find helpful and make you feel good.

PATIENT: No.

THERAPIST: No?

PATIENT: Well, last week I was also happy with your questions, and then I got mad because you should have left your "Interview in Progress" sign on. I was mad when that woman came in. Was she another of your patients, or a resident, or someone like that? She interrupted our session.

THERAPIST: So you were mad at me because our interview was interrupted by that woman last week. Of course, there is a reality in what you say. I should have turned my sign on. You are absolutely right. Isn't there something more, however, about this episode which is similar to what we were talking about a few minutes ago?

PATIENT: In what way?

THERAPIST: You and I get along well. I ask you helpful questions like your father used to do about your report card, and that makes you happy. Last week, however, this was also taking place until that other woman—due to my negligence—interrupted our session and you got mad at me.

PATIENT: Yes.

THERAPIST: Well, didn't the birth of your sister interrupt your good relationship with your father?

PATIENT: I see what you are saying. Yes, there is the exact set of circumstances and the same feelings, positive and then negative.

Clearly, a past–transference link has been made. The therapist asked very specific questions about the interaction between the patient and her father. The patient's statement, "This is quite helpful," brought immediate attention to the current transference situation. A therapist should always be on the alert when a patient expresses positive feelings about the therapist and then very quickly undoes the statement by bringing up something negative. In this case the patient picked on the "Interview in Progress" sign. Her annoyance at the woman who interrupted her session as well as at the therapist felt exactly like her anger with her father when her sister interrupted their relationship.

A woman who had expressed her appreciation about the progress of her therapy in the early part of a session suddenly stopped in the middle of a sentence.

PATIENT: —Oh, the thought just occurred to me that your driveway has not been plowed well and I had some difficulty driving up with my car.

THERAPIST: After telling me how much you appreciate the progress of our therapy, you seem to want to undo the expression of this positive statement by being annoyed at the state of my driveway. Now, in reality, sometimes the driveway is not as well plowed as it should be. But this sudden association about the driveway seems to point to a need to take back the expression of your positive feelings about the progress of your therapy and my role in it. Does this situation remind you of anything from the past?

PATIENT: No, it just occurred to me, and that is why I said it.

THERAPIST: Oh, of course. Don't get me wrong. I am not criticizing your bringing it up. Not at all. What I am referring to, however, is the paradox of a positive statement being followed closely by a negative one. We have seen this tendency of yours before. Why do you have to undo something positive?

PATIENT: It is to protect myself.

THERAPIST: Protect yourself? From whom?

PATIENT: From anyone who might take advantage of the expression of my good feelings.

THERAPIST: When did this hypersensitivity and protection of yourself begin?

PATIENT: From the time when my older brother, whom I liked, admired, and respected, started to abuse me.

THERAPIST: Abuse you?

PATIENT: Well, no, not in the way that you think. Not sexually.

THERAPIST: Why did you think that I would have thought that you were sexually abused?

PATIENT: Because we were talking about my sexual feelings for men last week. No, I did not say that, that is what you said, I don't put it on you, but—

THERAPIST: *(Interrupting)* Wait a minute. We were trying to figure out your need to undo the experience of expressing a positive feeling by substituting a negative one, as you did in reference to me. This inquiry of mine has reminded you of your brother, whom you "liked, admired, and respected." I quote your own words. Then you say that he started to abuse you and as a result of this you have to protect yourself whenever you experience a positive feeling. You also add that you are afraid that the same situation will repeat itself. Now you experienced this feeling here with me. You talked positively about the progress of your therapy and then suddenly, out of the blue, the idea popped into your mind about the bad state of my driveway. As I said already, realistically the driveway should have been better plowed. What is more important, in my opinion, was your need to undo your positive feeling for fear I might abuse you as your brother did, and therefore you felt a need to protect yourself.

PATIENT: Hmm.

THERAPIST: Tell me, how did your brother abuse you? And forget about my thinking that you were sexually abused.

The patient proceeds to describe how her brother enjoyed teasing her and how he minimized her intellectual achievements whenever she expressed admiration for him. The therapist, having made clear the present–past link between himself and the patient's brother, proceeds.

THERAPIST: Maybe your brother had the same problems you do—a tendency to undo his positive feelings for you by becoming easily annoyed and critical.

In another STAPP case, a past–present link was made with a patient for whom the focus of therapy was the resolution of feelings of separation and loss.

The patient was a twenty-year-old male college student whose parents had been divorced when he was eight years old. His mother had remarried one year later while the patient and his older sister were living with their father. The therapist was a female third-year resident who had elected to treat a STAPP patient. The therapy started in mid-May, and the resident had planned her vacation for mid-June.

The patient's sensitivity to the loss of his mother was thought to be crucial because it had affected his relationships with two of his girlfriends. He terminated his relationship with each woman after he thought that she rejected him by going to visit her family. In reality, however, the women had not rejected him at all; they were surprised and chagrined when he announced that he was ending the relationships. Because of his sensitivity in this area, it was decided during supervision that the therapist would bring up her forthcoming vacation plans at the second treatment session so as to anticipate his potential reaction to separation. She did so. The patient responded appropriately: he took out his notebook and wrote that there would be no sessions during the last two weeks of June.

The therapy moved along well. The patient had said that when his mother left he had not missed her very much because he was very close at the time to his sister, who was six years his senior. He also mentioned that he had accepted and agreed to work on the issue of his separation from his mother because the evaluator had presented him with some impressive arguments about how much this loss may have affected his relations with his girlfriends. Although he said that he had respect for the evaluator's expertise, nevertheless he had some reservations about the importance of his mother's departure and about any significance that she might have had in his life.

During the fourth session, the last one before the therapist's vacation, the patient came in and immediately brought up a financial complication. He said that the hospital clinic was charging him too much, and he wondered whether he would be able to continue his treatment after the therapist's return.

THERAPIST: I am surprised that you bring up the subject of your finances now. I thought that it had all been discussed with you during your initial evaluation.

PATIENT: Yes, it was, but now it seems to be a problem for me.

THERAPIST: "Now"? What do you mean by "now"?

PATIENT: I mean that I calculated my expenses and I find that it is difficult, if not impossible, for me to continue with you here in this clinic. [Since the patient brings up his relationship with the therapist, she immediately picks it up for clarification of his transference feelings.]

THERAPIST: Are you saying that you can't continue therapy with me because of the financial problems, or that you don't want to continue therapy at all?

PATIENT: *(Irritably)* Oh no, of course I want to continue therapy, but I cannot do it here because it's very expensive.

THERAPIST: You seem to be irritated at my question.

PATIENT: Of course I am. A lot of good work has already been done. I do want to get to the bottom of this business about my relations with my girlfriends.

THERAPIST: So why are you irritated with me?

PATIENT: Because you question my motivation for psychotherapy.

THERAPIST: Are you sure that that is all?

PATIENT: What else could it be?

THERAPIST: I don't know, but you bring up this financial problem at the time when you know that I will be going away for two weeks.

PATIENT: Oh, not at all. Your vacation has nothing to do with my financial problems.

THERAPIST: It may not, but the idea pops up into your mind all of a sudden.

PATIENT: You're making a big deal out of this. Of course you are entitled to a vacation like anyone else.

At this point the therapist is facing a problem if she insists on pursuing the issue of her vacation. So, having pointed out the patient's apparent irritation with her, she decides to approach the subject from a different angle, namely, to become very precise about the timing of his decision to discontinue his therapy.

THERAPIST: When did you calculate your expenses and find out that you might not be able to afford to continue therapy with me?

PATIENT: Two weeks ago.

THERAPIST: During our second session? [She had told him then about her vacation plans.]

PATIENT: I guess so.

THERAPIST: If so, why did you bring it up today? Why not then?

PATIENT: I still wanted to give this therapy a chance.

THERAPIST: You don't anymore?

PATIENT: I do, but as I told you, I can't afford it. How many times do I have to repeat it?

THERAPIST: Now you are angry with me.

PATIENT: You bet I am. You are making a mountain out of a molehill.

The therapist again is facing an impasse. She has two options. She could try to soothe the patient by volunteering to do something about decreasing his fee at the clinic. This would be a mistake, however, unless she was sure that there really was a financial problem. Her second option is to take an entirely different tack and inquire about the patient's past.

THERAPIST: So you are angry with me now, but weren't you also angry at your two girlfriends when they went to visit their families?

PATIENT: Yes, it is true, but you are not my girlfriend, and as I said, you are entitled to your vacation. Maybe you will also visit your family.

THERAPIST: *Oh?*

PATIENT: I didn't mean it that way. I don't care where you are going or what you plan to do.

THERAPIST: But why are you angry with me?

PATIENT: I feel irritated by your questions. Maybe I should find a therapist who charges less and also doesn't irritate me.

Again the therapist seems to be hitting at a stone wall. She tries to extricate herself from her predicament by bringing up the patient's girlfriends' visits to their families. She has no solid evidence, however, and in light of his irritation with her she must be very careful not to antagonize the patient too much and lose him.

THERAPIST: So, have you thought of finding another therapist who is not as expensive as I am?

120

PATIENT: Well, if you want to know, I know of a therapist. She is my roommate's therapist. She's good. She is in private practice, so she can afford to offer lower fees.

THERAPIST: What else do you know about your roommate's therapist?

PATIENT: Except for the lower fees, nothing, except that it appears that she is quite young. My roommate told me that she was only twenty-six years old.

THERAPIST: So she is just six years older than you?

PATIENT: Yes, but apparently she is good.

THERAPIST: Oh, I am not questioning that. Doesn't a six-year-older person and a woman mean anything to you?

PATIENT: What do you mean?

THERAPIST: I mean what I mean. I asked you a question.

PATIENT: I don't know what you mean.

THERAPIST: Come on now, she is six years older than you. Isn't that how old your sister is, to whom you became so attached after your mother left?

PATIENT: *(Remains silent)*

THERAPIST: You are silent. What are you thinking about?

PATIENT: When I discovered my financial difficulties, I talked with Jim, my roommate, and it was then that he told me about his therapist. Well, you know that the queer thing is, that very night I had a dream about my sister. She was not twenty-six, she was fourteen. She looked in the dream as she looked at that time.

THERAPIST: What else happened in the dream?

PATIENT: I was angry, and she was nice to me.

THERAPIST: So you are angry with me because I am going away and you go to another therapist who is six years older than you, as you did after your mother left. You turned for support to your six-year-older sister, who soothed you.

PATIENT: I must say, it is an interesting coincidence.

THERAPIST: Coincidence?

PATIENT: Well, not really, because although I have financial troubles, maybe they are not as bad as I make them out to be. The peculiar thing is that I obsessed about my finances. I suppose it had something to do with your leaving.

THERAPIST: Well, then, shall we try to look at all this now before deciding whether we should stop your therapy?

PATIENT: Yes.

THERAPIST: If the financial problems are realistic and not associated

121

with my leaving, I shall see what I can do with the clinic admini-
stration about possibly lowering your fee.

PATIENT: *(Sheepishly)* Maybe it won't be necessary after all.

The session continues uneventfully and the decision is reached to
continue after the resident's return from her vacation.

The transference—past link, which was expertly made by the therapist,
was instrumental, without doubt, in saving the treatment.

CHAPTER 10

Later Technical Issues and Termination

Avoiding Regression

Stapp patients are people with considerable strength of character, as established in the exploratory evaluation. Unlike patients who are psychologically more disturbed, STAPP patients are not expected to regress during their treatment. Then why discuss regression? Although we do not see true regression in STAPP, there can be a "pseudoregression."

As a result of the anxiety-provoking confrontations and clarifications and the activity of the therapist in keeping the treatment on the focus, the patient feels progressively more uncomfortable. It is understandable, therefore, that occasionally and in order to avoid temporarily the anxiety, patients may pretend that they are regressing when in reality they are not. This type of reaction gives the patient a sort of relief. But if the therapist does not recognize it and interpret it, it will eventually be antitherapeutic because it avoids a successful resolution of the problems and tends to perpetuate the patient's emotional conflicts.

To deal with such a situation, first, the therapist must be sure that the evaluation was correct. The patient should have fulfilled the criteria for selection, and the agreed-upon focus should have been the correct one. If there are doubts in the therapist's mind, especially about the patient's character structure, then of course he or she may be worried when confronted with a potential regression. Second, by the time such regressionlike reactions make their appearance, the therapist has had ample opportunity to assess the patient's strengths of character, how the patient deals with transference issues, how well the patient tolerates anxiety, the extent of his or her motivation for change, the success of the therapeutic alliance, and other aspects of the therapist–patient relationship. If the therapy is on track, signs of regressive behavior do not represent a true regression. Instead, the patient is attempting to avoid the unpleasant feelings that have been aroused by the therapist's relentless efforts to pinpoint his or her difficulties, to demonstrate maladaptive reactions, to encourage insight, and to enhance the process of a therapeutic conflict resolution.

A twenty-five-year-old man had gone through the evaluation process. He was seen by two senior members of the research team that was studying a group of STAPP patients with unresolved oedipal problems as the focus of the treatment. He was being treated by a gifted third-year psychiatric resident under weekly supervision.

The therapy had been going along well. The resident had been active and had amassed enough evidence from the patient's statements to confront the patient with his ambivalent feelings for his father. The patient resisted vehemently, having repeatedly professed his love for his father. In the next session the therapist announced that he could see the patient the following week but then would have to postpone the next appointment for two weeks. He told the patient that he had to attend a series of scientific conferences out of town. The patient said that he doubted that he could wait for two weeks because he had been feeling quite anxious; he asked if he could be seen by another therapist or if he could be given some tranquilizing medication. The therapist wisely said that they should discuss that request the following week and decide at that time how to proceed.

Immediately after that somewhat difficult session, the therapist called his supervisor to ask for advice on how to deal with the patient's request. He was told that because the patient had been thoroughly evaluated and had passed all the STAPP criteria for selection, it was thought that he was perfectly capable of withstanding the anxiety that emanated from the discussion of his ambivalent feelings for his father. The therapist was advised therefore not to give the patient any medication and not to have him be seen by another therapist. The resident hesitated, then said that he thought that it would not be such a bad idea if he gave some tranquilizing medication to the patient. The supervisor, having noticed the therapist's reluctance to accept his recommendation, went on:

> SUPERVISOR: You should know that each patient is seen by two inde-
> pendent evaluators who are members of our STAPP research team,
> consisting of five senior psychiatrists. Two evaluators, after seeing
> the patient independently, present their findings to our research
> team. A general discussion takes place about the suitability of the
> patient in terms of the five STAPP criteria for selection and the
> specified focus. If there are some discrepancies between the find-
> ings of the two evaluators, an attempt is made to clarify them. If
> these discrepancies persist, then the patient is referred back to the
> clinic to receive psychotherapy, but is not accepted for the STAPP
> research, which deals only with the evaluation and treatment of
> candidates who have been found by unanimous agreement of the
> research team to be indeed good STAPP patients. Now, your
> patient has been found unanimously by our committee to be an
> excellent candidate, so all this business of his regression is a form
> of acting out in order to test you. So, again I repeat that I recom-
> mend that you not give him any medication and that you not
> advise him to see another therapist while you are away.

As reported by the resident, the following exchange took place at the end of the next session.

> PATIENT: Doctor, have you decided what to do about my requests?
> THERAPIST: Yes, I have. It seems to me that seeing someone else while
> I am away will not be helpful to you, because a new person will
> not be in a position to know what you and I have been working
> on. So it seems that the only reason for seeing a new person will
> be to reassure you about your anxiety. Now, in reference to that
> anxiety, I feel sure that you are perfectly capable of withstanding
> it without tranquilizing medication.
> PATIENT: I'm disappointed. You seem to have much more faith in my
> capabilities than I do. I don't know what will happen while you
> are away.
> THERAPIST: If anything happens that makes you too uncomfortable,
> you can always come to our emergency unit. It is open twenty-four
> hours a day, and there is always a psychiatrist on call.
> PATIENT: Thank you, doctor. It is too bad that you don't understand
> my wishes. Have a good time, wherever you are going. I really

don't know what will happen. After all, you are just learning. I'm sure older doctors who saw me during the two evaluation interviews would know what I am going through.

THERAPIST: OK. I'll see you in two weeks, but if my schedule changes I'll give you a call and we can have our regular appointment next week.

As soon as this session was over the therapist immediately called his supervisor to ask whether he should cancel his plans to attend the scientific meetings because the patient was regressing. The supervisor told him not to change any plans and not to call the patient. He did, however, set up an extra supervisory hour the following day.

Consider what is transpiring in this situation. The patient gives the impression that he is regressing. The resident therapist treating a STAPP patient for the first time becomes understandably apprehensive, not having evaluated the patient himself. He is right not to trust someone else's impressions outright, but when his supervisor reminded him once more that the two senior evaluators who had worked for several years doing research on STAPP agreed that the patient was a good candidate, he should have felt relieved. In addition, the supervisor reminded the therapist that the research committee had also unanimously found the patient to be an excellent candidate for this therapy. Under these circumstances the supervisor thought that the resident had nothing to worry about.

The supervisor agreed that as a compromise it was appropriate for the therapist to have mentioned the hospital's emergency unit, but it was not all right to imply that he might change his plans, particularly after the patient mentioned the therapist's apparent lack of experience. He went on:

SUPERVISOR: It is clear to me that the patient is testing you, to see whether you trust him and whether you are qualified to treat him. Of course, he is *your* patient and you must do whatever *you* like about your plans. I, for one, recommend that you don't change your plans, that you do go to your scientific meetings, and that you don't call the patient to reassure him.

The resident again reluctantly agreed to follow these recommendations. When he came two weeks later for his supervisory session, he reported that the patient had greeted him with a smile. He described the session:

PATIENT: Doctor, you passed my test.

THERAPIST: What test are you talking about?

PATIENT: You trusted me, and you stuck to your opinion. I thought that you might not.

THERAPIST: Why did you think that I might change my mind?

PATIENT: As I told you, I think that maybe you are not as experienced and that you are learning.

THERAPIST: I assume you mean these questions of yours about medications and about seeing someone else were ways to test me?

PATIENT: Yes, exactly. Of course I wasn't too anxious to be able to wait for you for two weeks, and of course I didn't need any medication. If you had given it to me, I would have thought that you didn't trust me.

THERAPIST: OK. Let's return to the subject which created all this difficulty, namely your ambivalent feelings about your father, which you didn't like to face.

PATIENT: Except for one more thing. Why is it that you said that you would call me if your plans changed? Were you worried?

THERAPIST: To be honest with you, I was a little bit, but on second thought I felt that all would be all right.

PATIENT: I am glad to hear it. Everything was all right. OK, then let's go back to where we left off.

It is understandable that trainees may become anxious, particularly if they have been treating sicker patients over a long time, but adequate supervision helps them to learn to differentiate between seriously disturbed patients and STAPP patients.

Avoiding Transference Neurosis

Transference neurosis, a psychoanalytic concept, is not often discussed in relation to short-term dynamic psychotherapy. The term describes a state that develops during the height of the psychoanalysis of a neurotic patient (Glover 1955). At such a time the patient makes the analyst the recipient of all the emotional reactions the patient has experienced in connection with every relationship in the past. A transference neurosis develops as a result of the free-associative technique used four or five times a week in psychoanalysis. Short-term dynamic psychotherapy, with once-a-week, face-to-face sessions, uncovers only a limited number of memories, images, fantasies, and thoughts, generally related to the therapeutic focus. If the therapy lasts long enough, however, the transference neurosis will invariably develop; since the STAPP therapist does not have access to *all* of the patient's associations for key people in the past, it will be difficult to help the patient resolve the transference neurosis. As a result, the therapy is prolonged, the conflicts are not solved, and eventually everything bogs down. It is important, therefore, that the therapist help the patient resolve the emotional conflicts underlying the focus quickly, and then the therapy should be terminated as soon as possible.

Evidence of New Learning, Problem Solving, and Insight

As the therapy is progressing, the therapist must be alert to evidence of new learning and problem solving. New learning demonstrates that the patient is assimilating knowledge about the ways in which he or she deals with the emotional conflicts underlying the focus and is experiencing the feelings associated with the conflicts.

Learning is sometimes viewed as a strictly cognitive phenomenon, unrelated to dynamic psychotherapy. In a conference in London in 1968, a group of behaviorists and psychoanalysts spent three days discussing the role of learning in psychotherapy (Porter 1968). We had been puzzled by our experience with patients who had been offered STAPP during the mid-1950s: they stated in follow-up interviews that the most striking result of their therapy was that they had learned a great deal about themselves. At first we attributed this statement to the fact that many of them had been students. At that London conference, however, it became clear to us that both learning theory and psychoanalytic theory played an important role in psychotherapy of brief duration.

We concluded that new learning and problem solving were to a great degree responsible for the development of new insights. In addition, they contributed to reinforcing the patient's positive feelings for the therapist, which in turn help increase the patient's efforts to tackle and resolve new emotional conflicts. This series of events is associated with the patient's motivation for change and is instrumental in reinforcing the overall therapeutic problem-solving work. Thus any evidence of new learning and problem solving during the therapy means progress. Furthermore, even partial insight into the focal conflicts indicates that things are going well.

It follows that it is advisable for the therapist to raise questions often to ascertain what the patient has learned, what problems have been resolved, and how new insights have developed.

- "On the basis of the work that we have done during the past few sessions, do you feel that you have learned anything new about the focal problem we have decided to investigate and attempt to resolve?"
- "Could you give an example of what problems you have solved since you started your therapy?"
- "Since we have been able to understand and resolve your difficulties in your relationship with your mother, how can you use these insights in your current relations with other people?"

Questions like these denote interest on the part of the therapist and signal the patient that they are important components of his or her therapy. A periodic summary of the progress of the therapy underscores any evidence of partial insight, new learning, or problem solving.

A twenty-five-year-old man was seen because of difficulties in his relationship with his boss. He was afraid that he might be fired. He was treated by a male therapist. During the first three sessions he talked about his relations with women in general and with his wife and his mother in particular. He said that his relations with women were very good except that at times he felt afraid that some man might be able to seduce his wife, and this might lead to a divorce, which he wanted to avoid at all costs. At the end of the third session, the therapist had summarized the work which had been done up to that time. The therapist began the fourth session with a reminder.

THERAPIST: Last time, you may remember, I spent part of the interview summarizing the work we have been doing. Can you tell me what you remember about the issues I brought up?

PATIENT: Well, I must say that I have always been aware of having had good relations with women, like my wife and mother, but I had not thought as clearly about my tendency to bend over backward to please both of them.

THERAPIST: All right, but have you drawn any conclusions about your relations with women and your current problems with men? [The therapist wants to test whether the patient has done any thinking

129

on his own or was parroting what the therapist brought up during the previous session.]

PATIENT: Well, yes. You see, I remembered that when I was practicing the violin and my mother always sat next to me giving me instructions—which I always enjoyed—my father at times would get annoyed and he would call her. He would say—and I remember clearly his words—"Lois, you have spent enough time with Jim's violin lessons. Come here because I have a lot to talk to you about." At such times my mother would more or less apologize to me and say, "Now Jim, continue to practice your violin, but I think that your father is a bit irritated tonight, so I must leave you to see what he has in mind." Then my mother would leave, and I remember feeling kind of sad and annoyed with my father. What I figured out after our last session, was that my fear that some guy might seduce Suzanne [the patient's wife] and take her away from me had nothing to do with Suzanne. I figured out that it was that old fear and irritation at my father, when he would call my mother, take her away from me, and I was left alone to practice the violin.

This patient's use of the material connecting his mother and his wife, which came up during his therapy, was new learning and also produced a new insight for him. For example, it was very important for him to understand that the fear of losing his wife was associated with his father's succeeding in separating him from his mother at a pleasant time. This obvious problem solving on the part of the patient was a step in the right direction, enabling him to separate his feelings in reference to his father and mother from those for his wife and her potential seducer.

The therapist under such circumstances should encourage the patient to continue doing this type of work not only during the treatment session but also alone. Problem solving and partial insights help consolidate the therapeutic alliance, and they can be used effectively by both participants at times of resistance. They are like landmarks for a mountain climber who may be forced at times to retreat and consolidate a position before embarking on another climb toward the mountain peak.

Another male patient spontaneously brought up the value of what he had learned in reference to his feelings about his mother.

PATIENT: I never realized how ambivalent I felt about my mother until last week, when we talked about my tendency to create problems for my female secretaries. As I told you, I sometimes made them

130

work extra time when it was not necessary, or I would ask them to do a variety of things at the end of the day, when I knew that they were eager to go home. I have always felt a bit guilty about this mild form of sadistic behavior. Last week, when I told you that I got into an argument with the secretary of another lawyer who was much older than I and you asked me whom did she remind me of and I answered that she had the same name as my mother, I was amazed. All of a sudden I realized how unfair I had been, both to her and to my own secretary. I felt very bad about it, so this week I gave my secretary the day off.

STAPP patients often give this sort of evidence of new learning and problem solving during the course of therapy. The therapist should acknowledge the patient's progress and encourage more work along the same lines.

Recapitulation for Avoiding Resistance

Occasionally the STAPP patient's anxiety may become so intense that a strong resistance makes its appearance. Although the therapist may feel that his or her interpretations are correct, it is a mistake to insist that they are correct if the patient shows strong resistance. Any such insistence will invariably increase the patient's resistance.

Resistance may also set in as a result of an unorthodox therapeutic technique by which the therapist helps the therapy move more rapidly and reach an early ending. This technical maneuver involves interpreting a focal conflict *before* analyzing and dealing with the defense mechanisms that are used by the patient to avoid it. In classic psychoanalysis this technical device is considered to be inappropriate because it results in strengthening the defenses and increasing the resistance. Usually therefore it is advisable for the therapist to analyze the defense mechanisms first, arriving gradually at the emotional conflict that gave rise to the defenses. In psychoanalysis, of course, the analyst is not pressed to terminate early and there is ample time to analyze all the defenses slowly. In STAPP, however, the therapist must avoid the onset of a transference neurosis and therefore must proceed rapidly. Confident that the patient's motivation for change will prevail, the therapist must jump over the barrier of strong defenses to interpret the focal conflict. As is to be expected, such a maneuver will intensify the patient's resistance.

The therapist deals with this increased resistance through recapitulation.

The therapist quotes the patient correctly, using his or her exact words. By reviewing notes, the STAPP therapist can use during interpretation the precise information brought up by the patient, in the patient's own words. By quoting, and saying so, the therapist underscores the importance of the interpretation and relates it clearly to what the patient has brought up in the past. The patient hears familiar words coming from the therapist, not alien words or jargon.

A thirty-five-year-old businessman accepted for STAPP was very controlling in his relations with women. The problem resulted in the termination of two important relationships with women, and he became very depressed. Because of a fight with his current girlfriend, who accused him of being controlling, he felt very anxious and decided to seek psychiatric assistance.

During the first five sessions he talked at length about his relations with women in general and his mother in particular. His relationship with his mother seemed to have sexualized aspects. He was an only child and was his mother's favorite. At fourteen his mother had an affair, which led to a divorce. The patient lived with his father, to whom he felt very close, but he was competitive with him and he blamed him for his mother's departure. Her leaving had an enormous impact on him and had made him feel anxious and depressed for about a year.

During the fifth STAPP session the subject of the patient's sexuality in general—and the sexualized aspect of his relationship with his mother in particular—was brought up by the patient and was discussed at length. The patient felt very anxious while the therapist was confronting him with that aspect of his relationship with his mother. The therapist used information given to him by the patient, who had described feeling excited as he remembered various episodes of interaction with her. For example, he had described his seeing his mother undress. He once felt sexually aroused when she got in bed with him wearing her flimsy nightgown when he was sick with the flu. Toward the end of that session the patient mentioned that he had an urge to run away. He claimed that he had not heard the therapist's clarifications and that the whole subject of sexuality was very difficult for him to discuss with his therapist. When asked why, he answered that he associated his therapist, who was older than him, with his father.

The next session started with the patient's declaring that he had been very anxious during the week, and that he had felt on several occasions like being a little kid.

THERAPIST: Did you feel like being a little kid in order to avoid what we had talked about last week?

PATIENT: Well, maybe so.

THERAPIST: What did you remember about last week's session?

PATIENT: I remember being anxious and wanting to run away.

THERAPIST: Yes, that is true, and why were you so anxious?

PATIENT: Because *(hesitating)*, because of the subject we were talking about.

THERAPIST: Now, what was that subject?

PATIENT: It was about my sexuality as a child.

THERAPIST: Sexuality in reference to whom?

PATIENT: In reference to my parents.

THERAPIST: No. In reference to whom?

PATIENT: —to my mother.

THERAPIST: Precisely. so it was your description of these sexualized episodes with your mother that made you anxious and led to your wanting to run away.

PATIENT: Well, yes.

THERAPIST: Also you mentioned at the end of the hour that it was difficult to discuss this subject with me because I was older.

PATIENT: That is true.

THERAPIST: Let's not forget that on several previous sessions we had agreed that you had some feelings for me that reminded you of feelings for your father.

PATIENT: Yes.

THERAPIST: So today let us hear more of what you imagine that your father would have thought and done if he were to hear about all these sexualized episodes you talked about during last week's session.

PATIENT: I don't know.

THERAPIST: On the basis of what you told me about your relationship with your mother and about these sexualized experiences you had with her, you became a competitor with your father.

PATIENT: We had talked already about my competitive feelings for my father, but also about my love and devotion for him.

THERAPIST: Oh yes, but let us first look at the competition, particularly after all these sexualized episodes with your mother. In a sense, you became a competitor of your father's, even in this sexualized area.

PATIENT: What do you mean?

THERAPIST: I mean just what I said.

133

PATIENT: I don't understand.

THERAPIST: Tell me, what is it that you don't understand?

PATIENT: You mean that as a young kid I had sex with my mother? Is that what you mean? All this talk is absurd. I don't know what you are talking about.

THERAPIST: Tell me, what is it that I asked you about?

PATIENT: I don't know. I don't understand.

It should be evident that the therapist is faced with an anxious, angry, and very resistive patient. He doesn't hear anything. He doesn't understand. It seems absurd to hear his therapist assert that he was a sexualized competitor with his father. He is angry at his therapist—whom in the past he had associated with his father. Under such circumstances of massive resistance, the therapist must try to circumvent it, not by insisting that he is right, but by demonstrating to the patient why and how he arrived at his conclusion.

THERAPIST: OK, let us recapitulate.

PATIENT: Recapitulate what?

THERAPIST: Let us recapitulate how I arrived at my conclusion that you became a sexual competitor with your father because of your sexualized feelings for your mother.

PATIENT: (Hesitating) OK.

THERAPIST: What did we talk about last week?

PATIENT: My feelings for my mother.

THERAPIST: What kinds of feelings?

PATIENT: Feelings of being excited.

THERAPIST: About what?

PATIENT: About my mother's undressing, coming to bed with me when I was sick, and all that.

THERAPIST: Precisely. So if your mother was coming to bed with you in her nightgown instead of being in bed with your father, being his wife, wouldn't your father be upset?

PATIENT: Yes.

THERAPIST: And wouldn't you be, in a sense, taking her away from him, competing with him, as you had already told me that you competed with him in other areas?

PATIENT: Well, yes.

THERAPIST: Even in this area of sexuality?

PATIENT: I can see that this could be possible, in a sense.

THERAPIST: Therefore, if this might be the case, and if this whole subject is very difficult for you to discuss with me because I also remind you of your father, then the question which must be asked is, why is it so difficult?

PATIENT: Because I love my father.

THERAPIST: Of course! It is because you love your father. It is because you lived with him after your mother abandoned both of you. It is because of this love for him that you didn't want to compete with him and that you resist so vehemently my interpretation.

PATIENT: *(Becoming teary)* Yes, I love my father.

THERAPIST: I know that you do. What we have to look for here, however, is the truth. The truth tells us that you also felt very excited about your mother's seductiveness.

PATIENT: It is true.

THERAPIST: All right, then. Now, why do you have to deny all this, cover it up, and avoid it? As you say, it is because of your love for your father. But your love for your father has not changed in the slightest by all the revelations to yourself and to me. It has not changed by your looking at things realistically and truthfully. It is still as strong as it has ever been, and I, for one, am convinced of it.

PATIENT: Yes, this is true.

From then on the sessions proceeded smoothly. The patient described how he did not want to become a businessman as his father wanted him to be, but in order to appease his father he had considered going to business school. The therapist emphasized that since he was aware of his competition with his father on all fronts, there was no need to appease him, and it was therefore best for him to choose a career of his own liking.

It should be clear that in this session the therapist did not do what is classically recommended in long-term dynamic psychotherapy. He did not work on the clarification of the patient's defense mechanisms—his avoidance, his denial, his lack of understanding, and so on. Instead, he brought into the open the patient's basic conflict: namely, his sexual competition with his father, which produced an enormous amount of anxiety. This anxiety was dealt with appropriately by the therapist's technical tool of recapitulation, which gave rise to an insight and which bypassed the patient's strong resistance.

Supporting the Patient Who Is Anxious as a Result of Insight

Although STAPP uses anxiety-provoking techniques, the therapist may at times act in a supportive way. Clarification of this paradoxical situation is in order. First, the anxiety-provoking aspect of the therapist's attitude is not sadistic but serves the purpose of keeping the patient centered on the focus and the emotional conflicts underlying it. Despite the pain, the patient continues to be highly motivated and makes every effort to cooperate with the therapist to resolve the conflicts. It is precisely because of this hard work that the patient on occasion needs to be encouraged and supported. Just as the surgeon who needs to confirm a diagnosis of appendicitis has to palpate the patient's abdomen and cause pain, the therapist must cause anxiety when interpreting difficult conflicts. Both practitioners' goal is to eliminate the pain.

In the following example, during their sixth session a therapist talks with a man who is working hard to deal with his feelings about his childhood sexuality.

PATIENT: Everything that we talked about last week is difficult.
THERAPIST: I know that, but—
PATIENT: *(Interrupting)* I was hoping that this week you would give me some rest.

There are several issues presented to the therapist. For example, should he pick up the transference "give me some rest" issue? Should he be reassuring to help the patient recuperate? Should he pursue the subject until the patient's childhood sexuality has been clarified? Obviously, it all depends on what has been discussed during the previous sessions. If the therapist has not clarified the transference feelings by the sixth session, then something has gone wrong technically. Transference feelings, which are usually positive, appear quite early in STAPP, as has been discussed. In this case, the transference has appeared and a sexual past–present link interpretation has been made. The therapist has to weigh the other two options. He can continue the discussion of the subject of the patient's childhood sexuality, increasing his anxiety and relying on his motivation for change to continue that subject's elucidation; but he must expect to encounter strong resistance. He can, on the other hand, be supportive for a while to avoid resistance. All this depends on how satisfied the therapist is with the information that has been obtained thus far. If he is satisfied, then it is time to support and encourage the patient for his courage and for his hard work at resolving the difficult and anxiety-provoking conflicts. If he is not satisfied, then he should stay with the subject and pursue his anxiety-provoking interpretations. In this case the therapist continued with his interpretations.

THERAPIST: I think that you have worked hard at looking at all the different issues we have been talking about, but if I were to give you some rest, as you put it, the subject that is so important and that made you anxious will be covered up, but unfortunately it will not disappear. So let us go on. For example, of all the things we talked about last week, which made you anxious?

PATIENT: All this talk about my sexual feelings as a child. It is the most inner kind of issue. It touches the quick.

THERAPIST: Precisely. So if I were to give you some rest, as I already said, we would help make it go underground and continue poking its ugly head out at times.

PATIENT: I guess so.

THERAPIST: Don't you think, then, it is better to pursue the subject and get to understand thoroughly how it has affected you in the past and how by facing it, difficult as this may be, to get rid of its consequences once and for all?

Tangible Evidence of Change

As the therapy progresses and as the patient is able to gain more and more insight into the various underground emotional conflicts, the therapist should start to look for tangible evidence that dynamic changes are taking place.

A young woman tended always to date men who were dark, short, and stocky. During the eleventh STAPP session a great deal had been discussed about the patient's attachment as a young girl to her very tall, thin, blond, and somewhat dictatorial father. It had been made clear also that her choosing short, dark, and stocky men was a way of avoiding her own sexualized feelings for her father and competitive feelings for her mother, whom she felt she always tried to please. The following vignette is taken from the opening of the twelfth session.

PATIENT: I had a date with a new man whom I met at a cocktail party.

THERAPIST: Hmm.

PATIENT: Well, I thought I should bring it up because there is some difference in the way in which I dealt with Jim. I felt very relaxed, but there is also something special about him.

THERAPIST: What is that?

PATIENT: Jim is tall, thin, and has light brown hair.

THERAPIST: I see.

PATIENT: We have been talking all along about my choosing to go out with men who look very different than my father. I now have a very clear understanding about my avoidance of the old feelings I had for my father. What dawned on me was that I was excluding from my life so many potentially nice men who are tall, thin, and blond. I felt attracted to Jim, and I was also aware of all the old feelings I had for my father. They were in the open.

To the therapist this exchange with the patient is tangible evidence of change. Before deciding that it is time to terminate the therapy, he has to make sure that the patient knows why she has been able to alter her behavior. Her example has convinced him that she is ready to end therapy.

Insight about the Focal Conflict

The therapist should pursue tangible evidence of change to be sure that the patient's improvement is not an accidental event or a flight into health. Similarly, evidence of insight into the focal conflict must be confirmed.

THERAPIST: You said that you went to your boss and complained about your office. Can you tell me what made you decide to do it, something you had not done before? Was it accidental?

PATIENT: No, not at all. I had thought about it for quite some time.

THERAPIST: What did you think about?

PATIENT: I just thought that it was time to do it.

THERAPIST: [The therapist must insist in order to find out if the patient has developed insight, instead of just having some other reason for changing his attitude.] I repeat again: What did you think about?

PATIENT: Well, you know, we have been talking quite a bit about my earlier experiences with my father, who was very authoritarian. He preferred my younger brother, who was a good athlete, and looked down on my sensitivity and my interest in art. The other day, as I was thinking about all this, I decided that what belonged to my father belonged to my father and not to my boss. I therefore said to myself, "Stop being sensitive and take the bull by the horns." Right then and there I decided to see my boss about the office. What is amusing in retrospect is that he thought that it was I who did not want to have an office with a window.

This type of frank statement and the patient's assessment of his own psychodynamics indicate that the neurotic conflicts that interfered with his adult behavior in reference to men have been loosened up and eventually resolved. All this is evidence that the patient has obtained considerable insight as a result of his short-term dynamic psychotherapy.

It should be evident, then, that the therapist must always seek to obtain confirmation that the patient has indeed developed the insight necessary to terminate the treatment.

Another patient's focus was an unresolved grief reaction. She was a young woman who had lost her mother in adolescence. The following dialogue took place after twelve sessions.

PATIENT: I should mention that I have been feeling very much better lately. My depression has lifted, and I am glad that I refused to take the antidepressant drugs my general practitioner offered to me before I decided to get a second opinion at this clinic.

THERAPIST: Why do you think that you are feeling so much better?

PATIENT: It is because of my understanding of what we have been talking about lately.

THERAPIST: What specifically are you referring to? [Again, the therapist should be specific and should not accept her statement about improvement as an isolated fact.]

PATIENT: It was after our session three weeks ago, when all of a sudden I experienced all those sad feelings about my mother's death and when I cried most of the hour. What was so important was that I had not experienced such feelings for my mother's death because I was supposed to keep a stiff upper lip. But when you asked me if I felt guilty, your question hit me like a ton of bricks. Guilty? Yes, I was, because I felt so antagonistic, so competitive with her for several years. It was when I blurted out that I was glad when she died, to be free of her, I suddenly felt all the sadness which enveloped me and made me cry so much. When we talked about all the good things that had also taken place between my mother and me, and which I had denied, it all added up to realizing my true feelings for my mother.

THERAPIST: Do you think these realizations helped you to eliminate your depression?

PATIENT: Without doubt.

Termination of STAPP

The termination of any psychotherapy, including STAPP, depends on the joint decision by the patient and the therapist that the goal of therapy has been accomplished.

In STAPP, a clear delineation of the focus during the evaluation period, the patient's agreement to work on the resolution of the emotional conflicts underlying it, and the fairly modest expectations regarding outcome should all lead to an easy and early termination.

About 50 percent of our STAPP patients initiate discussion of the ending of therapy. They say things like: "I seem to be behaving in a different way"; "I understand the reason why I used to be anxious"; or "My relations with women in authority have improved greatly and I am not afraid of them any more." Then they ask: "Now, where do we go from here?" or "Is it time to stop?"

The therapist should be certain that the patient is not acting out, that he or she is not fleeing the therapy because of its anxiety-provoking component, and that he or she has not had a "transference cure." Then, when the patient brings up termination, the therapist will ask for clarification. The therapist may say: "You tell me that your relationship with your girlfriend has improved. Please give me an example of how it has improved"; or "You used to say that you were depressed and discouraged by your inability to improve your relations with older women because they reminded you of your grandmother, who loved and took care of you. Has this tendency changed?" The patient's response to such questions should be substantiated by specific examples to demonstrate that the changes are real.

In his paper "Analysis Terminable and Interminable," Freud (1950) pointed out that difficulties in termination could arise from traumatic environmental factors that set up very strong resistances and from defensive maneuvers. This is obviously not the case with STAPP candidates, who have been selected precisely because they have not experienced early traumas and have demonstrated that they posses a high degree of motivation for change. It is not difficult to terminate the treatment of STAPP patients.

The choice of focus makes some difference with termination. For example, some patients who had as their focus an unresolved oedipal problem talk about finishing therapy just before the end of the final session. They say: "I have done most of the hard work during this treatment, but I must also admit that I needed your professional competence. All in all, I can say that it was a successful treatment"; or "It seems that we have talked about all the important points. I don't think that there is much more to be discussed." Of course, if the focus involves loss and separation or an unresolved grief reaction, a few extra sessions should be made available to discuss the effect on the patient of separation from the therapist.

Any difficulties that arise in terminating a STAPP treatment are more likely to be caused by the therapist than by the patient. The problem is countertransference feelings. Because STAPP patients are such good candidates for psychotherapy, because they demonstrate convincingly the importance of psychodynamics, because they work hard, because they are motivated to change, because they are likable, and because they do improve in comparison with difficult borderline or narcissistic patients, their therapists usually do not want to give them up. Thus the therapist will look for excuses to prolong the therapy by imagining that he or she is indispensable to the patient's mental health or that the patient cannot function adequately without his or her help. The therapist may become convinced that some minor emotional problem, which was not considered to be of great importance, has not been worked through; so the therapist concludes that more therapy is necessary. This type of thinking has many sources.

Therapists in general and psychiatrists in particular emphasize psychopathology and minimize mental health. A therapist who does not believe patients' will be able to deal on their own with new emotional problems after STAPP underestimates the patients' capabilities. Furthermore, therapists have been brainwashed to believe that only long-term psychotherapy is effective—a wrong conclusion, unfortunately.

As Freud (1950) describes in "Analysis Terminable and Interminable," the analyst's own defense mechanisms can interfere with the termination of the treatment; the same principle may also apply to STAPP therapists who are unwilling to accept that enough is enough.

Michael Hoyt (1985) demonstrates that therapists' belief that more is better or that short-term therapy is not as good as a long-term approach, encourages them to recommend therapy without careful consideration of its necessity. These therapists ignore evidence from research that short-term therapy produces more lasting and successful outcomes. Some therapists may feel that they *need* to conduct long-term therapy, contrary to their patients' wishes. Perhaps economic considerations are behind this phenomenon. Also, the demanding work associated with short-term therapies, as well as countertransference problems related to the therapist's loss and separation issues, may discourage the offering of briefer treatments. Finally, the more rapid turnover in patients may also play an important role in why long-term treatments are chosen and recommended.

CHAPTER 11

A STAPP Technical Demonstration

THIS CHAPTER WILL FOLLOW the course of STAPP to demonstrate how the therapist handles various aspects of the therapist–patient relationship and how he uses the techniques of this form of therapy.

Although in this case example the emphasis will be on technique, I present in detail the whole evaluation interview with this patient to orient the reader to his basic psychological problems.

The patient, a twenty-six-year-old male graduate student, came to the psychiatric clinic complaining of being anxious because of his tendency to hide his feelings, to "camouflage" them, and to be defensive in his relations with people. All these difficulties stifled his capacity to relate well, particularly with women, as well as his ability to be creative.

During the initial clinic interview it was thought that the patient was very bright and insightful, and that he fulfilled the selection criteria for STAPP. He was therefore referred to our research team for further evaluation. Additional history was obtained by two independent evaluators. The patient was the oldest of three children. He had a brother three years his junior and a sister aged nineteen. His father, sixty-two, was a successful businessman who traveled extensively and had been absent for long periods of time while the patient was growing up. The patient felt, however, that he had always been his father's favorite. His mother was thought to have been closer to his younger brother. The patient was very fond of his brother but also felt competitive and jealous of him,

143

particularly when their mother paid too much attention to him. During his childhood the patient had suffered several accidents, two of which sent him to the hospital. In the first episode, he cut his knee on a broken bottle; the cut required several stitches and was subsequently infected. He remained in the hospital for a few days. In the second, he was crossing the street when he was hit by a bicyclist. His mother, who had witnessed the episode and who drove him to the hospital for a checkup, scolded him for not being careful enough. For a long time afterward he remembered her lack of sympathy in his time of need.

He had always been interested in and played with girls, and on one occasion he had experimented sexually with one of them. When his mother found out about it, she "screamed," reprimanded him, and told him never to do such terrible things again. As an adult he dated a lot of "beautiful" women who in his opinion were stupid. Academically he had always excelled. It was also of interest that during his adolescence he became his mother's favorite; on many occasions, while his father was away, she called him "the man of the house" and sought his advice.

The precipitating event for seeking help was the breaking up of a relationship with a fellow student who told him that she was tired of his pretentious mannerisms and how they were always used to hide his real self. She called him "a coward" for not daring to show his true feelings. These observations and her rejection pained him greatly because he thought that the first one was true and the second was its obvious consequence.

Both evaluators who saw the patient agreed that he easily passed the five STAPP criteria and thought the focus for the therapy to concentrate upon was an unresolved oedipal one.

Evaluation Interview by the Therapist

THERAPIST: What is your basic problem?
PATIENT: I have difficulty communicating with people, and this makes me anxious. This difficulty is more pronounced with women. My relationships are not real. I get easily bored and I try to cover it up, but invariably people find out and then they get mad. This is what happened with my latest girlfriend. She told me that I was "hiding my real self," that I was "a coward," and she ended our relationship. I was crushed. Because this thing has happened before, but not in a clear-cut way as with Ellen—that was her name—I felt

the need to get to the bottom of it, and that is the reason why I am here.

THERAPIST: So, what is it that you want help with—your anxiety, your problems in your relations with people in general and women in particular, your hiding your feelings, your being told that you are a coward? I can go on. [The therapist is testing whether the patient fulfills the first STAPP criterion.]

PATIENT: *(Interrupting)* No, I want to understand my relations with women. This is what makes me anxious. I want to understand why I put a facade on my feelings.

THERAPIST: All right. Now, do you know when that tendency of yours to hide your feelings originated?

PATIENT: It started when I was young, with my father.

THERAPIST: In what way?

PATIENT: I altered my behavior in order to please him. I did what he wanted me to do, and that gratified him. I was his favorite. He always approved of my behavior. I acted like a child.

THERAPIST: Is this still going on?

PATIENT: No, at thirteen I stopped pretending, but the same thing started to take place with my friends and particularly with my girlfriends.

THERAPIST: Let me take a history briefly and ask you some questions about your past.

PATIENT: I must say that I know I have to make an effort to understand myself. This treatment will make me anxious, but I am prepared to face it. [This fortuitous statement arouses the therapist's interest because it points to the patient's motivation for change.]

THERAPIST: I am glad to hear what you say. OK, then, how old are you?

PATIENT: Twenty-six. I am the oldest.

THERAPIST: Of how many?

PATIENT: Three. I have a brother who's twenty-three, Roger, and a sister who's nineteen, Donna.

THERAPIST: Are your parents in good health?

PATIENT: Yes. My father is a very successful businessman, sixty-two.

THERAPIST: Your mother?

PATIENT: She is sixty. They are both in good health.

THERAPIST: Is there a history of any medical or psychiatric illnesses in your family?

PATIENT: Not that I know of.

THERAPIST: What is your earliest memory?

PATIENT: A visit to the Bronx Zoo. We lived in New York when I was three years old. I remember a big lion roaring, and I was very scared. I remember my father consoling me, but my mother paid no attention to me.

THERAPIST: How did you get along with your brother?

PATIENT: Not very well. I was jealous of him when he was a baby. I thought that my mother liked Roger more than me. We fought a lot growing up, but I also loved him. Don't get me wrong. Once I gave him my favorite car to play with when he was sick. Now I am closest to him. He is getting married soon.

THERAPIST: Did you have any close friends as a child?

PATIENT: Oh yes. Chuck and I were inseparable for many years. We still correspond—now he lives in Texas.

THERAPIST: Would you make any special sacrifices for Chuck, as you did for your brother even though you were jealous of him?

PATIENT: Oh yes. Chuck was poor, so many times I gave him all my allowance. Once I also gave him a sweater of mine which he liked, and I lied to my mother when she asked me what happened to it. I said I had left it at school. Later she found out that I had given it to Chuck when she saw him wearing it. She gave me hell for lying, but I was glad I did it. [With these two altruistic examples, the therapist was satisfied that the patient had meaningful relationships during his childhood, thus fulfilling the second STAPP criterion.]

THERAPIST: Were you close to anyone else?

PATIENT: I was very close to my grandparents, who lived with us. Being the oldest, I was their favorite grandchild. When my sister was born, I was seven. From then on, she was my father's favorite.

THERAPIST: How did you do during grade school? [The therapist has the option of pursuing the patient's loss of the favorite's place with his father or getting more information about historical details. He chooses the latter because he will have a chance to return to the father later on.]

PATIENT: I was always an excellent student, yet I had trouble with my sixth grade teacher, who didn't like me because I was flirting with a female classmate. Actually, it was an unfortunate situation because a jealous classmate reported me and my teacher punished me. I lost on all counts. I think it was then that I started hiding my feelings as I do now.

THERAPIST: You've told me very little about your mother except about her not consoling you at the zoo.

PATIENT: As I told you, Roger was her favorite when we were little, but later on I became my mother's favorite.

THERAPIST: Later on? When?

PATIENT: When I was thirteen. From then on she treated me more as grown up; being the oldest helped.

THERAPIST: How did you do in high school?

PATIENT: I did very well. My father seemed to be away a lot and my mother turned to me many times for help. She used to say that when Dad was away I was the man of the house.

THERAPIST: And how did you feel when she said that?

PATIENT: I felt very proud.

THERAPIST: So you were the center of attention when your father was away, you were your mother's favorite, and you were the man of the house, which made you feel good.

PATIENT: Sure I was.

THERAPIST: So why did you start hiding your feelings?

PATIENT: To avoid trouble.

THERAPIST: With whom?

PATIENT: With everybody.

THERAPIST: Well, we must look much closer into all this. Now where did you go to college?

PATIENT: In New York.

THERAPIST: And now you are studying here?

PATIENT: Yes, I am working on my Ph.D.

THERAPIST: In your opinion, where do all these difficulties with hiding your feelings and getting in trouble with others emanate from? Of course you may not have the answer, because if you did you wouldn't be here, but what comes to your mind, what do you think?

PATIENT: I think it has to do with my relations with my parents, but I don't exactly know how.

THERAPIST: Yes, I think that the focus of this treatment should center on our understanding your relations with your parents and how they affected your relations with people in general and women in particular. We must also understand how it led to your hiding your feelings, camouflaging them, and feeling anxious.

PATIENT: Yes.

THERAPIST: Tell me, how motivated are you to do this work, which as you already know may be anxiety provoking?

PATIENT: I am very motivated. I want to understand this behavior of mine at all costs, because if it goes on it will ruin my life.

THERAPIST: So you agree to work on this focus that I have mentioned?

PATIENT: Yes, I do.

The interview continues with a discussion of the patient's finances, the fee to be charged by the clinic, the appointment time, and consent for videotaping. The patient signed an informed consent form.

At the end of this session, the therapist agreed with the other two evaluators that the patient was an excellent STAPP candidate, psychologically minded, relating very well, and motivated to change and to work on an unresolved oedipal focus.

First Session

PATIENT: I have been thinking a lot since I saw you last time about what we talked about. I discussed my feelings about this camouflage with a friend of mine. I talked about having conflicts with people in authority, even here last time.

The therapist is presented with two important points. First, the patient's motivation is high, because even after only one evaluation interview he does a lot of thinking about it. This is a good sign. Second, he is faced with a transference issue when the patient mentions that he has conflicts with people in authority, including the therapist. For the therapist both points are significant, but the transference issue must take priority.

THERAPIST: You say that you were aware of having conflicts with people in authority as well as with me here last week?

PATIENT: Yes. Your role versus my role. I envy your authority.

THERAPIST: Hmm. What is my authority over you?

PATIENT: I assume that you are a good therapist. A friend of mine said that you have a very fine reputation.

THERAPIST: So it is because your friend praised me?

PATIENT: Yes, but also because of your profession, this hospital, Harvard, and all that.

THERAPIST: So it is that my credentials impress you?

PATIENT: Yes, but also that I feel the same urge to hide my feelings

148

as I did with my parents. I hide them not only from my parents but also from both men and women. I felt like hiding them from you last time.

THERAPIST: When you experience your feelings for your parents and hide them, as you say you felt like hiding them from me, which parent comes more to mind, your father or your mother? [Two of the technical aspects of STAPP have appeared already in the early part of the first therapy session—the transference and a potential past–present, or parent–transference, link.]

PATIENT: My father. My father's authoritative role, like yours.

THERAPIST: What is my authoritative role vis à vis you? In reality there is none.

PATIENT: Yes, but you are very perceptive, from what I observed about you last time.

THERAPIST: OK, you say I am authoritative in the same way as your father was and that you try to hide your feelings, but last time you emphasized that this camouflage was more in reference to women. Are you saying that you put on two different kinds of facades, one for men and one for women?

PATIENT: The camouflage is the same thing with both men and women, but the problems with women have a top priority now, and this is what brings me to therapy. I try to impress females.

THERAPIST: I am still interested whether the hiding of feelings is different for men and women, since you mentioned that it occurred with both of your parents. I wonder if there are certain things that should be hidden from your father or from authoritative men like me, and whether there are other things that have to be kept from your mother's or women's knowledge.

The therapist tries to differentiate the patient's feelings for his parents. Patients invariably try to lump together feelings for their parents to avoid differentiating them. It is important, therefore, to insist on trying to find out what feelings were aroused by which parent.

PATIENT: With authoritative figures I tend to rebel. With my father, he always wanted me to be a leader of men—a role which I didn't want to take—but with women . . .

THERAPIST: Maybe you wanted to be a leader of women instead.

PATIENT: *(Laughs)* I want to be intimate with women, not to lead them.

THERAPIST: It depends what the words "to lead women" mean.

149

PATIENT: There is an image that Don Juan or Errol Flynn reflects. This comes to mind.

THERAPIST: What does that image mean to you?

PATIENT: A very cavalier attitude . . .

THERAPIST: and . . .

PATIENT: I try to be spontaneous, but it is hard, very hard.

THERAPIST: Now you are trying to get away from my question. What does the image of Don Juan mean? [The therapist actively uses anxiety-provoking questions, which the patient tries to avoid by pleading that they are difficult to answer.]

PATIENT: Well, Don Juan is a very attractive man and gets along very well with beautiful women. I also love to go out with beautiful women. My girlfriend must always be an outstanding beauty.

THERAPIST: So Don Juan equals you. You both love beautiful women. Now, what did Don Juan get out of his interactions with these women?

PATIENT: I enjoy being with beautiful women. There is an element of status being with them. Peer group status, social status.

THERAPIST: Was Don Juan getting "peer group status" when he went out with beautiful women?

PATIENT: I think so.

THERAPIST: Nothing else?

PATIENT: He got some pleasure. I like a degree of intimacy.

THERAPIST: Now, look what you do: you intellectualize when I draw a parallel between you and Don Juan. You both like beautiful women. Now as soon as I raise this parallel, you start bringing in "peer status," "social status," and all that stuff, to get away from my questions. There is something more direct, isn't there?

PATIENT: You strain my brain.

THERAPIST: Come on, now. There is nothing wrong with your brain. What comes to mind?

The therapist is not being supportive by making this statement. He tries to humor the patient by showing him that he is resisting and evading his anxiety-provoking parallel. If the therapist had tried to be supportive realistically and did not pursue the confrontation, he would have missed the opportunity to investigate the meaning of the patient's identification with Don Juan.

PATIENT: Well, you are stressing your point. Will you please repeat your question?

THERAPIST: No. My question stands as is. You heard it perfectly well. You need no assistance, I am sure of it.

PATIENT: Well, there was Karen. She was a beauty. She had a lovely face and a superb figure. I was fifteen when I tried to date her, but I thought that she wouldn't go out with me because she was so beautiful. I anticipated her rejection. [The therapist is rewarded with an interesting association from the patient's past.]

THERAPIST: This is a non sequitur. Why should a girl who is beautiful necessarily reject you? This is your assumption. If so, why? All this gets us nowhere. It gets us away from my question, my very simple question, namely, What did Don Juan get out of his interactions with beautiful women? [Again the therapist insists on having the patient associate to his question by repeating it and not allowing him to avoid it.]

PATIENT: Well, I assume he got sexual pleasure. I have an image of beautiful, shapely breasts in these women. Is that what you wanted me to say?

THERAPIST: I don't want you to say anything. I am asking. I am interested in your association. Is this part of your facade? Is this image of the shapely breasts a way to please me? I am not here to be pleased.

PATIENT: No. I see Errol Flynn and all these women in my mind. Women with low-cut dresses, very shapely breasts, very beautiful . . .

THERAPIST: And what associations do you have with this image?

PATIENT: *(Remains silent)*

THERAPIST: What comes to mind?

PATIENT: A memory . . . an image of my mother nursing my younger sister. I was very attracted to that image. A very intimate image.

THERAPIST: You were how old, seven or eight?

PATIENT: Eight or nine.

THERAPIST: Do you say this because you think that this is what I like to hear, or is this spontaneous?

PATIENT: No, it is spontaneous—images racing through my mind. It was a warm feeling, yet it was not a natural kind of love. It was somehow a different feeling. We talked with my mother about nursing. She explained nursing to me, breastfeeding and all that.

THERAPIST: Yes, and this association originated from our talk about Don Juan, Errol Flynn, beautiful women like Karen, and finally your mother nursing your sister.

PATIENT: Are you saying then that there is connection between all these things?

THERAPIST: I am saying that there is a connection between you and Don Juan in reference to the beautiful women like Karen, as well as to this association with Errol Flynn, women with low-cut dresses, and your mother nursing your sister, shapely breasts, and all that.

PATIENT: I reject that.

The anxiety-provoking clarification is being resisted, although the therapist presents the patient with the exact information that was supplied to him by the patient. The therapist faces a dilemma very early in the therapy. Should he continue pressing the patient, or should he retreat? From what has been described in this book, the answer will be obvious.

THERAPIST: What do you mean by rejecting all this?

PATIENT: I don't believe in this oedipal relationship complex.

THERAPIST: Let's forget about terms, books, Freud, Oedipus complex. Tell me, why do you reject this parallel of mine?

PATIENT: I didn't have any sexual feelings for my mother.

THERAPIST: Where does "sexual feelings" come from? You talked only about a warm feeling for your mother during the nursing of your sister.

PATIENT: It popped out of my head (laughs).

THERAPIST: Hmm.

PATIENT: I wanted, I guess, to replace my sister.

THERAPIST: Do you view a nursing baby as being sexual?

PATIENT: No . . . but I was allowed to feel my mother's breasts, to see if they had enough milk. Actually, before my sister's birth, when she was pregnant, she allowed me to touch her abdomen.

THERAPIST: So we have two feelings—warmth and then a feeling which you resisted at first but then described as "sexual." So what does the word sexual mean to you? Don't say what you think that I want to hear.

PATIENT: I just feel a sexual relationship is the most intimate and warm relationship that one human being may have with another person—a person who allows it and opens himself to another. Shall I go on?

THERAPIST: There you go again, asking my permission. What comes to mind, to *your* mind, in reference to my question about the word *sexual?*

PATIENT: Sex is taboo. I want to hide my thoughts about it. When I was six I played with a girl in the cellar, and we took our clothes off and were curious about each other. My mother discovered us. I was spanked by my mother. I was also caught later on when my cousin Mary came to visit us. I went into the woods with her, we undressed, and . . . well . . . nothing happened; actually, we just assumed sexual positions but we didn't know really what to do. I was about eleven at the time. Then my mother found out—maybe from her sister, who was Mary's mother—and she made a big scene about it. She cried and mentioned that sex and intercourse were very intimate, sacred acts. She told me never to do such a thing again. She implored me. She appealed to my morality.

THERAPIST: So the first time you were punished and spanked. The second time, when you were older, your mother cried and implored you never to do it again and appealed to your morality. So it is clear that you had an interest in sex, both times, earlier and later.

PATIENT: I remembered also that my mother said that my father's interest in sexual matters didn't arise until he was twenty. When I asked my father about this later on, he was mad.

THERAPIST: So your mother told you that your father was not interested in sex until he was twenty, while you had a great interest in sex much earlier, when you were eleven. So you were different from your father as far as sexual issues were concerned, your interest was much earlier and greater than his.

PATIENT: Yes . . . but later on in high school, I was interested in girls yet I had no dates and there was no sexual stuff.

THERAPIST: So you followed your mother's advice? Did you want to be a good boy in her eyes and hide your sexual feelings, which were of such importance to you from very early times? [the therapist is able to tie together the information given to him by the patient and is able to associate it with the patient's chief problem—hiding his feelings from women.]

PATIENT: I remember Mary had large and shapely breasts. She still does.

THERAPIST: OK, then, let us summarize what we know from this interview today: you have an interest in beautiful women. From Don Juan and Errol Flynn we went to your relationship with your mother, which at first you described as warm, and later on you introduced the sexual component. This also implied curiosity and sexual interest in girls. At eleven you experimented with sex with Mary. Your mother cried, implored you not to pursue such interests, and told you that your father was not interested in such subjects until he was twenty. Therefore you were nine years ahead of your father in this sexual area as far as your mother was concerned. Since your interest persisted, you seem to have tried to submerge it in order to please your mother. Another possibility is that you and your mother had an intimate secret which was kept from your father. So after all this, it seems there is a great deal to think about during the coming week, as you said that you did during last week.

PATIENT: Yes, indeed.

This type of summarizing helps to consolidate what has transpired during the session and encourages the patient to continue doing some of the self-inquisitive work outside of the therapeutic hours. It should not be interpreted, however, as giving the patient a special task.

After the patient left, the therapist summarized what he thought were the highlights of this first therapy session and made short-term predictions of what he expected to take place during the following session. This is what he dictated:

This session starts with some transference feelings but rapidly the patient associates to some interesting aspects of his relationship with his mother. I am aware that this aspect of his putting on a facade or camouflaging his feelings will also occur within the transference. It is also possible that these interesting associations may be viewed as gifts to me in order to please me. Once he got going, however, he became genuinely involved, and the use of the word *sexual* slipped out and took him by surprise. It is striking that these incestuous associations gave rise to strong feelings which he was not prepared to face even if he had anticipated dealing with such issues intellectually. All in all, the therapy seems to have started very well.

Second Session

PATIENT: I had a freak accident last week. I slipped and fell and injured my leg.

THERAPIST: Was it a bad injury? [Obviously the therapist should step out temporarily from his psychotherapeutic role and inquire about the medical details.]

PATIENT: No, it is OK. I went to the hospital emergency room. The X-rays were negative, and with a little aspirin I feel better.

THERAPIST: OK, I am glad to hear it. Now what about our last session?

PATIENT: The whole incest taboo area is difficult. [The patient continues describing the problems and feelings he experienced. The therapist listens to him for a while, but soon realizes that the patient is avoiding the difficult subject of his relations with his mother.]

THERAPIST: It may be difficult, but let's go right back to it.

PATIENT: Well, this whole sexual issue is the most difficult one. The sexual feeling stunned me.

THERAPIST: You used the word *warm*, and then the word *sexual* popped up. So what comes to mind today in reference to these two words?

PATIENT: *(Remains silent)*

THERAPIST: You seem to be silent.

PATIENT: I expect you to ask me some questions to stimulate my thinking.

THERAPIST: Hmm.

PATIENT: I try to gather my thoughts. I can't formulate them . . . too much . . .

THERAPIST: Yes, yes, go on.

PATIENT: I remember sleeping in my parents' bedroom when I was four or five years old. I had nightmares, so my mother took me to their room for security because I was crying. I had recurrent dreams about running over a bridge and falling to the shore below. I was so scared.

THERAPIST: You seem to be the victim today—accidents, dreams. Anyway, what happened?

PATIENT: My mother took me into their room.

THERAPIST: So by having nightmares you got a reward?

PATIENT: Hmm, well, yes.

THERAPIST: Where did you sleep?

PATIENT: Between them. [The therapist continues to be precise, to try to get all the information he can despite the patient's efforts to avoid talking about such episodes.]

THERAPIST: Can you tell me more?

PATIENT: It is vague, very vague.

THERAPIST: You made your point: it is vague. Let's hear more about it, even if it is vague.

PATIENT: Sometimes they refused to let me sleep with them.

THERAPIST: Why do you think?

PATIENT: I didn't need the security. I mean, they thought that I did not need security.

THERAPIST: Anything else?

PATIENT: No. Well, I would also imagine that at times they would want to have sexual relations. After all, they eventually had two children.

THERAPIST: So that would have been a good reason to be refused.

PATIENT: Of course.

THERAPIST: But you seemed to be reluctant to bring it up.

PATIENT: Sex is a taboo subject.

THERAPIST: Yes, but you are here for us to look into this.

PATIENT: Everything that had to do with sex in my family was always negative. Everything was taboo.

THERAPIST: Yet there were times when sex was not always negative—for example, when your mother was nursing your sister and you looked and touched her breasts.

PATIENT: (Interrupting) Sex—premarital sex—was viewed otherwise. It was not OK. This became very clear when my mother gave me a lecture about this episode with my cousin that I described to you last week. My mother not only told me that such behavior was prohibited, she also cried. It was an emotional scene. She mentioned the Bible. It was something not to be done until I was married. It never should take place premaritally. I felt this way until late, until I was nineteen or twenty. This influenced me greatly.

THERAPIST: So it was a way to please your mother?

PATIENT: That talk influenced me greatly.

THERAPIST: Yet your curiosity didn't disappear. Your curiosity was great between five and twelve. All these episodes you talked to me about, with Mary and so on.

PATIENT: Something also popped into my head. When I told you about sleeping in my parents' bed, I always assumed my father's position. I assumed my father's role.

THERAPIST: Interesting. What does it mean?

PATIENT: I wanted to be the dominant force, the man of the house. I wanted to take his role. As you know, he traveled a lot. I didn't want to knock my father out of his dominant position, because I loved him, but I also wanted my share. I wanted to have influence

156

when my parents went out. I exercised a ruthless position with my siblings. I sometimes beat them up.

THERAPIST: Was your father ruthless?

PATIENT: No, not at all. Sometimes, but very rarely, I saw him being angry. He was very benign in general, however.

THERAPIST: You wanted to take his role, but his role was benign. Yet your role of authority with your siblings was very different than your father's. Isn't this a paradox?

PATIENT: I am straining to think about it.

THERAPIST: Don't strain too much. What comes to mind?

PATIENT: I can't think about it.

THERAPIST: Is that your "facade"?

PATIENT: Maybe . . . yet I remember an episode. Once my father reprimanded me for not doing what I was supposed to do. I was scared.

THERAPIST: You now give me an example of your father not being benign. Why?

PATIENT: I didn't want to give the impression that everything was rosy between us.

THERAPIST: Of course. We know that there was competition between the two of you. Competition with someone whom you loved. How did you deal with this competition?

PATIENT: Keeping things to myself.

THERAPIST: What is your basic problem? Why did you come to the clinic?

PATIENT: For my feelings.

THERAPIST: Yes, camouflaging your feelings.

PATIENT: I could hide what I wanted, and what I felt. I still do . . .

THERAPIST: What are you thinking about now?

PATIENT: I find this subject of competition difficult.

THERAPIST: Of course, because you want to hide your feelings, your actions, even here from me.

During the rest of the session the patient reminisces about various episodes from his past which seem to be unrelated to his competition with his father. The therapist points out his evasive techniques, but the patient continues in the same vein. At the end of the hour the patient goes back to discussing the episode with his cousin.

PATIENT: There were several incidents when I touched my cousin's vagina.

THERAPIST: Interesting association! How did this thought come to mind? What were your feelings about all this?

PATIENT: I was scared that my mother would find out. I tried to hide my feelings and my actions from her.

THERAPIST: So, what we can say is that your curiosity about sexual matters continued, but it had to go underground to be hidden because of the puritanical attitude of your mother. It is important, of course, to say that this curiosity of yours was very healthy, but the way in which your mother dealt with it may have created problems for you.

At the end of this session the therapist dictated that he felt the treatment was proceeding well, particularly after the patient's sexualized feelings for his mother had been discussed and his competitive feelings for his father, whom he loved, emerged.

Third Session

PATIENT: Not much new . . .

THERAPIST: You are quiet today.

PATIENT: *(Remains silent)*

THERAPIST: It's your hour.

PATIENT: I need some direction. Would you ask me some questions?

This type of exchange is not unusual in the early part of a session. After an anxiety-provoking session, the patient may communicate to the therapist a need for relief from the pace of the psychotherapy. The therapist may choose to back off from pressure to deal with the emotional conflicts surrounding the focus, or the therapist may continue to provoke anxiety. Clearly, the second option is the one to pursue.

THERAPIST: No.

PATIENT: Last week's session was difficult.

THERAPIST: Which part?

PATIENT: Those sexual episodes with my cousin, and all that. You said that my sexual curiosity was healthy, yet I have tremendously strong guilt feelings about it.

THERAPIST: Guilt . . . is this guilt feeling associated more with the competition with your father or with your sexual feelings for your mother?

PATIENT: Oh, invariably in reference to my mother.

THERAPIST: I see.

PATIENT: My father was always afraid to talk about sex.

THERAPIST: If sexual feelings are more associated with your mother, why is it so? How are they related to your mother?

PATIENT: Well, she would be disappointed in me. I told you last week about that emotional scene when she cried and implored me not to have premarital sex. I was afraid that she would reject me.

THERAPIST: Your mother would be "disappointed" and would "reject" you. But why should she?

PATIENT: I defied her moral code.

THERAPIST: What was this code—this moral code?

PATIENT: Sexual taboo.

THERAPIST: Did you think that your mother's motivation was *only* moral?

PATIENT: Are you referring to what I talked about two weeks ago, this sexual aspect?

THERAPIST: Don't worry about what I am referring to, just associate to my questions.

When a patient implies that he or she knows what the therapist wants to hear, it should be made clear that it is not so. The therapist must persist in clarifying that he or she wants to hear the patient's spontaneous associations, that there is nothing of particular interest.

PATIENT: Well, as I said, this sexual aspect is difficult to talk about.

THERAPIST: Yes, I know. You repeated that several times, but it is important because if we can understand some of your difficult feelings about this subject—which you have tried to avoid—then we can get down to the bottom of it all. This will help us understand the need to camouflage your feelings, which is really the reason you came to therapy and which causes problems for you now.

The therapist is supportive when the patient is experiencing difficult feelings but also seems to be working hard. After all, in this case it is the patient who again brings up the word *sexual*, but because the subject is painful he attempts to retreat.

PATIENT: Yes, that is what I was thinking. The first thing is that moral aspect, but I also know that mothers are often close to their sons.

THERAPIST: Let us not generalize. Let us stick only to *your* story and the sexual feelings for *your* mother. [Again the therapist becomes anxiety provoking by avoiding the generalization and focusing on the patient's relations with his mother.]

PATIENT: There was a strong bond between us. For example, if I had sexual—

THERAPIST: *(Interrupting)* If?

PATIENT: Well, *when* I did, I had the feeling that maybe such feelings made my mother feel youthful.

THERAPIST: Can you give me an example?

PATIENT: My mother was concerned about aging.

THERAPIST: What does your mother look like?

PATIENT: She's relatively heavy, not extremely so, but she is also attractive. As you know, I love beautiful women.

THERAPIST: To avoid your feelings for your mother? If you go out with a young woman who is very slim and very beautiful, then she would be very different from your mother. *But* if you went out with a somewhat heavy and not so attractive woman, then these feelings about your mother might again be aroused and might make you feel guilty.

PATIENT: But there is always the feeling that the very beautiful woman would reject me.

THERAPIST: Of course! So you can be free to go back to your mother.

PATIENT: *(Laughs, but looks anxious)* Recently I met a young woman. She is a little like my cousin. She's very attractive . . . but I have that feeling of rejection again.

THERAPIST: You place the rejecting responsibility on her. Last week we saw your own curiosity about sex. Are you placing the emphasis of rejection on someone else to absolve you from your own sexual feelings for your mother? What about this young lady— does she have a name?

PATIENT: She's nice. Her name is Cindy; she's very attractive. [The patient spends some time describing his relationship with her, emphasizing its relaxed quality.]

THERAPIST: Is this relationship different, or are you camouflaging your feelings for Cindy?

PATIENT: No, what struck me is that I feel more open with her. It seems to be a bit different. It might be associated with what we are doing here.

THERAPIST: Are you saying that to please me?

PATIENT: No, no, not at all. I met her just ten days ago. When I am honest here it makes me feel good. [The therapist wants to make sure that the patient is not using his neurotic tactics again. On the basis of his answer, however, it appears that this may be viewed as an early evidence of change in his behavior. It remains to be seen.]

THERAPIST: Go on.

PATIENT: I also have the fear, however, that you may reject me if I don't work hard.

THERAPIST: Reject you? Where does that feeling come from?

PATIENT: Because you mentioned that the therapy will be short term.

The therapist is presented with an interesting situation. The patient is bringing up some information about a new relationship in his life, but he also introduces the transference in terms of the therapist's potential rejection. Because of the use of the word *rejection* the therapist chooses to investigate the transference.

THERAPIST: You mean I might "reject" you, like your mother?

PATIENT: Hmm. The same feeling is here.

THERAPIST: If you view me like your mother, why will I be disappointed in you and reject you like your mother?

PATIENT: You may dismiss me and stop the therapy.

THERAPIST: So then you will be free to go back to your mother and not to examine your sexual feelings for her as we have been doing here? Do you see how subtle all this becomes?

PATIENT: Oh boy, I really do! Because really I view you more like a father figure.

THERAPIST: Maybe I can represent both aspects of your parents. If I remind you of your father, we must look at it and try to understand it, but if I also am viewed like your mother, that should be kept in mind. Both aspects are important. [This is a beautiful example of a past–transference link, which appears during this third STAPP session.]

PATIENT: It is all so intricate. [He goes on intellectualizing for quite a while. The therapist feels that it is appropriate to listen to these intellectual associations.]

THERAPIST: You have been talking for some time about all these intellectual realities of yours. Are they associated more with your father or with your mother?

PATIENT: Oh, clearly with my father. When I went to school I felt other kids were intellectually my superiors. [He continues at some length.] My father said that they were superior to me.

161

THERAPIST: Did he?

PATIENT: Yes. This also reminds me of my third grade math teacher, who humiliated me in front of the whole class.

THERAPIST: So you associate your father and this teacher as both being intellectual and humiliating you?

PATIENT: I always felt my father was an intellectual giant, when I was three feet tall I thought that he was eighteen feet tall.

THERAPIST: Hmm.

PATIENT: I remember I used to ask my father the meaning of words. He knew all these big English words. He was like a dictionary. Once I do remember an episode when we were watching TV and the announcer said that some character was "infamous." It was a triumph for me because my mother asked my father what the word *infamous* meant. My father said it meant "not famous." I jumped up then and said that he was wrong, *infamous* did not mean "not famous," it meant "a very bad person." My mother was impressed with my knowledge. She beamed when I challenged my father. We looked it up in the dictionary, and of course I was right.

THERAPIST: So intellectually you challenged your father?

PATIENT: My father is a successful businessman, but he is a salesman. He doesn't get straight to the point. He goes around and around.

THERAPIST: You mean like you do? Avoiding issues?

PATIENT: Well, yes, in a way.

THERAPIST: Now let us look at what you just told me. You described your father as an intelligent giant, eighteen feet tall, yet in this example of the word *infamous*, you teach him a lesson. He tumbles from his eighteen-foot height.

PATIENT: It's hard to resolve all this, isn't it?

THERAPIST: Before we resolve it, let us say that you were competitive with your father even in the intellectual realm, but at the same time you also admired and loved your father and that was a conflict— hard to reconcile.

PATIENT: I feel pity for my father. He has no control over his destiny except in business. My father was tremendously afraid of his own father. He was intimidated by him. This is why I came here, in order to understand my feelings for him.

THERAPIST: What kind of a husband is your father?

PATIENT: Very faithful, very gentle, very loving of my mother; but I know that he would like to be more spontaneous, more creative, and not to just try to make a living and support his family.

THERAPIST: What role does your mother play in all this?

PATIENT: My father denies a lot.

THERAPIST: You avoid my question.

PATIENT: She dominated him, and he gave in to her wishes. He was trapped. I felt and feel sad about it.

THERAPIST: One gets trapped if only one wants to. This is also the case with you when you try to avoid and camouflage your feelings by putting up a facade.

PATIENT: Yes, yes. This is why I am here. I don't want to repeat the problems my father had to deal with.

At the end of the session, the therapist dictated:

It was my impression that this interview was not as anxiety provoking as the previous ones. The patient seems to want some breathing space. He brought up an example of a new female relationship. It is too early to attribute this to the therapy, but it is of interest. Also the "infamous" episode is very significant. He is showing off in front of his mother in his father's area of expertise, but at the same time he experiences both sympathy and compassion for him.

Fourth Session

PATIENT: You do the talking today. I feel like "eye-contesting" you. I was circuitous last week.

THERAPIST: Hmm.

PATIENT: Well, I was eye-contesting you last week.

THERAPIST: So there is something going on between you and me in the same way as it did between you and your father. You are eye-contesting me so we have this feeling aroused here between us. Can we hear more about it?

As a result of the patient's opening remarks, the therapist has an opportunity to pick up the transference feelings as well as to make a past–present link interpretation. Which aspect of the patient's response to follow should depend on getting more information.

PATIENT: When I was a teen I developed an ability to contest people in eye-to-eye confrontation. I always wanted to challenge people in authority. I want to challenge your authority.

THERAPIST: This is of interest. In reality, what is my authority over you? [Since the transference is what seems to be primarily on the patient's mind, the need to challenge the therapist's so-called authority should be pursued.]

PATIENT: You are a professional. You also know a lot about me.

THERAPIST: Hold it. By virtue of being a professional, I do know something about people's behavior. But my having authority over you is another matter. I have none, because I depend on information that you give me. So if there is anyone who has authority over you, it is *you*. [The patient attempts to disagree with this statement and there are some further explanatory statements made by the therapist. But after a while the patient agrees that he has exaggerated the therapist's authority over him.]

THERAPIST: If you *perceive* me as authoritative, however, this is what counts. Let us then pursue this association to see where it leads us.

PATIENT: Well, it is true that there is a contest here between us. I enjoy it. Maybe it is a sadistic sort of a pleasure that I feel when I put people on the defensive. So I want to put you on the defensive for you to lose your authority. I do know that all this sounds silly, because I always fail.

THERAPIST: Don't call it names. Let me see, where does this tendency to compete with me come from?

PATIENT: Well, I start at a level below you. You are in an elevated position, but as the contest develops, you remain stationary while I move higher and higher, and finally I am way up in a higher position than you are.

THERAPIST: So, how do you feel and what associations does this elevated position bring up?

PATIENT: I like to use big words to impress people.

THERAPIST: You mean, like *infamous?*

PATIENT: Right.

THERAPIST: You put your father down while you elevate yourself to great heights above him.

PATIENT: Yes.

THERAPIST: And you do this here with me?

PATIENT: Yes.

THERAPIST: So I have certain characteristics similar to your father's in this contest.

PATIENT: It is apparent.

THERAPIST: What thoughts does this situation, this similarity, bring up?

PATIENT: Wish to endear myself to you. Wish for a friendly relationship, rather than a professional basis. A friendly relationship is more enduring and long term.

THERAPIST: Are you saying the reason for the friendship is that it is not terminated?

PATIENT: Yes.

THERAPIST: Yet I wonder if a professional relationship that turns into a friendship is of any value at all.

PATIENT: Well, I suppose not, but the contest is exciting.

THERAPIST: Let's look into this contest. You have a friendly relationship, which is what you wish to have because it lasts long. At the same time you turn it into a contest when you elevate yourself higher than your father or me and you win. The question is, what happens then to that friendly relationship?

PATIENT: It reminds me of an episode in seventh grade. I had a friend who had a girlfriend whom I liked, but I was also close to him, so I started pushing him around. I became brutal because I was bigger than he was and I got sadistic pleasure from it.

THERAPIST: So there was a contest between you and your friend over this girl? So we have a triangular relationship.

PATIENT: I wish I didn't like to do what I did to him.

THERAPIST: The notion of having a contest between you and me and putting me down, which gave you sadistic pleasure like you experienced with your friend, involves a contest between two men over a woman. Now between us where is the woman?

PATIENT: *(Laughing)* But we saw that I saw you as my father.

THERAPIST: Yes, but in the "infamous" episode there was a contest between you and your father over a woman—your mother.

PATIENT: Hmm, true.

THERAPIST: So, coming back to the contest between us, where is the woman? Any thoughts about any person here, a female, whom you may know and whom I may also know?

PATIENT: Yes, there is the clinic receptionist.

THERAPIST: So, there is Ms. Johnson who knows me and who knows you.

PATIENT: Oh, I don't think that she knows you.

THERAPIST: Hmm—interesting. I have been in this department for several years, and the clinic receptionist does not know who I am?

PATIENT: I asked her if she knew you, and she said she didn't know you very well.

THERAPIST: She may not know me very well. What do you mean by "very well"?

PATIENT: Hmm. Well, I mean intimately.

THERAPIST: [The therapist has two options: to get more information about the use of the word *intimately* or to find out what the patient's thoughts are about the receptionist.] What are your thoughts about Ms. Johnson?

PATIENT: She is very nice, a pleasant person. She is also attractive, but she doesn't know you well.

THERAPIST: So there is someone here who is a "nice," "pleasant person," and "attractive," who knows you and who knows me.

PATIENT: I took her to my apartment some time ago, after one of our sessions. The only thing that we had in common was this clinic. We talked about your professional status and your reputation. It was small talk.

THERAPIST: Wait a minute! How could she talk about my professional status and my reputation if you say that she doesn't know me?

PATIENT: *(laughs)* You caught me. I didn't think of it.

THERAPIST: Very interesting! Now, how would you feel if you were caught in the same way by your father? We established that you view me like your father.

PATIENT: It's funny. I need to escape.

THERAPIST: How do you feel right now?

PATIENT: Funny. I haven't thought of it in this way.

THERAPIST: This example is helpful, because now every time that you have a feeling of competing with a man and you want to elevate yourself in this "sadistic" way, you should always raise this question to yourself: "Where is the woman between the two of us?" This association you talked about, you and your friend and the girl, was most interesting.

PATIENT: Indeed, she was very attractive and he was my best friend. There is another friend who is very close to me now, a very successful engineer in L.A. If I were to think about a woman between us it must be Jill. She is very attractive. He says that he can see the games that I play, the camouflage of my feelings when there are the three of us. He is very perceptive. [The patient goes on talking about his friend's perceptiveness and says the friend called him psuedophilosophical.] When Jill was present, he said that I was playing games and that I covered my feelings.

THERAPIST: You mean, what you did with me earlier this hour?

PATIENT: Yes *(laughs)*.

THERAPIST: Can we hear more about Jill?

PATIENT: She is very attractive. She has a gorgeous face, an outstandingly nice figure. She's a nice, charming woman. [He goes on describing Jill in detail. The therapist, having heard enough and suspecting that the patient is trying to run away from his competitive feelings with men, interrupts him.]

THERAPIST: What is her relationship with your friend—what is his name?

PATIENT: Bob.

THERAPIST: So?

PATIENT: Well, he and Jill are very intimate—very, very intimate.

THERAPIST: Hmm, like my being "intimate" with Ms. Johnson in your fantasies? [The therapist is rewarded for postponing his inquiry about the word *intimate*.] What are your thoughts or fantasies about Jill?

PATIENT: In my sexual fantasies it is always Jill who comes to mind.

THERAPIST: Let's hear about them. Don't forget that I am not your father. [The therapist encourages the patient so as to gather more information about this subject.]

PATIENT: Very debonaire, feeling that I am—well, you know—Errol Flynn with her.

THERAPIST: What is the outcome of the fantasy?

PATIENT: I suppose sexual intercourse, wonderful sex and then "au revoir."

THERAPIST: "Au revoir" after intercourse?

PATIENT: I don't want to dismiss her, like "Slam, bam, thank you, m'am." After intercourse I must dismiss her by saying "au revoir." I like to terminate the relationship.

THERAPIST: Things don't fit. If you are Errol Flynn and you have sexual intercourse and then you say "au revoir"—"au revoir" means "I'll see you again." So it does not terminate the relationship at all. The implication is that "we shall repeat the sexual relationship when we see each other again." In a conscious way you wish to end it. So there is a conflict. Do you see what I mean? You have a conflict with Bob and a sexual wish for Jill.

PATIENT: Hmm.

THERAPIST: So why do you want to end the relationship?

PATIENT: So as not to hurt Bob.

THERAPIST: Of course! But then why do you say "au revoir"?

PATIENT: So as to see Jill again.

THERAPIST: Yes, yes indeed! Going back to this conflict with a man, with your father and with me, when you rise like the thermometer. You succeed and you defeat the man. As soon as this happens, however—let us say, as soon as you have sexual intercourse in your fantasy with Jill—immediately you want to terminate the relationship. The reason is because you like Bob, you like me, and you like your father. So when you have fantasies about your mother, you don't want to hurt our feelings. You want to reestablish the relationships with us men, so as not to hurt us. Do you see what I mean?

PATIENT: Yes, more or less.

THERAPIST: You need to reestablish relationships with men whom you like because you have performed an act which they *don't* like. Now, if they knew, *they* would terminate the relationship with you, or they would even possibly . . . ?

PATIENT: Hmm.

THERAPIST: What would Bob possibly do if he knew you had sexual intercourse with Jill?

PATIENT: He'd be angry.

THERAPIST: What would he do?

PATIENT: Well, I am bigger than him, so it won't be a physical contest.

THERAPIST: You may be bigger, but things might not be settled with a physical fight. He may use a gun. Your relationship ends, but also there is a fear of punishment. So this fear motivates you to end the relationship with the woman.

PATIENT: [The patient starts again to intellectualize, to avoid the impact of the therapist's confrontations.] I see, more or less.

THERAPIST: More or less? Now, let us recapitulate. [Because of the patient's resistance, a recapitulation is in order. The therapist must review and repeat what has already been said.] Now, this is the way I see things, but if you disagree, tell me in what way you interpret what we have talked about.

PATIENT: I don't see that there is any other way of looking at it. I only want to emphasize that what you said is vague.

THERAPIST: It is vague because you don't want to see it.

PATIENT: This is a possibility.

THERAPIST: Look at the facts simply. Jill and Errol Flynn, which is you.

PATIENT: I like her, but presumably my interest is in Bob because *he* is my friend.

THERAPIST: Are you saying your interest in Jill is because of Bob? If Jill was available, what would happen?

PATIENT: Well, she is attractive!

THERAPIST: So there is a clear-cut attraction for Jill herself?

PATIENT: Yes.

THERAPIST: But there is something special about her because she is also Bob's girlfriend?

PATIENT: Yes.

THERAPIST: There is also the fantasy that you and she have a sexual relationship. After it ends, you say, "Au revoir," meaning "I'll see you again," and yet you wish to end the relationship, which creates a paradox. Now what is it that you don't understand?

PATIENT: I see it. It is clear, but emotionally I am distant.

THERAPIST: OK. Again, tell me, how would you explain this paradox?

PATIENT: My brain is with you but . . . Now, I rarely remember dreams, but I had this dream last night. I remember it extremely well. My brother, Roger, is getting married later this month. It was a strange dream: I was lying in bed. My brother was sitting next to me and Martha, his fiancée and future wife, was in bed with me. Just the three of us.

THERAPIST: What do you mean, Martha was in bed with you?

PATIENT: Martha is lying somewhat lower in bed. Intercourse is not exactly possible. She is lying on top of me. I envy Roger for marrying such a nice girl. I am closer to him. I love him dearly, as you know.

THERAPIST: One thing is clear: in a situation where there is a triangle of two men and a woman, and when you are obviously fond of that man and feel close to him, you always win. In the Errol Flynn fantasy, you win, and you seduce Jill. In this dream, Martha is in bed with you, and your brother sits on the side, so you win again. In the "infamous" episode, with your talk you also win. So we must conclude that when conflicting feelings get stirred up, you avoid them. It is a pity that you camouflage them because they lead to the problems that brought you here for therapy.

PATIENT: It was a very interesting dream.

THERAPIST: Indeed, it was a perfect dream. It was a perfect crowning to a perfect hour!

PATIENT: Yes *(laughing).*

THERAPIST: OK. I'll see you next week.

The therapist dictated the following postsession notes:

The transference feelings and contest with me came up in terms of a triangular situation, involving a woman between us. Then came the interesting association about his friend's woman, Jill, followed by the "au revoir" association and finally the perfect dream about Martha and Roger at the end. All this points to clarification of the focus and signifies very meaningful progress in the STAPP. The therapy has clearly reached its height during this fourth session. His defense mechanisms of isolation and avoidance seem to predominate. I think he is experiencing more feelings than he is willing to acknowledge. It is clear that the therapy is moving at a quick pace.

The therapist is too optimistic. Although this was without doubt an excellent session, and the focal oedipal conflict was in evidence and was revealing, one should be cautious. The therapist fails—possibly because of his enthusiasm—to make a short-term prediction of what is likely to take place during the following session. One should anticipate either a confirmation of the therapeutic work that took place or a temporary slowing of the pace. After such a meaningful session, the latter is more likely. One could say that the patient, having overextended himself, needs some time to catch his breath.

Fifth Session

PATIENT: Not too much to talk about today . . .

THERAPIST: It's your hour. Nothing to talk about?

PATIENT: I need more direction to go ahead.

THERAPIST: You know better than that. You know that it is not up to me to tell you what to talk about.

PATIENT: Yes, I know, but last week's was a difficult session.

THERAPIST: What aspect was so difficult?

PATIENT: The last few minutes. Issues of sexuality. I felt quite ridden. This issue of my sex drive. I was not able to totally repress it. Sex is a terribly taboo subject.

THERAPIST: Is this taboo about sexuality associated more with your father or with your mother?

PATIENT: Oh, mostly with my mother. With my father we never talked about sex. I think he was afraid of the subject. Sex is mostly associated with my mother.

THERAPIST: Why is this the case? How are these guilt feelings associated with your mother?

PATIENT: She was the one who disciplined me, as I told you. She'd be disappointed in me. I'd be afraid that she'd reject me. I don't want to use the term too often because it is too much of a cliché.

170

THERAPIST: Let's forget if it is a cliché or not. You use the terms *disappointed* and *rejected.*

PATIENT: Yes. So I put on a facade to avoid all those feelings. My mother taught me about sexual morals. The notion was that sex was something to be experienced only when you are married.

THERAPIST: We have talked about all that stuff already. Do you think that your mother's motivation was only moral?

PATIENT: Moral . . . you must clarify that for me.

THERAPIST: You used the word *moral.* We talked also about some of your mother's exhibitionism, didn't we? Is it also possible that the disappointment and the rejection was also motivated by other than moral reasons?

PATIENT: Yes. I have been thinking about that, but it is a difficult subject.

THERAPIST: Yes, I know it is, and I know it is hard. [After making an anxiety-provoking confrontation the therapist feels it is important to encourage the patient to continue talking about this difficult subject.]

PATIENT: The sexual aspect hasn't solidified as yet.

THERAPIST: It hasn't because you resist it. Now, your mother's disappointment was not only on moral grounds. There was also the other aspect which you talked about, the "warm" as well as the "sexual" components. Do you think that these warm and sexual aspects played a role in the disappointment? That's my question.

PATIENT: Mothers are attracted to their sons.

THERAPIST: Don't generalize.

PATIENT: OK *(hesitating)* I gave my mother a feeling of youth by being interested in her.

THERAPIST: Interesting point.

PATIENT: She is attractive, but maybe not beautiful. I am interested in beautiful women, as you know.

THERAPIST: As a reaction, as an avoidance?

PATIENT: Well, maybe.

THERAPIST: Are these the difficult aspects that have to be avoided?

PATIENT: I have the feeling that a very attractive woman will reject me because she is popular.

THERAPIST: So, if she does, what happens?

PATIENT: What happens?

THERAPIST: Yes. If she rejects you, you are free to go back to your mother, who will not reject you, who will love you, who will accept you.

PATIENT: Oh, my God, yes *(laughs)*.
THERAPIST: Your laughter means a lot, doesn't it?
PATIENT: Yes.
THERAPIST: What are your current relationships like?

The therapist feels that the patient's wishes for his mother, with their difficult sexual aspects, have been confirmed amply by his hearty laughter. Thus it is safe to change the subject. The patient proceeds to say that he has met a young woman, Rose, who is not like his mother and who is not very beautiful. It is a surprise to him because it has defied his usual pattern. The therapist sees the event as a possible indication of tangible change. Perhaps he no longer has to go to the extreme of choosing very beautiful women who will reject him so that he can continue to be attracted to his mother. The patient describes Rose as timid, intelligent, and nice.

THERAPIST: In what way do you relate to Rose?
PATIENT: I am much more open. No camouflage. It probably has much to do with our work here.

For the rest of the session the patient talks about his relationship with Rose and reminisces about the girlfriend he had during his adolescence.

As expected, this session was not as exciting as the previous two interviews; a pause was necessary. It was important, however, to observe the appearance of a new relationship in which the patient felt more relaxed and had no need to put on a facade. This occurrence may not be a result of the therapy, but it should be followed and scrutinized carefully because it may mean that the STAPP is already producing some meaningful results.

Sixth Session

PATIENT: Thinking is a good thing.
THERAPIST: Hmm. Let's hear about it.
PATIENT: I have done quite a lot of thinking this week. We covered a great deal during the last five times we met. It takes time to assimilate all that stuff.
THERAPIST: What did you assimilate about these sessions?
PATIENT: All these triangles we talked about two weeks ago. I was quite resistant then, but when I came up with that dream about Martha being in bed with me and Roger sitting on the side looking

172

sad, I really felt that what we have been talking about makes a lot of sense. The more I thought about it during the week, the more sense it made. Actually, despite the dream I want to tell you that I love Roger. When we were kids we had some fights and I thought that maybe my mother preferred him to me. As grownups, however, we are very close. When I went home after our session two weeks ago, I felt guilty about my dream. You know, Roger is getting married on Sunday. I like to tease him a bit. I asked him if he was ready to get married. I pulled his leg a lot this week *(laughing)*. I also like to tease Martha. I joked with her. I asked her if she was sure that she wanted to marry Roger. She said yes. So, where do we go from here? What do you want me to talk about?

THERAPIST: There you go, asking me for questions and guidance. I am pleased that you did not forget the session two weeks ago. Carry on. What about Roger's wedding? [Any discussion of this transference request might obscure information about Roger's marriage and the dream that came up at the end of the fourth session.]

PATIENT: As you know already, Roger is three years younger than I. He was the first baby I had seen. I remember him when he was an infant. He was so ugly. Later on, when he was two or three, he was a cute kid. At that time, or maybe a couple of years later, we lived on a farm. My dad bought a farm in Connecticut. We had a lot of fun playing, but . . . well, I remember once Roger hit me with a rock. I tried to run after him, but he was too fast for me, so I went and I complained to my mom. She laughed and laughed. I was mad and I told her that from now on Roger must "play with himself" alone. She laughed again and she said, "He'd better not." I didn't understand it then, but later I knew that she was thinking about masturbation. As you know, sex was taboo with my mother.

THERAPIST: I am not so sure about that.

PATIENT: *(Ignoring him)* I always protected Roger in school from the other kids. I liked being in the big brother role, but when he misbehaved, I'd whack him once or twice.

THERAPIST: Is that why he hit you with the rock?

PATIENT: That was earlier, but maybe you have a point there. I don't remember why he hit me. I must have done something to annoy him. Maybe I bossed him too much, I guess.

THERAPIST: How did you get on later?

It is a mistake on the part of the therapist to inquire about a later episode when the patient is going merrily along reminiscing. Such an interruption may interfere with some special association. I do not mean that the STAPP therapist should encourage free association; STAPP is not psychoanalysis. The therapist must be active and directive about the focal conflicts. However, the therapist should also be careful not to interrupt the flow of the patient's spontaneous associations about material relating to the focus. The exact timing will depend on the style of the therapist.

PATIENT: While we were at college—we were both at the same school—he was a freshman when I was a senior. We had fun that one year together . . . I forgot to tell you that when he was ten he had appendicitis.

THERAPIST: Oh? [The therapist, realizing the prematurity of his question, backtracks.] He had appendicitis when he was ten?

PATIENT: Yes. I don't know how he contracted it. He was in severe pain. The funny thing about it was that he doubled up, and when a nurse tried to get his legs down, he grabbed her and he tore her dress. My father described that to us. It was so funny, a small kid tearing the nurse's dress (laughs).

THERAPIST: I see nothing funny about it. [Clearly, the therapist should point to the paradoxical situation. The patient is describing his brother's painful experience, but he finds it funny.]

PATIENT: Well, a little kid grabbing the nurse, a big woman, by the stomach and tearing her dress off . . . (giggles).

THERAPIST: Now, just a minute. What do you know about appendicitis?

PATIENT: It is an inflammation of the appendix and can cause peritonitis.

THERAPIST: Thank you. Now, tell me, what does the appendix look like?

PATIENT: Well, the appendix is a useless organ. You must have it removed when it gets inflamed.

THERAPIST: I asked you, what does it look like? [The therapist senses that the patient is becoming a bit anxious about the subject and proceeds with anxiety-provoking questions.]

PATIENT: It is a small, wide body, about two or three inches long— kind of like a pouch. I remember something like that from my anatomy course in college.

THERAPIST: Thank you for being a good college student, but I am interested in your associations and not in your knowledge of anatomy from your college years. [The therapist is not trying to be sarcastic but rather wants to find out what is really making the patient anxious.]

PATIENT: I just told you what I know about it.

THERAPIST: Can we go back to my question: What does the appendix look like, from what you know about it?

PATIENT: It is a small body that looks like a stomach or a liver or an intestine.

THERAPIST: You mean that the appendix looks like a stomach?

PATIENT: No. It's a small, flaky body that is located in the right lower part of the abdomen. I don't remember what color it is . . . I . . . This is what I remember. I know it is very painful when it gets inflamed.

THERAPIST: Yes, but how long is it?

PATIENT: Very small, long, narrow—not very narrow . . . oblong . . . Well, I am all confused.

THERAPIST: So Roger has appendicitis. He is in pain and has this episode with the nurse which you found so funny. Any thoughts about the operation? [It is clear that the patient resists the subject of the appearance and length of the appendix. The therapist therefore tries to bypass the resistance by shifting the emphasis back to Roger; with more information, he will confront the patient again.]

PATIENT: Well, I also had an injury that I had to be hospitalized for. *(Holding out his hand)* As you can see, I have a scar on the palm of my hand.

THERAPIST: Yes, I see. [The patient is also resisting the subject of Roger's hospitalization, but the therapist decides to let him describe what he wants. There is time to get him back to the subject of Roger.]

PATIENT: I fell on a piece of glass. It was painful. I remember the incident very well. My mother was hanging clothes. There was a glass cover that you put on baby's bottle to protect the nipple and to keep it clean. I picked it up. My mother demanded that I give it back to her, but I didn't. I ran away to avoid her. As I did, I slipped and fell down. The glass cap shattered and cut my palm, and I bled profusely. My mother panicked. My grandfather was there. He put a tourniquet on, then drove me to the hospital. My father was not there. In the hospital I was put in a crib; I had just graduated from one a few months before, so I was insulted at being treated like a baby. My mother called my father to tell him about my injury. My father came to visit me later on and I demanded that he take me out of the crib and get me out of the hospital. I was glad to see my father.

THERAPIST: Just a minute. Let us summarize. You and your mother were doing something together. You got injured; your mother gets panicky. There is a lot of blood. You are taken to the hospital and put in a crib, which you dislike. Your father comes to visit you. You are pleased to see him and you demand that he let you out of the crib and also out of the hospital.

PATIENT: That's the most positive image I had of my father. He was going to be my rescuer. It was an extremely positive picture. I didn't think it was his fault.

THERAPIST: Why do you put it this way? His fault? You view your father in such a positive way and now you blame him? His fault? [Paradoxical statements should always be clarified.]

PATIENT: He could have gotten me out . . . I am afraid we go on too long at times . . . I screamed at my father to take me out of the hospital.

THERAPIST: Why did you scream at your father?

PATIENT: I was angry.

THERAPIST: Angry?

PATIENT: Yes. He was too busy to bother with me and relieve my pain.

THERAPIST: So you view it as a punishment?

PATIENT: Maybe, or putting it better, as frustrating me.

THERAPIST: If he was frustrating you, maybe he didn't punish you. [The therapist should have avoided this tentative statement.]

PATIENT: It's possible. Maybe he wanted to be rid of me as long as possible and that is why he kept me in the hospital.

THERAPIST: To be rid of you? Hmm.

PATIENT: Well, yes. Let's leave it at that. Yes, to be rid of me. Even then I was a burden to my father. Later on, I became even more of one.

THERAPIST: In your mind you viewed his keeping you in the hospital as a wish to be "rid" of you, in your words. I would call it a punishment, however. How else would you view it? Why would he want to do this?

PATIENT: I don't know; I just have these thoughts. I am too slow.

THERAPIST: You are not. Don't run away from my questions. Let's go back. What caused your injury?

PATIENT: My stubbornness. I guess Father used to criticize and blame me when I was stubborn.

THERAPIST: OK. How were you injured?

PATIENT: As I told you, by the baby bottle.

THERAPIST: Yes. You told me that this is what your mother didn't want you to touch.

PATIENT: Yes. Because I took away the bottle's glass cap.

THERAPIST: "Bottle," you said?

PATIENT: The baby bottle cap. The cap on top of it. I ran holding the bottle's glass cap. I fell down and I cut my palm, as I told you.

THERAPIST: Yes, but you said something special in your description of that glass bottle cap.

PATIENT: The glass cap covered the . . . the nipple of the baby bottle.

THERAPIST: *Nipple* is an interesting word.

PATIENT: *(Laughing)* I repressed it completely. I blanked it completely.

THERAPIST: Of course you did, but I remember that you used the exact word *nipple* a few minutes ago.

PATIENT: The nipple is of course very important because of the connotation of a woman's breast.

THERAPIST: And also about

PATIENT: My mother's.

THERAPIST: Yes. If your mother was using a bottle to feed a baby, who was the baby?

PATIENT: Oh! It must have been Roger, of course *(laughing)*.

THERAPIST: *(Also laughing)* Yes, of course, it was Roger.

PATIENT: My God. Isn't this something *(laughing)*.

THERAPIST: Well, this is called the unconscious! Some people don't believe that it exists. [At times good humor can be very helpful in relieving a tense situation.]

PATIENT: *(Still laughing)* How could I have blocked it? Wow, it is amazing! [The patient proceeds to talk about his stubbornness. The therapist after a few minutes interrupts him.]

THERAPIST: Now don't run away; you have a tendency to do that a great deal today. Why did you steal that nipple cap?

PATIENT: Well, to take something away from Roger that I didn't have.

THERAPIST: Precisely. So you were jealous, and this motivated you to take it away?

PATIENT: Yes. I took something away from Roger. He needed it to survive, and if he didn't have it he could have died. I wanted to be rid of him.

THERAPIST: The words to be "rid of" also came up before. You used them to describe your father's attitude.

PATIENT: My father's? Did I?

THERAPIST: You forgot already? Your father at the hospital. So being "rid of" is a punitive reaction. You get rid of Roger by taking his nipple away, and your father keeps you in the hospital to be rid of you. So the term I used before, *punishment*, is correct, isn't it?

PATIENT: Yes, yes, it is a punishment, all right.

THERAPIST: OK, then, the whole situation involves your mother, you, and Roger. A triangle. At the hospital it involves your father, you, and your mother, who called to inform him about your injury. Your mother describes your injury involving the cap which protected a nipple. So why did you think that your father wanted to be rid of you?

PATIENT: *(Laughing)* I assume that my father wanted—

THERAPIST: *(Interrupting)* Don't assume. What are *your* thoughts?

PATIENT: I wanted to take something Roger had.

THERAPIST: You were jealous, but in your mind it is your father who punishes you by getting rid of you because of the information your mother gave to him on the telephone. The information was about the nipple, about your stubbornness and your injury. Now, why would your father be punitive? At face value there is no reason for it. If anything, your father is anxious about his son's injury. He follows the doctor's orders, and that is why you remain in the hospital. In your mind, however, it is all different. You feel guilty about your feelings for your mother and Roger. You assume that your father knows about it and you decide that this is the reason he wants to be rid of you.

PATIENT: There are other implications also.

THERAPIST: Such as what?

PATIENT: Well, what we have been talking about the last few sessions, challenging my father's authority, taking over his role, my interest in my mother, and all that—the bottle, nipple, mother's breast.

THERAPIST: This may be true, but it has an intellectual quality to it. [It is important for the therapist not to miss a patient's defensive attempt to be intellectual.]

PATIENT: Yes, it is.

THERAPIST: But your hearty laughter a few minutes ago—was that intellectual also?

PATIENT: *(Laughing again)* No, that was strong. That was emotional. That was true.

THERAPIST: OK. Let's go back to Roger and his appendix, and being the center of attention in the hospital. [The therapist now must come back to the subject of the appendectomy, which was left unresolved.]

PATIENT: His appendectomy?

THERAPIST: Yes.

PATIENT: It must have been terrible.

THERAPIST: Roger was put in a difficult position in your mind because you had been in the hospital before and you knew that it was an unpleasant experience. Yet there is a difference between what was going to happen to Roger and what happened to you. What were your thoughts as to what was going to happen to Roger?

PATIENT: He was going to have his appendix cut off.

THERAPIST: What thoughts did you have about that appendix, that useless organ which was to be cut off?

PATIENT: He was put on a table. He was anesthetized.

THERAPIST: Don't be medical.

PATIENT: I am drawing a total blank . . . You know . . . you know . . .

THERAPIST: I don't know. Go on.

PATIENT: Roger was the center of attention.

THERAPIST: But when you were the center of attention, that ended in disaster for you. What was going to happen to Roger?

PATIENT: I don't know.

THERAPIST: Was the operation going to be Roger's punishment?

PATIENT: I am vague about it.

THERAPIST: Again you are trying to run away.

PATIENT: I remember Roger in pain and suffering.

THERAPIST: OK, you are trying, and have succeeded in wiggling out of a difficult situation.

PATIENT: Yes, this was a difficult hour.

THERAPIST: The time is up, but I must say that your laughter was worth the whole session.

PATIENT: *(Laughing)* Yes, indeed it was.

The therapist's notes were as follows:

For an interview that appeared to have started in a nonspecific way, it certainly ended in an extraordinary way. Clearly the patient's competition with his brother Roger appeared in a very interesting way, particularly in relation to his mother as well as his father. The relationship with Roger he had described during the evaluation interview in very positive terms. The competition with someone whom he loves, in the same way as with his father, always occurs in the presence of women in general and his mother in particular. The question is, what form will his resistance take after his brother's wedding? It seems that the therapy is proceeding exactly in the same way as one would have expected with an excellent STAPP patient.

Half an hour after the end of the session, I was told by my secretary that the patient was on the phone and wanted to talk to me. I asked her to inquire what he wanted to talk to me about. If it was something that had to do with a change of appointment, I was going to talk with him, but if it was something, as I suspected, that he wanted to discuss about the content of the session, then she should tell him that it could wait until the following week.

This type of situation arises at times with patients who resist and manage to end an anxiety-provoking session still avoiding the conflicts that made them anxious. Because they are well motivated and recognize that such maneuvers on their part are antitherapeutic, they call back and want to talk to the therapist on the telephone. This is acting out. It is not a good idea to deal with these situations on the telephone because it reinforces the patients' acting-out behavior. With reinforcement the patients will repeat the action. It is best, therefore, to wait and discuss the problems during a subsequent session.

Seventh Session

PATIENT: *(Looking sheepish)* I am sorry about my phone call.

THERAPIST: Why? What about it?

PATIENT: Well, you see . . . you asked me what the appendix looked like? Well, you know.

THERAPIST: No, I don't know. Let us hear what you have in mind.

PATIENT: Hmm. Roger and the appendix that we were talking about last week.

THERAPIST: Yes. [The therapist is not going to be supportive and give the patient a chance to escape from the anxiety-provoking component of his associations, knowing only too well that the patient is trying again to avoid the difficult subject.] Now that you are here again, let us hear about your thoughts on that subject.

PATIENT: Hmm . . . you see . . . I thought at the time . . . but I avoided . . .

This type of fragmented association, which indicates continuous anxiety, is associated with the psychological conflicts underlying the central focus. At the height of STAPP the focus should be pursued relentlessly. If not, the patient will try to run away, the opportunity will be lost, and the therapy will bog down and may even have to be unnecessarily prolonged.

THERAPIST: [The therapist becomes somewhat supportive.] I know that this subject may be difficult, but you avoided it last week. Let us therefore get back to it and deal with it once and for all. What do you think?

PATIENT: Yes . . . yes. I thought about the appendix last week during the session. I thought about its phallic aspects, but I decided not to say anything regarding that. I was, shall we say, resistant. I was very ambivalent about it. I was, and I am, very much attached to my family. I am aware of these feelings, but I am also aware that by evading talking about them I am not doing any good to myself. You see, I thought of dropping out of therapy after our last session. I was scared. I wanted you to help me, to encourage me, to talk, but I realized that if you did, it wouldn't do me any good. It was up to me to have the courage to look at this stuff I have swept under the rug for years. You are a good doctor, you trusted me, you didn't support me to make me feel good and to reassure me because I was weak. You trusted my strength to deal with all this.

THERAPIST: As I said already, I know that it is difficult, but I also know that you can deal with it. [After the patient's moving statement relating to his motivation for change, the therapist is supportive and encourages the patient to go on.]

PATIENT: Although I felt lonely, anxious, and I had a wish to run away, I also had some very positive feelings about this treatment. I knew that I had to do the work. Yes, I thought that the appendix looked like a penis . . . a penis of a little boy, but I skirted the subject during the hour. After I left, I felt angry at myself for being evasive, for being a coward, and I thought that you would be fed up with me and end the treatment. That's why I called you.

THERAPIST: You were thinking of ending the therapy, yet now you say that I might have been the one to do it. Which is it?

PATIENT: I was frustrated at holding back. I thought I was childish.

THERAPIST: Don't call yourself names. Let us hear what went through your mind.

PATIENT: Roger is a difficult subject. He was married this week and

. . . we had a good talk before his wedding. He is shy and quiet, but he is so dear to me. I love him very much, but it is difficult to talk to him because of my fear of homosexuality . . .

THERAPIST: Now, what is this fear of homosexuality all about?

The therapist senses that the patient is avoiding the issues both of castration—appendix and surgery—and of his feelings for Martha, which appeared so clearly in the dream. He is using homosexuality—pseudohomosexuality—as a way out of his conflicts. This the therapist is not prepared to let him do, but there are already too many balls up in the air. This type of situation can occur quite often in STAPP. It is hard to recommend one path to pursue. Eventually, however, all roads lead to Rome. Any one of these issues in time can be dealt with appropriately.

PATIENT: Well, I also had the feeling that I would be a threat to him, being older and more experienced, as we saw in the dream.

THERAPIST: So this fear of homosexuality—or, to put it better, "pseudohomosexuality"—is a way out of your wishes for Martha. If Roger were to know about them you would say, "Who, me, Roger, interested in your wife? For heaven's sake, I am gay, so you don't have to fear any competition from me. I only like men."

PATIENT: (Laughing) Yes, there is that. It was a lovely wedding reception. Roger and Martha were a beautiful couple.

THERAPIST: So you felt envious?

PATIENT: Yes.

THERAPIST: And lonely?

PATIENT: Yes . . . you see, I have no special relationship with any woman at present. There is Rose, but she is not special, not ideal.

THERAPIST: You don't because you are too interested in attached women, like Jill, Martha, and so on, to women whose men you love and admire, like Roger and Bob.

PATIENT: Yes. I look for the ideal woman. [The patient spends quite a bit of time describing the ideal woman, until the therapist interrupts.]

THERAPIST: Who is this ideal woman?

PATIENT: From our previous talk, it is my mother.

THERAPIST: Is it? Or are you saying this to please me?

PATIENT: No. This feeling of looking at the perfect woman comes from my feelings for my mother.

THERAPIST: Yes. That relationship with your mother was warm, loving, and sexual, as we have already seen. So is it then that no other woman can measure up to that relationship?

PATIENT: The funny feeling crossed my mind as you were talking of cutting you off . . . slicing . . .

THERAPIST: You mean like surgery, appendectomy, like poor Roger? You want to cut me off because with my interpretations I interfere with your special and sexualized relationship with your mother?

PATIENT: Oh, go to hell.

THERAPIST: Yes, because you know that what I say is the truth. The unfortunate thing, however, is that the time has come to an end and there are many aspects that are left up in the air. The whole issue of Roger's appendectomy, the appendix looking like a penis, which you avoided so much. Roger and Martha's wedding, the so-called homosexuality of yours, the perfect woman, your mother, and your anger at me. Don't worry, however, we can look at all these things again next week.

The therapist's postsession summary notes that too many issues are unresolved, which makes it difficult to decide which one to work through in more detail. This type of situation occurs often in STAPP: material is brought up by the patient easily, actively, and massively.

Eighth Session

PATIENT: It was nice to have a week's rest from what we are talking about. I feel relaxed. There is nothing in particular going on.

The patient goes on for quite some time talking about his work and various of his previous week's activities. The therapist allows him to go on for a while and then decides to reintroduce the subject of homosexuality and to concentrate on it. Another therapist might consider some other aspect—for example, the details about Martha and Roger's wedding or about the perfect woman—more important to talk about. Any subject the therapist picks is appropriate as long as it is related to the focal conflicts.

THERAPIST: What was the most important point about homosexuality for you?

PATIENT: It was important last week, as I remember, but today it doesn't seem to be so vital. Right now I feel relaxed. I almost feel like going to sleep.

THERAPIST: Well, don't. Are you calm because the subject is in the open and it doesn't make you so anxious after our discussion, or is your calm a way to go to sleep and to run away?

PATIENT: It is more the former. After our talk last week I felt that I had to help Roger during this difficult time. He is shy and was anxious about the wedding. [The patient continues describing in detail helping Roger with furniture moving and relates various other efforts to help his brother.] You see, Roger and Martha are an idyllic couple, a perfect relationship.

THERAPIST: You mean Roger has found an "ideal," a "perfect" woman?

PATIENT: Hmm . . . I completely forgot about that.

THERAPIST: I see. Is this the reason why you are so calm today?

PATIENT: Oh, yes, now I remember what we talked about. My mother appears to be apprehensive when I mention my dates with women.

THERAPIST: Apprehensive?

PATIENT: Yes. She always asks if I have been intimate with any of them. She also asks me what a woman that I choose to go out with looks like, and stuff like that. She gives me the impression that she feels threatened that another woman will take me away from her.

THERAPIST: Jealous?

PATIENT: Yes, indeed . . . it is her tone of voice. I can see her feelings coming up.

THERAPIST: Give me an example of your mother's behavior.

PATIENT: Yes, of course. Now, because my father travels a lot for his business, she said, "Why don't you move in and stay with me? It would save you money and you can keep me company."

THERAPIST: And what did you say?

PATIENT: I said, "No, no, no."

THERAPIST: Why did you say no?

PATIENT: Well, it is as a result of our work here. All those triangles that we have been talking about. I don't want to lose my identity. I want to know who I am. A part of me knows that it would be nice and easy if I moved in, but I know that I must grow up and not give in to all my mother's wishes and temptations.

THERAPIST: Yes. Let us hear more about this.

PATIENT: With this young woman I talked to you about, I was completely unspontaneous because she was too easygoing. She was too attainable. I became critical of her, yet I knew that this attitude

184

was neurotic. In the past I wouldn't even have noticed it. I was cold, I was uninterested because she was not the perfect woman, but this time I was aware of it and I am glad I was. [This episode may be viewed as a partial tangible example of change. Although the patient performs as he did in the past, at least he is aware of what he is doing.]

PATIENT: *(Continuing)* But with Martha it was different. You see *(hesitating)*, before the wedding I was—well, I had a talk with Martha on the phone. You know . . .

THERAPIST: No, I don't know.

PATIENT: Well, you know . . . Martha is shy, so I talked with her on the phone so that I could prepare her for her wedding night. They say that for a woman the nights before and after the wedding are the most difficult.

THERAPIST: Oh?

PATIENT: I also had a violent fight that night with my father and mother.

THERAPIST: What about?

The therapist has a chance to inquire about the fight with the parents as well as the telephone call to Martha. He chooses the first, which, as it becomes clear subsequently, is a mistake. Yet there is no sure way to know exactly what aspect of the patient's associations should be pursued. Because the time is so limited in STAPP, a review of session notes is always helpful to the therapist because he or she can find out if the focus has gone astray. Of course, the therapist can always return to the subject that was missed.

The patient proceeds to describe at some length his arguments and his disagreements with his parents. He also talks about the role of being the best man at his brother's wedding. All in all, as the therapist discovers belatedly, the fight with his parents was inconsequential and the narration appears to be a diversion on the patient's part.

PATIENT: My father is an unhappy man. I have pity for him because what he aspired to do in his life he hasn't achieved. He is a successful businessman, yet he looks down on business. What he really wanted to be was an artist. Art, my God! It is the opposite of business, with all its bureaucracy, with all the time wasted on details, with money, with time requirements, with accountability, and all that crap . . . excuse me. That is what my father does all the time, and he hates it. Poor guy, what he wanted he never was able to achieve. He got married and he had to support us all. I feel sorry for him, yet I despise him for not doing what he liked . . . I love the guy.

THERAPIST: So your ambivalent feelings for your father are evident. I never doubted that you loved your father. It is precisely because you do that you get into conflicts with him, and it is then when you begin to compete with him over your mother.

PATIENT: I must also add that my mother was angry with me because she said that I was cold to her. You see, I didn't want to walk down the aisle with her. This was what the argument was all about. I thought that she should walk with my dad. She said that she should walk with the best man. She complained later to Roger about it, saying that this treatment of mine is making me act in a remote way and I am not as close to her as I used to be.

THERAPIST: I see.

PATIENT: Well, yes, these sessions here have helped me get some insight and some distance into my relations with my mother. I must admit that I like my sessions here. I guess it is time to stop.

THERAPIST: No, we have a few more minutes. Why do you want to stop, when you just said that you liked these sessions?

PATIENT: I think that I have covered all the important points.

The patient continues to talk for a while about how his parents had coerced Roger to be like what they wanted him to be. The therapist feels that there is something more to the patient's wish to end the interview early, but he is unclear what the reasons might be. He noted this in his dictation. In retrospect, he thought that he should also have inquired about the content of that telephone conversation with Martha.

Ninth Session

PATIENT: I want to work on the whole issue of my alternating interest and lack of interest in my work. I'm not at all clear about it. It is kind of hazy.

THERAPIST: Don't forget that we have a focus on which we agreed to work. This is short-term therapy. We cannot and shall not work on everything which creates problems for you.

A blunt statement by the therapist is often necessary in STAPP. Although the patients are clearly aware of the necessity to work on the specified and agreed-upon focus, because they enjoy the therapeutic process and because positive feelings for their therapist predominate, they tend to want to prolong their treatment. Thus they often bring up other issues to investigate. Our research findings on the outcome of STAPP have shown that if one area of emotional conflict is resolved, such as the specified focus, patients learn to use their knowledge to solve other emotional difficulties by themselves.

PATIENT: You demand a lot from me, but I am said to demand a lot from others. So we are in conflict. [The patient is annoyed by the therapist's statement, so he reintroduces the conflict between the two of them. The therapist under such circumstances should deal immediately with the conflict in the transference.]

THERAPIST: Can we hear more about this conflict between us in terms of who demands what from whom?

PATIENT: I wish you saw me for fifty rather than forty-five minutes. I wish you were more guiding in your approach and did not ask so many questions that make me anxious, like about my feelings for my father, my mother, Roger and his appendix, and all that. I don't doubt your ability or your very fine reputation, but at times I wish for another, more supportive, therapist who does not limit the length of the session or of the therapy as a whole. I know that there are therapists like that.

THERAPIST: Yes, of course they exist, but don't forget that I am your therapist. I see that there is a conflict here between us, and we know quite a lot by now about conflicts between two men. One eighteen-foot-tall man becomes defeated by you and falls from his pedestal while you grow taller and taller . . .

PATIENT: I don't know. The first person I saw in this clinic I thought was learning. He was a novice. You are an expert. You are causing me a lot of anxiety. I ask sometimes, what is this therapy doing for me? I know that there are subtle changes, but when I feel anxious I forget about all that.

THERAPIST: So, what is the verdict? Is this therapy which causes you all this anxiety good or bad? [The therapist senses that the annoyance the patient is expressing is a camouflage.]

PATIENT: [The patient does not answer the question.] Let me give you an example. I was very anxious on Saturday. We went to the beach. It was a lovely day. We had a cookout. I was with my sister, Roger, and Martha. We had a great time, but when Roger and Martha got into their car to leave, I felt anxious, just like being in a void. Roger and Martha seem to be so happy with each other.

THERAPIST: So the question is, why were you anxious?

PATIENT: Why?

THERAPIST: Yes.

PATIENT: Possibly because of my role with my brother and his wife.

THERAPIST: We have discussed your brother and his wife. Let us see if there is something new that took place on Saturday in reference to them that made you anxious.

PATIENT: Not really.

THERAPIST: But you remember, don't you, the dream you had about Roger and Martha when you took Roger's wife into bed with you and he was sad.

PATIENT: I feel that at times I frighten Martha. You see, before their wedding I related to Roger and I related to Martha separately. Now I have to relate to the two of them as a unit. The marriage union is very strong with them. Before their marriage, when I was lonely, I would do something or other with Roger, and my loneliness and anxiety would go away.

THERAPIST: Are you saying, then, that if Roger hadn't been married, on Saturday when you felt anxious you would have gone out together and your anxiety would have disappeared?

PATIENT: Yes.

THERAPIST: In that case, Roger would have been anxiety-suppressive, like a pill, and you say that you don't need such supports any more. Now, are these the thoughts that went through your head on Saturday when Roger and Martha were leaving, namely a wish that Roger was unmarried and that the two of you could have gone out together?

PATIENT: Yes, more or less.

THERAPIST: Was that all, or was there another thought?

PATIENT: Well, there was another thought. I wasn't anxious before they left. I was at my parents' home on Friday and I felt secure and comfortable and . . . and—

THERAPIST: (interrupting) Now, let us repeat what happened to you on Saturday exactly. You were on the beach. You had a cookout. It was a lovely day. Now when did you feel anxious? Exactly at what point were you aware of the change in your feelings from pleasure to anxiety? [The therapist is aware that the patient is becoming anxious and wants to change the subject, so he interrupts to return to the focus.]

PATIENT: It was in my apartment. Roger and Martha came to pick up a chest of drawers which belonged to them and they wanted to have it moved to their apartment.

THERAPIST: Did they stay with you for long?

PATIENT: For a few minutes and . . .

THERAPIST: And then?

PATIENT: Then they left.

THERAPIST: When did you start feeling anxious?

PATIENT: When they were ready to leave.

THERAPIST: So, what did you think exactly at that point?

PATIENT: I thought that it would have been nice if they stayed for a while to entertain me. It was then that I started feeling anxious. I was out at their car and I said farewell and so on. Roger said, "Why don't you come with us and have dinner?" But I declined because I didn't want to use them as an anxiety-suppression pill. I knew that I was going to be anxious, but I wanted to face this feeling with my renewed insights from our work here. Yet it bothered me to think that I'd be alone in my apartment in the city. I felt lonely and anxious.

THERAPIST: Any other thoughts?

PATIENT: Not really . . .

THERAPIST: Any other thoughts? [Again the therapist is aware that the patient is trying to avoid something, so he insists. When a therapist becomes aware that a STAPP patient is trying to avoid the focus, he or she should persist doggedly in efforts to remain on the focus.]

PATIENT: That evening I went visiting a neighbor across the street.

THERAPIST: No, I meant at the point of separation.

PATIENT: Hmm.

THERAPIST: Didn't Martha come to your mind at all? [From the previous information about Martha, the therapist feels that he is not far afield.]

PATIENT: In a strange sort of a way. As I kissed Donna and Martha good-bye, a strange feeling occurred to me, that I hoped my kissing Martha would not upset Roger. I didn't think that it would, but the thought did occur to me.

THERAPIST: "Strange feeling." [The therapist uses the patient's exact words to reinforce his point.] Can we hear more about this "strange feeling"?

PATIENT: It is a conflicting feeling. I do not want to make Roger anxious, and I also want to be as close to Martha, as well as to

Mother, not in a fantasized way or as it was in that dream that I spoke to you about, but in a realistic way.

THERAPIST: I understand.

PATIENT: But I also do not want my brother to think that I am making a play for his wife.

THERAPIST: Why should he?

PATIENT: Maybe it is my own fantasy, but I also think that people do perceive what one is feeling. So I had an active wish that he would not perceive that I was making a play for his wife, but I was afraid that he might.

THERAPIST: If he might, what would he conclude? That you were making a play for his wife?

PATIENT: Yes, that I was making a play for his wife. That would be a possibility, but Roger would dismiss it, I'm sure.

THERAPIST: But we know that you had some thoughts along those lines about Martha, and as we said before, you had that dream about her. So has that thought come to your mind at all? Let's try to see what happened. Did it come to your mind?

PATIENT: No.

THERAPIST: At that time on Saturday, didn't you have any such thoughts about Martha?

PATIENT: Yes. As I was saying before, I do have nice thoughts about Martha. I consciously always think about Martha.

THERAPIST: But why is that completely left out from our discussion?

PATIENT: (Sheepishly) I forgot about it.

THERAPIST: Oh, come on, now. How can you forget it when we have been talking about it in great detail?

PATIENT: I know.

THERAPIST: Do you really want to find out why you were feeling anxious on Saturday? Do you want to find out the *real* reason?

PATIENT: Yes.

THERAPIST: OK, then, let us recapitulate. [Recapitulation is a way to deal with a patient's resistance when anxiety and the defense mechanisms used to deal with it make the patient forgetful.]

PATIENT: OK.

THERAPIST: Saturday was a lovely day. You went to the beach for a cookout with your sister, Roger, and Martha.

PATIENT: Yes.

THERAPIST: Everybody was happy.

PATIENT: Yes, everyone was content.

THERAPIST: Then you all drove to your place so that Roger would get back his chest of drawers. At that point Roger asked you to accompany them. You started feeling anxious, but you refused because you would have viewed going away with them as being an anxiety-suppressive act. You didn't want other people to help you decrease your anxiety because as a result of your therapy, as you said, you wanted to deal with such an issue by yourself. So you decided to stay at your apartment and to feel lonely, which took courage on your part. [The therapist is not patting the patient on the back, but he acknowledges that his behavior under those circumstances has been courageous and that it has demonstrated evidence of change as a result of their psychotherapeutic work.]

PATIENT: Yes.

THERAPIST: At that point, when they were about to drive away, you kissed Donna and Martha.

PATIENT: Yes.

THERAPIST: But at that precise moment, you had a "strange" feeling that Roger could have perceived that you might be making a play for his wife, which you didn't want him to perceive. Furthermore, however, you thought that at times people do perceive such thoughts, although you don't know how they do it.

PATIENT: Uh-huh.

THERAPIST: We also know that you had some feeling of attraction for your sister-in-law, which we have talked about.

PATIENT: Yes.

THERAPIST: What were these thoughts you had about Martha that you forgot completely to bring up until now, and when do they occur?

PATIENT: Any time that I get into physical contact with Martha, I have a thought that maybe Martha and I can get together. I told you that I talked to her before her wedding on the telephone.

THERAPIST: Yes, you told me about it.

PATIENT: What I didn't tell you, however, was what the talk was all about. [The patient's statement confirms that the therapist was mistaken for not having inquired specifically about the nature of the patient's communication with Martha.]

THERAPIST: What did you talk about?

PATIENT: Well, you know . . . you know.

THERAPIST: No, I don't know. Go ahead.

PATIENT: Well, she is shy, as you know.

THERAPIST: I don't know.

PATIENT: She is shy and anxious. I told her that the wedding night is

191

a difficult one, so I offered to initiate her so that she would become sexually experienced.

THERAPIST: You mean that you offered to have sex with her?

PATIENT: Yes, to help her out.

THERAPIST: I see!

PATIENT: She refused.

THERAPIST: I can certainly understand that she did.

PATIENT: So the thought occurred to me that I didn't want Martha to perceive that I still wanted her to have sex with me now that she is married.

THERAPIST: You didn't want Roger to perceive, you didn't want Martha to perceive, that you were going to make a play for her. What is of importance is that if there is anyone who is going to make a play for Martha, it is *you*.

PATIENT: Yes, I know.

THERAPIST: So now let's see what your wishes were.

PATIENT: My wishes?

THERAPIST: Yes, your wishes at the very moment that you were having physical contact with Martha.

PATIENT: Well . . .

THERAPIST: Was it at the time when you were giving Martha a kiss?

PATIENT: Probably.

THERAPIST: Not probably.

PATIENT: I would say yes. Is that what you want to know?

THERAPIST: I want nothing. What I want is that *you* want to know what was happening to you, so that we can understand what made you anxious at that moment on Saturday.

PATIENT: When I anticipated saying good-bye to Martha I thought, "I hope she does not remember our telephone conversation." She does have a good memory, however, so she couldn't have forgotten our telephone conversation. But I didn't want her to think now that she was married to my brother that I still wanted to pursue my sexual interest in her. I assume that such a thought would also make her anxious.

THERAPIST: Yes, I understand. So go on.

PATIENT: It was at that point that I started wishing to go with them, when Roger asked me to accompany them. It was then that I started to feel anxious.

THERAPIST: So one thought would have been that by going out with them you wouldn't have felt lonely. There was, however, a second reason for you to wish to go with them. That wish was to be with Martha.

PATIENT: I would like to say with Roger and Martha.

THERAPIST: Was that the thought that convinced you not to go with them?

PATIENT: Yes, I suppose so, primarily.

THERAPIST: Yes?

PATIENT: The feeling right now is that my family . . .

THERAPIST: *(Interrupting)* Don't run away.

PATIENT: No, I am not trying to digress, I know. The only people I communicate with now are my family.

THERAPIST: Yes, I know.

PATIENT: The thought was that if I went with Martha and Roger on Saturday afternoon, it would have been like going to my parents' home and I would have felt well and my anxiety would have disappeared. The second thought, however, was that I wanted to be with the two of them because of the wish to change my relationship with them.

THERAPIST: OK. So at that time you decided to give Martha a kiss?

PATIENT: Yes.

THERAPIST: What about that physical contact that you talked about?

PATIENT: Well, at times of physical contact with her I get the wish to call Martha and carry on the way I described to you, when I spoke to her on the telephone.

THERAPIST: So what were your specific thoughts on Saturday when you were having physical contact with Martha?

PATIENT: Of our previous communication, that is, of engineering something so we could get together again.

THERAPIST: Did that thought occur to you then?

PATIENT: Yes.

THERAPIST: On Saturday?

PATIENT: Yes.

THERAPIST: You are not saying that because you think that that is what I want to hear?

PATIENT: No, it really did.

THERAPIST: So, that was the thought that Roger might have perceived and that you didn't want to talk about here today?

PATIENT: Yes.

THERAPIST: Tell me, did you have the same thought when you were kissing Donna?

PATIENT: No, Donna is my sister.

THERAPIST: Of course! If your thoughts were different between Donna and Martha, then it means that the kiss for one was of a very different quality than the kiss for the other. It was not that

193

you were kissing innocently your sister and sister-in-law to say good-bye. The kiss for one had a very different meaning than the kiss for the other.

PATIENT: Yes.

THERAPIST: So the immediate thought that followed was, "Roger might perceive this during my kissing of Martha."

PATIENT: Yes.

THERAPIST: So when did you start feeling anxious?

PATIENT: When they were going to leave.

THERAPIST: Before or after the kiss?

PATIENT: A little before.

THERAPIST: Specifically when?

PATIENT: It was when Martha was getting in the car after I kissed Donna, who had already entered the car. It was then that I thought of engineering some kind of a plan to get together with Martha. It was at that point that I started getting anxious.

THERAPIST: So the specific point when you started being anxious was when the thought occurred to you of planning to go with them. Now we know why you wanted to go with them, not so much for the sake of feeling better like the old times but . . .

PATIENT: (Interrupting) Yes, it was when I had the thought of having some contact with Martha—to be together and have some physical contact with her.

THERAPIST: To have sexual contact with her.

PATIENT: Well . . . to be honest, yes.

THERAPIST: So it was then that you decided not to go with them, but you felt that maybe only a kiss would do. Is that so?

PATIENT: (Nods his head)

THERAPIST: Don't nod your head. Tell me if it was so or not. I don't know. I was not there.

PATIENT: You were not there (laughs sheepishly). Of course, when you bring up the point that a kiss for Donna and a kiss for Martha are very different, it is absolutely true. It is also true that Martha is a very attractive woman.

THERAPIST: Yes, I understand, and that is why we try to be so precise in order to understand these feelings rather than have them go underground—which invariably leads to all kinds of difficulties and acting out. [In this way the patient is encouraged to look at the anxiety-provoking quality of the therapist's task, which is aimed not at making him uncomfortable but at helping him understand his conflicts and his behavior. Precision is also an important technical tool of STAPP.]

194

PATIENT: Yes.

THERAPIST: What we were interested in here today was to understand your anxiety on Saturday.

PATIENT: Yes.

THERAPIST: So let me summarize. I think that you become anxious, from what we know now, precisely at the point when you had a desire to go with Roger and Martha. If you did, you might be able to engineer some plans to meet with Martha in the future, the Martha who is a very beautiful young woman and to whom you are attracted very much.

PATIENT: Yes.

THERAPIST: At that very moment you started feeling anxious. That anxiety stopped you from going along with them. It stopped you from going along with them so that in the same old way you would get support as you did with your parents. That feeling of anxiety stopped you from going along with them, but it did not stop you 100 percent. Something within you said no, but it said, "No, I won't go" 99 percent.

PATIENT: No, 80 percent *(laughing).*

THERAPIST: *(Laughs)* Eighty percent. So that twenty percent was equivalent to the kiss to Martha, which was so different from the kiss to Donna.

PATIENT: Yes.

THERAPIST: And then they left and you felt sad, forlorn, and lonely.

PATIENT: Yes, very lonely.

THERAPIST: Because you were not with Martha.

PATIENT: I would like to say Martha and Roger. [The patient makes a desperate attempt to diffuse the impact of the therapist's interpretation.]

THERAPIST: No, no, no.

PATIENT: OK.

THERAPIST: Now we understand the whole thing, the whole issue about Saturday's anxiety in a different way completely. You remember that dream. You and Martha were in bed together, and Roger was on the side. It is not that you don't love your brother. It is precisely *because* you love your brother that all this is difficult. Of course you want to have a new relationship with both of them, but also you are honest enough to admit that you have some sexual feeling for your sister-in-law, which existed in the past and which still exists. If that had disappeared completely, I would have been surprised, and so would you.

PATIENT: Yes.

THERAPIST: As we know, you have a tendency to be attracted to unavailable women because you enjoy being in that situation. We also know that this tendency originated in the past in reference to your relationship with your mother. It was repeated in your relations with women in general, and it was the motivating force for you to seek psychotherapy.

PATIENT: Yes.

THERAPIST: Is this clear now?

PATIENT: Yes, very clear.

This is an interesting session because it shows the efforts made by the patient to use what he has learned in his therapy. He is not completely out of the woods, however: he was telling the truth when he admitted that his old desires for unavailable women had not completely disappeared. It was that realization that prompted him to give a kiss to his sister-in-law. Therapists should not expect total, miraculous cures. Our STAPP investigation has demonstrated that changes do take place fairly quickly, however.

Another point about this session is that the therapist talks much more than the patient. Like the lawyer in a cross-examination, the therapist must look for the truth, which may be hidden by a mountain of defense maneuvers. This truth is the key to helping patients liberate themselves from their neurotic chains.

Tenth Session

PATIENT: I have been thinking about my therapy, particularly after last week's session.

THERAPIST: What specifically have you been thinking about?

PATIENT: All these triangular relations that we have been talking about—Roger and Martha, Bob and Barbara, my mother and father. I was thinking in particular about all the times that I competed with him, about the use of the word *infamous,* and so on. Now I am much more aware of my feelings when I compete with a man for the sake of the woman. I must also add that for the last two weeks I have been dating a new girlfriend. You will ask her name, I know, but I was going to tell it to you anyway. Her name is Dorothy.

THERAPIST: Can we hear more about Dorothy? [The therapist, having dealt with the transference explicitly and repeatedly, lets this reference about the name of the new girlfriend go by. Actually, he wants to hear about the new relationship. Is it again one of the "perfect," "unattainable" women, or not? If not, tangible change is taking place.]

PATIENT: There are many changes taking place within me. First, she is only twenty, while all my previous girlfriends were much older; secondly, she is not attached to anyone. She is shy but she is sweet. I used to go out with older women to prove a point, to be macho and to show off. Well, there is more taking place with Dorothy. By the way, she is far from being a beauty. She is plain looking. She is smart. She is lively, but she is far from being unattainable. I like to help her grow. I think my therapy has contributed a great deal to my understanding about the need I had to go out with perfect women and to put on a facade.

THERAPIST: I am glad to hear it.

PATIENT: Another thing about Dorothy is that I feel very uninhibited with her. We talk a great deal together, and when we are with other people I don't feel the urge to show off or flirt with other women as I used to.

THERAPIST: What you are describing is quite important. [The therapist obviously wants to reinforce the patient's improvement and the change in his interpersonal relations with women.]

PATIENT: Yes, I know. You see, Dorothy comes from a large family and she wants to escape from their pressure. She is the youngest. I also want to escape from that old spell I had with my mother.

THERAPIST: "Had"?

PATIENT: Yes, *had*. I saw how much that attachment to my mother interfered with my relations with women. Putting my mother on a pedestal made all other women second best, so I used to find excuses either that they were too perfect, so they would reject me, or that they were not good enough. So I was playing games, as we saw so clearly last week. I want to be honest, doctor, I am tired of my game playing.

The patient continues to describe his new relationship with Dorothy. The therapist lets him go on and on because he feels that the patient exhibits considerable insight and demonstrates significant evidence of change. He also notes that if, as seems to be the case, the patient's relations with women have changed as a result of his insight about his attachment to his mother, then what is left to be clarified is his relationship to men in general and to his father in particular.

197

THERAPIST: All that is very interesting, but it is only one side of the coin. What about the other side?

PATIENT: What do you mean?

THERAPIST: I mean your relationships with men, and with your father.

PATIENT: Oh, I see . . . Well, there is one episode with my father which I haven't mentioned here. It was some years ago, when he and my mother had a fight, and my father took off without saying anything to anyone and without calling or letting my mother know where he was. He always called her when he was away on business. After a couple of days, my mother got very nervous. She called her brother for advice. He suggested that she should talk to me, but she did not do it for a while. After a week however, my father called her and told her that he was not coming back. My mother got panicky and she spoke to me. She said that now I should assume the role of the man of the house since I was the oldest. She said that I should be responsible for everything, including finances. I was scared to have all these responsibilities at first, but then I started liking that idea.

THERAPIST: What were your feelings like at that time?

PATIENT: *(Remains silent)*

THERAPIST: You are silent.

PATIENT: I drew a blank.

THERAPIST: What about? What comes to mind?

PATIENT: Nothing . . . I was thinking that my father was not happy. He was not a vital force in the family. He avoided his responsibilities to our family. He was just a good businessman who wanted to be independent and simply to support us.

THERAPIST: And he left you to take all the responsibilities, which you say you liked. But why did you draw a blank?

It is always advisable for therapists, when confronted with a patient who draws a blank—provided, of course, that the patient is not psychotic—to inquire about the nature of the fantasies or thoughts that preceded this experience. Drawing a blank usually signifies an important association or a feeling that the patient wants to avoid, to repress, or to deny.

PATIENT: Well, my father was not, as I said, a viable force. He diminished in my estimation; I really beat him. He was no competitor. I really felt better, superior to him.

THERAPIST: All right, but then why did you draw a blank? [The therapist insists in a typical STAPP way.]

PATIENT: I don't know. I feel tired.

THERAPIST: No, tiredness is a way to escape. Something crossed your mind before you drew a blank. What was it? What comes to mind?

PATIENT: Nothing.

THERAPIST: What comes to mind after all these thoughts of being better, superior, and defeating your father? You are now feeling eighteen feet tall and—

PATIENT: *(Interrupting)* I had a flash thought: "patricide."

THERAPIST: Patricide?

PATIENT: Yes. If father were not coming back, if he were away, then I'd be free. I'd be free to reach to that magnetic pole. I wished that he would vaporize—not get hurt, not to be killed, but just vaporize quickly.

THERAPIST: I can see that you don't want him hurt, but would his vaporizing solve your problems?

PATIENT: Then, yes. Now I know better. No, it would not, because I could not live with the guilt. I loved and I do love my father. Now I know that there is a way out of my problems and I owe it to my therapy. You should know that he came back after being gone two more weeks, and I was very glad to see him.

THERAPIST: I think your being glad to see him means that you didn't want him to vaporize. OK, I'll see you next week.

As the therapist said later:

This tenth interview points clearly to tangible change, not only in terms of the patient's resolution of his feelings for women and his mother but also in reference to his competition and love for his father. I am ready now to introduce the subject of termination during the next session.

Eleventh Session

THERAPIST: When shall we terminate?

PATIENT: Terminate what?

THERAPIST: Psychotherapy, of course.

PATIENT: Oh no, I like it. I learned a lot.

THERAPIST: This is precisely why I bring the subject up. I do know that you like it and that you have learned a great deal. The example which you gave me last week about your new relationship with Dorothy is evidence that the pattern of your relations with women has changed. Hasn't this camouflage of your feelings, this facade, which prompted you to seek therapy, changed? From what you told me, Dorothy is an available and nonattached woman. So, don't we have it all here? Haven't we accomplished what we were supposed to?

PATIENT: I know what you are saying is true.

The therapist summarizes what has been learned during the ten previous sessions. This is a useful way to recapitulate and to underscore the insights and understandings that have been achieved. Such a summary helps solidify all that has been learned during the course of STAPP.

The session ends with the therapist asking the patient whether he agrees with the assessment. The patient proceeds to describe his accomplishments, giving numerous examples.

PATIENT: I understand completely now my need to seek unavailable women and the source of this neurotic tendency of mine, emanating from my wishes for my mother as a child and my competition with my father. I understand how I repeated this with my friends and even with my beloved brother, Roger. This therapy has been a great emotional realization for me. It has been, however, hard work.

THERAPIST: Yes, it has, and you have persevered in your efforts despite the anxieties that were aroused. It is because of this that I think it is time to terminate this therapy. When do you want to do it?

PATIENT: OK. Let's have one more session.

THERAPIST: Fine.

Final Session

PATIENT: I know I'm ready. I feel sad, and I also feel proud and happy for having achieved what I did.

THERAPIST: I am glad to hear it.

PATIENT: I know I have hard work ahead of me, but I feel prepared to do it and to do it alone. Of course there are areas which I still have to work on.

THERAPIST: What are they?

PATIENT: It has to do with my parents. I have changed, but they have not. Now I realize so many things I was oblivious of before.

The patient describes and gives examples of his mother's seductive behavior, her tendencies to pit him against his father and to treat him as her favorite. He goes on to express his amusement at behavior that once seduced him. He relates stories of challenging his mother by refusing her invitation to stay with her when his father was on business trips. He states that he has criticized his mother for her tendency to put down his father. When his mother complained about the change in his behavior, he proudly told her that he was not a kid anymore. He finally points out that he no longer has much desire to compete with men in general and his father in particular.

PATIENT: I am savoring the last few minutes of our final session. I've liked you as my therapist. You gave me a rough time, but I knew it was for the best. I am pleased with what I have accomplished.

THERAPIST: It is like a graduation, isn't it?

PATIENT: Yes, exactly.

THERAPIST: OK. In retrospect, what were the highlights of your therapy?

PATIENT: The "infamous" episode with my father, and—despite my competition with him my wishes for him to "vaporize"—my love, my great love for him *(becoming teary)*.

THERAPIST: What else?

PATIENT: The episode with Roger's appendicitis, and the Roger and Martha dream, and the Saturday anxiety episode, and how I could clearly see its source.

THERAPIST: Anything else?

PATIENT: Yes. The triangular situations and seeing that I don't need to be in similar situations with people that I like. Oh, I forgot to tell you, I have a nice new job making more money and leaving more time to study.

THERAPIST: I am glad. I would say it was good therapy. Of course, we would like to see you in a year's time to follow up, so that you let us know how the therapy looks to you then. Is that OK?

PATIENT: Oh, yes, of course. Thank you very much, doctor.

THERAPIST: You are very welcome. I also enjoyed very much working with you.

Follow-Up

The patient was seen after one year by his therapist and two different evaluators. The evaluators' impressions are summarized in the following paragraphs.

The first evaluator listed these impressions of the follow-up interview.

1. The patient was unclear about what prompted him to seek psychotherapy at first, then he said, "Oh, yes, 'camouflage' and 'facade.' Now these problems seem vague, silly, and nonexistent."
2. His relationship with Roger and Martha has been fine, with no sexual feelings for Martha persisting.
3. He describes that he has been close to his father but can view both parents more objectively. He says he gets irritated at times by what he considers to be his mother's seductiveness.
4. His relationships with women have been greatly altered. He had a relationship with an attractive, available twenty-five-year-old woman for six months. No Errol Flynn fantasies. No ideal women. His most recent relationship with another young woman seems to be developing into a serious one.

The second evaluator thought that the patient's relationships with women had improved. He had no further need to go out with beautiful, unavailable women or to be the "greatest." He did not feel threatened as much, and had no need to put on a facade. He mentioned that he was working in the same office with Roger and their relationship was fine. His relations with his parents he defined as being much more realistic and mature.

He said that he was able to use his anxiety to resolve his problems when faced with conflicts and claimed that he had become much better able to define emotional problems.

All in all, both evaluators thought that the patient had recovered from his emotional difficulties.

This case was not presented to claim universal success for STAPP. As mentioned already, we have had patients who failed to improve, although they are few. Instead, the presentation is meant to demonstrate the techniques of STAPP by allowing therapists to observe the process. I hope that others will incorporate the techniques of STAPP in treating the patients who are evaluated and found to be good candidates for such therapy. I am sure that they and their patients will find the encounter as worthwhile and pleasant as I always do.

Epilogue

THE PRACTICE OF SHORT-TERM DYNAMIC psychotherapy as set forth in this manual has its critics and detractors. For example, practitioners of long-term psychotherapies may find fault with the strict focus and time limitation. Researchers may not be satisfied with an approach that relies basically on clinical observations. Some therapists may be shocked by the active anxiety-provoking quality of this brief treatment, in which patients are seen as capable of handling unpleasant feelings and willing to stand on their own feet. Yet, although STAPP and other common brief psychotherapies have come under fire in recent years, they continue to grow in popularity. I would like to address particularly the biological controversy.

Biologically oriented therapists may object that my presentation of STAPP alone—without the extensive use of medication—is outdated. It seems to me that some biological psychiatrists and psychopharmocologists doubt the value of psychodynamic theory and have become more royalist than the king, thinking that they possess the only scientific answer for the treatment of mental illness. A dichotomy between the biological and psychological aspects of medicine expressed in the form of "hard" versus "soft" scientific data has persuaded psychiatrists to choose biological or psychological ways of dealing with their patients, rather than to attempt to combine judiciously both aspects for their benefit.

Although it goes without saying that every human activity is biologically rooted, it is also true that psychological functions cannot be explained at the present time in biological terms. Unfortunately, the familiar "organic" versus "functional" controversies have not resolved the issue. It follows, of course, that psychopharmacology is the therapeutic part of biological psychiatry, while dynamic and behavior modification therapies are part of psychological psychiatry.

In previous writings I have emphasized that specific psychiatric treatments should be made available for well-selected patient populations. For example, for the sicker patients—those suffering from psychoses or very severe personality disorders—psychotropic medication is the treatment of choice for the immediate relief of symptoms, and supportive psychotherapeutic interventions of brief or long duration are required for eventual rehabilitation. On the other hand, with healthier patients, dynamic or behavior modification techniques of long or short duration can be used effectively. All forms of treatment should be described clearly and should be based on specific criteria for selection and outcome.

The use of a more focused approach for patients who are now being treated with long-term psychotherapy should be investigated because it is possible that they may be helped to learn how to circumscribe their expectations, anticipate potential difficulties, concentrate on a specific area of emotional conflict, and achieve meaningful results over a short period of time. For example, we have occasionally seen a borderline patient who behaved in a typically disorganized way, yet who has been able to function exceptionally well in one emotional area. Technically speaking, it seems that by becoming more active a therapist may be able to demonstrate over and over to such a patient how to set the limits the patient has lacked. Staying within a specified area, the agreed-upon focus, may help such a patient remain within the confines of a setting that has been provided by the therapist, thus learning how to anticipate difficulties and circumscribe an area of problems that may be overcome.

I have given this example to demonstrate that certain technical principles developed in short-term dynamic psychotherapy, such as focalization, can be used effectively to shorten the treatment of more seriously disturbed patients—those who consume the greatest amount of time devoted to the treatment of mentally ill persons. Efforts of this kind, if they originate with mental health professionals and are not imposed upon them by third-party payers, might demonstrate the value of efficient and effective psychotherapeutic interventions. Taking the initiative will also free therapists from arbitrary administrative rulings by outsiders whose views are financially motivated. Above all, the sickest patients will benefit.

The value of STAPP needs no further defense. The great enjoyment that I as a therapist have derived from treating eligible patients, from seeing them work hard to free themselves from their neurotic constraints, I have tried to convey in this manual. STAPP has made my professional life worthwhile. I hope that those who offer STAPP to their eligible patients as a result of reading this manual will experience the same exhilaration and pleasure.

APPENDIX 1

Results of STAPP

SEVERAL STUDIES ON THE OUTCOME OF STAPP have been described previously (Sifneos 1972, 1975, 1987). Suffice it to say that these findings have been encouraging, particularly once we started using videotapes in follow-up interviews. In some of these interviews we asked patients whether they would like to view a past therapy session. Our follow-up tapes show the therapy session on one-quarter of the monitor; on the other three-quarters the patient can be seen commenting on the changes that have taken place since the end of therapy. Observers can see the change very dramatically.

Another trait that follows from STAPP is the development of what I have called an internalized dialogue inside the patient's head. It seems that one hemisphere raises questions similar to the ones the STAPP therapist used to ask during treatment, while the other hemisphere seems to answer, to associate, to remember, and to experience appropriate feelings. In this way the former STAPP patients are able to recreate the old therapy and use what they learned during its course. They can apply the technique to resolve new emotional conflicts.

It is to the therapist's advantage to keep in mind the outcome criteria and to be sure that the agreed-upon criteria for improvement have been met at the end of the therapy.

The following are the STAPP outcome criteria that are used by our research evaluators who have seen their patient in a follow-up session:

1. Improvement in psychological or physical symptoms
2. Better interpersonal relations
3. Increased self-understanding

4. Evidence of learning
5. Development of problem-solving strategies
6. Enhanced self-esteem
7. Better work or academic performance
8. Development of useful new attitudes

The evaluator does not simply ask for a yes-or-no response to questions about these criteria. Rather the patient should give specific examples that document changes.

The eight criteria account for half of the outcome assessment. The other half involves the patient's psychological vulnerability in terms of the predisposing factors that caused his or her problems. We call this vulnerability specific internal predisposition (SIP). It signifies that the patient's specific emotional conflicts were responsible for the difficulties and were resolved by STAPP.

The following scoring system is used for the eight outcome criteria and the SIP:

7 to 6 recovery
5 to 4 much better
3 to 2 little better
1 to 0 unchanged
−1 to −2 worse

Take the total from the first eight criteria and divide it by 8. Add to this average the score from the SIP and divide the total by 2. This division gives the final score of the patient's change. For example, let us say a patient's eight outcome criteria are scored, respectively, as 6, 4, 5, 6, 7, 5, 4, and 5. The total is 42, which is divided by 8 to yield 5.4. The SIP score is 6, so the two combined are 11.4. Divide that by 2 for the final outcome score, 5.2. By the same scale as used for the eight criteria, the patient is rated "much better."

Although numbers cannot capture the psychological complexity of a human being, for practical purposes, quantification is useful for looking at a large number of patients. Of forty-six patients with an unresolved oedipal focus who were treated with STAPP (Sifneos, 1989) twenty-nine, or 69 percent, were scored by two evaluators as "recovered," and eleven, or 23 percent, were "much better." In this most recent study, 92 percent of the patients had achieved very good results. Appendix 2 is a sample follow-up questionnaire.

It should be noted that in an impressive 2- and 5-year follow-up study of short-term dynamic psychotherapy in Norway, Husby (1985), in a series of articles, described outcome findings similar to ours.

APPENDIX 2

Follow-Up Questionnaire

Patient's Name _____ Date _____
Interviewer _____ Time elapsed since termination _____
Address _____
_____ Telephone _____

PART 1 Patient's Statements   Interviewer's Opinion
                                   (if different, please note and underline)

A. *General*

1. What was the chief difficulty that made you seek treatment?

2. How do you feel now?

3. Changes in *physical health?*

B. *Symptoms*

1. Initial:

2. Present status (including intensity):

C. *Changes in Interpersonal Relations*

1. With: Father
              Mother
              Brother
              Sister
              Spouse
              Friend
              Children
              Key people at work or school
              Other

2. New relations:

3. Changes at work or school:

D. *Understanding (verbal ability); please give examples*

1. Changes in *self-understanding:*

2. *Learning* during treatment:

3. Use of learning in treatment to understand more recent situations:

4. Other new attitudes:

E. *Problem solving; give specific examples*

1. While in treatment:

2. More recently and now:

F. *Self-Esteem*

1. Changes in self esteem (including appearance):

Appendix 2

G. *Focus of Therapy*

1. What was the focus of your psychotherapy?

H. *Treatment Experience*

1. What took place?

2. Differences from previous treatment:

3. How did treatment help?

4. Attitudes toward therapist during treatment and now?

5. Termination: how decided on; how experienced?

6. Was treatment sufficient?

Criteria for Outcome

1. Has specific predisposition changed?

2. Specific nature of dynamic change; give evidence:

3. Reasons for success or failure:

4. Diagnosis:

Motivation for Change

	Yes	No
a) ability to recognize that symptoms were psychological	___	___
b) introspection and honesty in reporting about himself/herself	___	___
c) participated actively in treatment	___	___
d) is curious about himself/herself	___	___
e) has changed	___	___
f) expectations of results achieved	___	___
g) reasonable sacrifices made	___	___

score _____

213

Appendix 2

SCORES

	Recovered		Much better		Little better		No change		Worse	
	7	6	5	4	3	2	1	0	−1	−2
1. Symptoms										
2. Interpersonal relations; with whom (average the scores of the different relationships for the final score)										
3. Understanding										
4. Problem solving										
5. New learning										
6. Self-esteem										
7. Work performance										
8. New attitudes										
Score										
Specific internal predisposition (SIP)										

Total score (Add score of 1–8 =   ; divide total by 8 =   ; add score of SIP =   ; divide by 2 =   .)

Characterological Criteria

	7	6	5	4	3	2	1	0	−1	−2
dependence										
passivity										
narcissism										
sado-masochism										
acting out										
other (specify)										

References

Alexander, F., and T. French. 1946. *Psychoanalytic psychotherapy.* New York: Ronald Press.

Brusset, B. 1983. De la psychothérapie à durée limitée et de la technique de l'évaluation et possibilités de changement. Symposium sur psychothérapies analytiques brèves, 22–25 Juin Symposium, Lausanne, Switzerland.

Davanloo, H. 1978. *Basic principles and techniques in short-term dynamic psychotherapy.* New York: Spectrum.

Ferenczi, S. 1978. *Further considerations on the theory and technique of psychotherapy.* New York: Spectrum.

Freud, S. 1949. The dynamics of transference. *Collected papers,* vol. 2, 312–23. London: Hogarth Press.

———. 1950. Analysis terminable and interminable. *Collected papers,* vol. 5, 316–58.

Gilliéron, E. 1983. *Au confins de la psychanalyse.* Paris: Payot.

———. 1990. Les psychothérapies brèves modules, 2nd ed. Paris: Presses Universitaires de France.

Glover, E. 1953. *The techniques of psychoanalysis.* New York: International Universities Press.

Hoyt, M. F. 1985. Therapist resistances to short-term dynamic psychotherapy. *Journal of the American Academy of Psychoanalysis* 13:93–112.

Husby, Ragnhild, et al. 1985. Short-term dynamic psychotherapy. *Psychotherapy and psychosomatics* 43:1–32, Basel, Switzerland: S. Karger.

Malan, D. H. 1976. *The frontier of brief psychotherapy.* New York: Plenum.

Mann, J. 1973. *Time limited psychotherapy.* Cambridge: Harvard University Press.

Porter, R. 1968. The role of learning in psychotherapy. London: Churchill.

Sifneos, P. E. 1971. Change in patient's motivation for psychotherapy. *American Journal of Psychiatry* 128:718–22.

————. 1972. *Short-term psychotherapy and emotional crisis.* Cambridge: Harvard University Press.

————. 1975. Criteria for psychotherapeutic outcome. *Psychotherapy and psychosomatics* 26:49–58, Basel, Switzerland: S. Karger.

————. 1987. *Short-term dynamic psychotherapy evaluation and technique.* New York: Plenum.

————. 1990. Brief dynamic and crisis therapy. In *Comprehensive textbook of psychiatry,* vol. 2, section 30:10, pp. 1562–68, ed. H. I. Kaplan and B. J. Sadock, Baltimore: Williams & Wilkins.

Index

Acting out, 194; motivation for change questioned due to, 109; termination desired by patient due to, 140; therapist resisting, 180

Active techniques, by therapist, 102

Adolescence, questions about, in developmental history, 12

Adulthood, questions about, in developmental history, 12

Affect deficit, in alexithymic patients, 36–40

Alcohol abuse: in alexithymic patients, 37; STAPP not appropriate for patients with history of, 14

Alexander, F., 33, 112

Alexithymic patients, 36–40

Altruism. *See* Meaningful relationship(s) in childhood

Anxiety: capacity to withstand as ingredient for STAPP, 26; divorced mother complaining of, 7–8; loss of father causing, 53–65; in patient with unresolved oedipal problem, 190–91; resistance in patient due to, 131; STAPP for patient with, 10; termination desired by patient due to, 140

Anxiety-provoking quality of STAPP: of confrontations and clarifications, 107–12,

171; therapists shocked by, 205; as therapist's task, 160, 180–81, 194

Anxiety-provoking questions: to candidate for STAPP, 48; patient avoiding, 150, 152; to patient with unresolved oedipal problem, 150, 152, 174–75; support from therapist along with, 136–37

Appointment time, kept unchanged, 90

Authority, patient having conflicts with people in, 148–49

Avoidance, evaluation hindered by, 28

Biological controversy, over STAPP, 205–6

Blank, patient drawing a, 198–99

Boss, patient complaining to, 138–39

Boyfriends: brief relationships with, 56–57, 59, 60, 61, 63–64; history noting difficulties in relationships with, 15–18

Brother, relationship with, 57, 58, 59, 60, 61, 64, 65

Castration, patient with oedipal problem having fear of, 182

217

Psychosomatic illnesses, in alexithymic patients, 37
Psychotherapy, therapists believing in long-term, 141
Psychotropic medication, for sicker patients, 206
Puberty, sexual experiences in, during history, 11, 15

Questions: motivation for change assessed with, 42–43; types of, in developmental history, 12–13. *See also* Anxiety-provoking questions
Quoting, during interpretation, 132

Realistic expectations for outcome, assessment of patient's, 44–45
Recapitulation: interpretation solidified by, 32; resistance avoided by, 131–35, 168, 190–91
Regression, avoiding, 123–27
Relevant information. *See* Important information
Repetition, by evaluator, 79, 85
Requirements, for STAPP, 90
Research, patient's willingness to participate in, 45–46
Resistance, 96; to anxiety-provoking questions, 150, 152; of patient with oedipal problem, 168, 190–91; problem solving and partial insights used during, 130; recapitulation avoiding, 131–35; transference, 97
Rewarding patient, 83
Running away from home, by man complaining of depression, 84

Sacrifice, assessing willingness to make tangible, 45–46. *See also* Meaningful relationship(s) in childhood
School years, questions about, in developmental history, 11

Second opinion: countertransference overcome by, 35; for woman complaining of migraine headaches, 69
Selection criteria, 19–46; for anxious patient who lost her father, 53–57; circumscribing presenting complaints, 21–23, 144–45; favorable interaction with evaluator, 26–35; intelligence and psychological mindedness, 35–41; meaningful relationship during childhood, 23–26; motivation for change, 41–46; for woman complaining of migraine headaches, 66–69
Self-entertainment, motivation for change associated with, 41
Self-sacrificing, STAPP not appropriate for excessive, 25–26
Senior consultant, of evaluation intake team, 2
Separation difficulties. *See* Loss and separation issues
Sequence, in developmental history, 13
Setting, of STAPP, 91
Sexuality, in developmental history, 2, 14–18, 136; of anxious patient who lost her father, 59–60, 61, 63–65; brother and, 59, 65; father and, 71–77; of man complaining of depression, 81–82, 83–84, 85–86, 88; mother and, 132–35; patient formulating complaint about, 6–7; of woman complaining of migraine headaches, 71–75. *See also* Oedipal problems
Siblings, questions about, in developmental history, 11. *See also* Brother, relationship with
Sifneos, P. E., 11, 19, 42, 50, 100, 209, 210
SIP. *See* Specific internal predisposition
Slips of the tongue, during first interview, 82
Social workers, 1
Sophocles, 51
Specific internal predisposition (SIP), 210
Spontaneous associations: attention paid to, 72; need for, 159; therapist not interrupting, 173–74; working alliance intensified by, 80
Suicide attempts, STAPP not appropriate for patients with history of, 14